Gita Mehta

WRITERS OF THE INDIAN DIASPORA

Series Editor
Jasbir Jain

Available Titles in this Series

Jasbir Jain	: WRITERS OF THE INDIAN DIASPORA: INTRODUCTORY VOLUME
R.K. Kaul	: NIRAD C. CHAUDHURI
Manjit I. Singh	: V.S. NAIPAUL
U. Parameswaran	: KAMALA MARKANDAYA
Jameela Begum	: CYRIL DABYDEEN
Mala Pandurang	: VIKRAM SETH
C. Vijayasree	: SUNITI NAMJOSHI
R.K. Kaul & J. Jain	: ATTIA HOSAIN
Nilufer E. Bharucha	: ROHINTON MISTRY
Akshaya Kumar	: A.K. RAMANUJAN
Frank Birbalsingh	: NEIL BISSOONDATH

Writers of the Indian Diaspora

Gita Mehta

Writing Home/Creating Homeland

USHA BANDE

Series Editor

Jasbir Jain

RAWAT PUBLICATIONS

Jaipur • New Delhi • Bangalore • Mumbai • Hyderabad • Guwahati

ISBN 81-316-0205-2

Published by
Prem Rawat for **Rawat Publications**
Satyam Apts, Sector 3, Jawahar Nagar, Jaipur 302 004 (India)
Phone: 0141 265 1748 / 7006 Fax: 0141 265 1748
E-mail: info@rawatbooks.com
Website: www.rawatbooks.com

New Delhi Office
4858/24, Ansari Road, Daryaganj, New Delhi 110 002
Phone: 011 2326 3290

Also at Bangalore, Mumbai, Hyderabad and Guwahati

Typeset by Rawat Computers, Jaipur
Printed at Chaman Enterprises, New Delhi

For

Jasbir Jain

in affection and admiration

Contents

Series Editor's Preface

It is a pleasure to be writing this preface for yet another volume in *Writers of the Diaspora* series and this one happens to be on Gita Mehta, a much-read, much talked about writer inhabiting two worlds with equal ease.

Gita Mehta's work offers and defines its own problematics. It raises questions related to location: first of the writer, then the world of her fiction and then of the historical underpinnings of the fictional world. One looks at her titles with suspicion and curiosity. What is it that compels her to juxtapose two different cultural worlds and summon forth oppositional and at times contradictory memories, spaces and philosophies? The contours of these divisions are never a straight line – they form a jagged edge like the flowing waters of the sea as they play with the shore. *Karma-Cola* evokes images of Hindu mysticism as well as the fizz of the western drink whose popularity has travelled beyond the west.

Usha Bande poses the question: where does Gita Mehta belong? This question has been a major concern in diasporic studies as theories of diasporic aesthetics are formulated over and above the writer's physical location; the choice of subject, the perspective, the lens chosen to define this perspective all acquire importance. The location of the text in a particular stream of writing is an additional issue; that is in which direction does it expand horizontally. In Gita Mehta's case the point of origin, the thematic choice and her relationship to the unknown reader display a certain ambivalence right at the beginning, she occupies a border zone and stands literally in two worlds. I am reminded of the demarcations line at Greenwich where one can stand in two time zones by standing across it. Living on the border is not necessarily a no man's land. Instead the experience of simultaneity can be very enriching. For one she does not believe in character contrasts, they are delineated in subtle hues. Again the issues at stake are multiple and complex as structures of power and strategies of resistance are explored and put under the scanner. *Karma-Cola, Raj, A River Sutra* – each is different from the other but all respond to western engagements with India and its traditions of meditation, mysticism and naturelore. Europe's fascination with the Empire and with eastern culture compels attention to two different historical perspectives, journeys into the past and the minds of men, even as these unfolding themselves relate to contemporary issues of resistance strategies, power struggles, empowerment and feminism. Mehta moves amazingly quickly from the intrigues of the palace to the isolation of a forest resthouse, the world of sadhus – fake or genuine – and then to an interrogation of the nature of reality and the value of experience.

This volume, like the preceding ones, places the writer's work in diasporic space and then works through the individual differences and issues. Usha Bande has engaged with Mehta's simultaneous location in two worlds, a hybrid sensibility and with the layered narratives, opening them out in various directions and turning the mirror around. Gita Mehta constantly plays a trick with the mirror – she looks into the outer world, then looks at India through the eyes of the other, estranging herself; then indulges in self-mockery, and then reveals a hidden depth. Usha Bande similarly follows Mehta as she travels these different worlds, but then distances herself from the writer and standing outside gives an interpretation which makes us recognize Mehta's complexity.

I would like to express my gratitude to the writer of this volume for taking up this responsibility and fulfilling it so wonderfully well. Thanks Usha.

Jasbir Jain

Preface

> Shifting images pass before me: Victorian, Civil Service, English India, with tremulous whispers about sex and with smoking-room banter. Political India, with curious legislatures. Intellectual India, with a Sanskrit text. Indias are endless.
>
> —Ved Mehta

It was the time I was reading Gita Mehta and was under her spell when Jasbir Jain suggested I choose some diasporic writer from the list for the series she was editing. I opted for Gita Mehta and I do not regret my choice. I am still fascinated by her writings. I had read her works almost in a reverse order: *A River Sutra* captivated me with its scintillating style and flow of language like the flow of the Narmada; then *Raj*, the story of princely India and then *Karma Cola* with its tongue-in-the-cheek style. *Snakes and Ladders* was in the market but I was yet to read it. It may be mentioned here that Mehta's latest work *The Eternal Ganesha* is out but it could not be procured; hence I have not included it in the present study.

What I find interesting about Gita Mehta is the newness of her approach, simplicity and the variety of her themes. After a long stint at reading and writing on feminism, the open sky and the serene river looked refreshing. No more social/familial sagas, no more women's sighs and no more delving into the inscrutable and irreparable ways of the patriarchy! Here was the cool jungle of Narmada valley and a bewildered seeker with whom you could identify; the inebriated world of "instant Nirvana" maniacs, as colourful as the seekers we often saw in Kullu-Manali or in Goa; the ups and downs of *Rajniti*; and the eternal paradoxes of the Indian scenario – "the assault on the senses and caress of the senses." Jaya (of *Raj*), Uma (the minstrel of the River) and Narmada (the river) are the women peopling her world but they are not stereotypes. Jaya is able to stand for herself, Uma is in the bliss of an ascetic and Narmada is the primordial presence. A kind of soothing effect, if not profundity, is what wafts through these pages.

Between the offer to write this book and the actual execution of the work there has been an inordinate delay which may be justified but cannot be condoned. Dr. Jain, herself a high-speed worker, accepted my justifications and excuses with magnanimity. I am grateful to her not only for the offer to write and her confidence in me but also for bearing with me as I struggled through the framework – theory, analysis and all. After all Gita Mehta's works are not as facile as they appear to be.

When it comes to diaspora, it also means postcolonialism, and postcolonialism in its turn implies postmodernism. One has to sift and arrange the material carefully before one starts justifying its applicability to the author. It means delving into theory and theory takes time.

In writing a book we all have to rely on people and institutions for support. I express my thanks to the library staff of Indian Institute of Advanced Study, Shimla, State Library, Shimla, R.K.M.V. Library, Shimla, and Sahitya Akademi Library, New Delhi.

As a friend once said, "the books you write are not yours, mind you. You can't overlook the sacrifices of the people at home in giving you time and space to work and keeping you free from responsibilities." I thank my mother Sushila Bande and brothers Avinash and Vilas, and Vilas' family – Shashi Bande and little Himanshu.

Shimla **Usha Bande**

My India, I carry with me wherever I go

— Raja Rao

One

Introduction

There's so much more which cannot be touched by the pen.

— Amrita Pritam

At a time when it has become a general trend to look for feminist leanings in any work written by women, and for the sense of loss and rootlessness in any work coming from the diaspora, it is delectably a different experience to read Gita Mehta who looks at life from refreshingly new perspectives. Not that she is unaware of women's problems or that she is impervious to the diasporic displacement, only she finds many more interesting themes to write about. Her first book *Karma Cola* (1979), a non-fiction-fiction, attracted critical attention for the satirical treatment given to the hippie influx in India and its repercussions on both Western and Indian societies, while her two succeeding novels *Raj* (1993)[1] and *A River Sutra* (1993) were specially acclaimed for the novelty of approach with which familiar themes are tackled. The issues raised are recognizable: issues of identity, exile and diaspora, and of history and postcolonial politics, but she manages to give them a pleasant spin with the skillful handling of the narrative technique, keeping these concerns crucial to the text, yet making them interactive participatory exercises. In 1997 Mehta brought out a collection of her essays meaningfully titled *Snakes and Ladders: A View of Modern India*. She observes India in all its colours; and with keen insight and by the flow of her language she is able to make the familiar appear unusual – sometimes glamorous, at others mysterious The book also provides a glimpse of her early years.

Daughter of the well-known freedom fighter Biju Patnaik of Orissa, Gita was born in Delhi in 1943. The family was active in India's freedom struggle and was always on the run, going often times underground because of their political leanings and anti-British activities. At her birth Gita's godmother suggested that the child be named Joan of Arc but somehow it did not work out and she was named Gita, so the author tells us. Gita means song and in that particular year it denoted the 'song of freedom'. It could also be, let us conjecture, that she was named Gita because her parents were fighting for a just cause and Lord Krishna's *Gita* is a treatise on Karma/action. Whatever be the case, Gita probably had something of Joan of Arc intrinsically in her which she gives to her protagonist Jaya in *Raj* – self-assurance and frankness.

Young Gita was growing up in the thick of political activities that always created fluid situations. Her father was often in jail and her mother followed him 'from jail to jail ... smuggling letters into the jail' (*Snakes and Ladders* 1997: 6), and running around offices to get him released. In order to ensure stability for their two children, particularly in their education, the parents decided to send them – Gita and her brother – to a boarding school. Gita received her early education in India; she graduated from Bombay University, and thereafter was sent to Cambridge for a Masters in English Literature. She met her future husband Ajai Mehta while at Cambridge where Ajai, "Sonny" to his friends, was also a student. After their marriage they settled in London and in 1987 shifted to New York where Sonny joined as the Editor-in-chief of the world renowned publishing house Alfred A. Knopf. Because of Mr. Mehta's position in the publishing industry, the family holds a prominent place in New York's literary and publishing circles. In her piece "Making India Accessible" published in *Publisher's Weekly* in 1997, Wendy Smith describes the Mehtas' home thus: 'Gita and Sonny Mehta's apartment is an oasis of tranquility in midtown Manhattan.

Outside on a chilly March day, Park Avenue traffic is at its mid-afternoon worst, and the chatter of kids from a school next door nearly drowns out the honking horns and screeching brakes. Inside, all distracting sounds seem to be absorbed by the crammed floor-to-ceiling bookshelves, custom-built when the couple moved to New York from London in 1987 when Sonny replaced Robert Gottlieb as Knopf editor-in-chief' (Wendy, 1997:53). Gita and Ajai Mehta have a son who lives in London and the family maintains residences in Delhi, New York and London. Despite their otherwise busy schedule, the Mehtas spend at least three months in India. In fact, every winter is a homecoming for them. This time is reserved for family visits and get-togethers. Gita says she does not write during these visits as it is a period reserved for accumulation of experience and assimilation of ideas.

Gita Mehta had been writing journalistic pieces and directing documentaries about India for BBC and ITV before she embarked on her career as a novelist. Writing fiction, she says, is not easy, particularly if you are dealing with facts and composing factual pieces. Non-fiction writing provides a kind of 'safety net' beyond which one does not go; not so in fiction where the imagination is at play. However, the experience in making documentaries gave her freedom to move about, to collect data and to amass information. As a war correspondent with NBC (USA), she got an opportunity to tour Bangladesh and cover the Indo-Pak War 1971. She saw the birth of the nation. She also made a documentary on elections in the erstwhile princely states. This first-hand knowledge widened her horizon further and her own experiences plus her family background moulded her vision of India and gave her keen insight to understand India's problems, her strength and weaknesses.

When she started writing books, fiction and non-fiction both, she did it with the self-confidence of an insider's familiarity. 'Because of this journalistic background, all of her books feature keen political insight founded in thorough investigation. Because of the intelligence and family history that follows Mehta into her writing, her books are smart investigations into the ideas, people, history and personalities that have determined what has shaped modern India and ultimately, who she is as a woman of Indian descent' ("Voices from the Gaps").

Karma Cola was the starting point of Gita Mehta's literary career. It was by chance that she came upon the idea which she later developed as a theme for her book. The incident behind the decision to write something on 'Karma' is interesting. It was 'sparkled by Mehta's annoyance at being seen as an automatic India expert' (Smith, 1997: 53). At a publishers' party an informal discussion was going on about the Karma philosophy when Gita Mehta entered the room. Seeing her in a sari, someone just grabbed her arm and said, 'here's the girl who's going to tell us what karma is all about.' Taking her for granted as an 'India expert' just because she was dressed in a sari irritated her and she retorted, 'karma isn't what it is cracked up to be.' Hearing this piece of conversation, Marc Jaffe of Bantam Books suggested that she should write a book on the theme. The topic was still hot in the 1970s after it had picked up in the 1960 with the Hippies making a beeline for India in search of Nirvana. Writing a book on the concept would be, Gita thought, 'taking the Mickey out of cultish spirituality at a time when people were really scared about it' (Smith, 1997:54). She wrote *Karma Cola* within three weeks and when the book came out it got a warm response. Its sub-title, *Marketing the Mystic East* is self-explanatory. The work is a satire on both the Indian fake mystics and the western naive seekers.

The idea for *A River Sutra* came to her when she was sitting on the bank of a river and thinking of the flow of time like the flow of the river. In this novel she thought of bringing together 'mythological time, historical time, contemporary time, and narrative time – all into say one paragraph' (Wallia, 1997: 3).[2] But when she actually came to writing, Mehta was skeptical about the subject and wondered if it would be palatable to the western readers. She was secretive about it and wrote it privately. But she was surprised to find that this novel in which she blended Indian mythology with contemporary realities was warmly received by the readers. Her next *Raj* took a long time – nine years – because it involved research, travel, interviews and delving into old historical records and also because of difference of opinion with the publisher. Apart from visiting libraries, browsing through dusty documents and watching the footage of Queen Victoria's diamond jubilee celebrations, she interviewed the Rajmatas of Jaipur and Tehri Garwal to understand what it meant to be from the family of rulers, and how it felt to throw off the veil and jump into the political fray. All this went into the depiction of Jaya.

Though Gita Mehta's heart is in India, as she often confides, she is not sentimental about it, nor is she unmindful of the present day realities existing in modern India. With her incisive wit and frank assertions she paints India as it is fifty years after independence in *Snakes and Ladders* with corruption, nepotism, chaos and self-serving politicians, all forming a part of her vignettes. There seems no hope for the country and yet like the game of 'Snakes and Ladders,' things are set right again to slide down once more, vacillating between hope and despair, progress and regress; and within less than 250 pages she paints her India with the strokes of an artist.

Thematically, Gita Mehta's works are varied, dealing with subjects such as experience of ennui, nostalgia, historical/political changes in India and the perennial theme of east-west encounter. India is at the centre of each work and the author takes care not to allow any of the themes to be so overriding as to shift the focus from India. Usually it is alleged that the migrant writers create 'imaginary homelands, Indias of the mind' and that their representation of India and Indianness is hybrid, meant for the western readers. And Gita Mehta is no exception. Her literary and cultural allusions to India's geography, mysticism, religions, history and the existing political situations are substantial and candid but they are at times too romanticized and exoticized to be acceptable to the indigenous readers. Between 'real' India, and India of the 'mind' there is but a thin line. Her works have a living immediacy that creates an authentic, recognizable milieu but when she depicts 'high culture' and traditions of the land as in *A River Sutra*, she slides into pseudo-philosophy, in trying to keep its contemporary relevance intact.

The theme of *Karma Cola* is the inflow of thousands of questing westerners 'clashing cymbals and ringing bells' in search of the mystic India, ready to gulp down her philosophy, appropriate her 'shakti' and delve into her esoteric realms. Places like Haridwar, Banaras, Manali and the beaches of Goa were flooded with these so-called seekers, who seemed gullible enough to imagine that Karma is an all-inclusive panacea for the ills of the world. When a wave like this spreads in a land, it also has its ramifications on the local population. The influx gave rise to dubious ashrams selling hallucinatory drugs and equally dubious gurus bartering their superficial spirituality for material gains. Most of the western 'instant spiritualists' were duped by the opportunists, thus creating an atmosphere of distrust and conflict, tarnishing the image of the country. Not that the west lacks genuine scholars and intellectuals seeking to understand Indian philosophy; nor does India lack really profound scholars and real philosophers who could expound the tenets of Indian thought to the satisfaction of rational seekers. But the trendy seekers who came with the waves of the Beatles, the Rolling Stones and the Hippie movement were here for instant kicks and more often than not ended in clinics.

It is this wave that catches Gita Mehta's attention after Marc Jaffe suggested that she should write a book on the theme. In a series of inter-connected essays she presents her own observations with ironic wit and sarcasm and weaves them with the impressions and experiences of many others. *Karma Cola* is a work of nonfiction but Mehta's terse and brisk prose and her ability to knit various episodes into a whole give the book the flow of a novel. If the author satirizes the western 'cultish' onslaught on Indian culture, she also takes to task the half-baked philosophers and 'gurus' who do more harm to the culture than the spurious seekers.

Raj is a serious work, a historical novel dealing with the turbulent period in Indian history from 1897 to 1947. Starting with 1897, the novel concludes with the end of an epoch when India attained freedom and the princely sates were merged with the Indian Union – some willingly, others unwillingly. The novel maps and dramatizes within its narrative framework the important events with which the century set in – the famine of 1898, the ever-increasing British interference in the affairs of the native rulers, emergence of Gandhi and other national leaders, their clarion call to the nation, the two wars, awakening of the democratic spirit among the masses and finally Independence. Apart from history, the novel presents the story of a woman – Jaya, the princess of Balmer and Maharani of Sirpur – her awareness, her fight and her victory.

In many ways *Raj* can be termed 'just one more novel on the much-explored theme' of the princes and colonial India. It has all the ingredients and stock themes – court intrigues, life in the harems, the tiger hunts, the neglected Ranis and the glamorous mistresses. There are also elaborate descriptions of the exotic life-styles of the Indian princes: eccentric, decadent and extravagant. Despite these, *Raj* is the saga of triumph – the triumph of 'the people', of democratic principles and of a woman who accepts the political change gracefully.

Structurally, the novel is divided in four books: 'Balmer,' 'Sirpur,' 'Maharani,' and 'Regent'. It has a "Prologue" and an "Afterword." The Prologue sets the pace of the story as it opens with little Jaya going hunting with her father Maharajah Jai Singh of Balmer, which in turn shows the training Jaya is going to receive, the affection and regard the public has for their Maharajah and finally the 'fear' which had become a part of the colonized psyche. Maharajah Jai Singh's insightful remarks, 'Rulers are men and men are always frightened. A man cannot govern unless he confronts his own fears' (*Raj*, 1993: 5), resonate the frightened psyche of the Rajas and Maharajahs, worried for their survival. 'Afterword' documents the abolition of the privy-purses, agreed upon at the time of merger. One cannot miss the undercurrent of indictment of 'breach of faith'. What the British could not or did not do, Independence did to the rulers – liquidated their identity.

The novelist has skillfully used her historical material to carve out convincing and real characters in their strength and weaknesses, whims and fancies, and pride and prejudices. Without being involved in their world, Mehta lets them expose themselves by the roles assigned to them rather than letting the rhetoric tilt in favour of one or the other. It is for the reader to judge whether the British were oppressive or the Nationalists were a 'boring lot'; whether the rulers were effeminate, inefficient or ineffective; or the manner in which the British succeeded in their game of giving the rulers a long rope and then strangulating them with the same rope, accusing them of excesses and moral laxity and then using it against them as an excuse to annex their kingdoms.

Jaya, though docile and passive in the beginning emerges as a spirited character, feminine yet brave. Charming and bold, she impresses her husband Pratap by her handling of Esme Moore affair, her ability to outdo the men in the masculine game of Polo, and in fact by creating favourable ripples in London. Maharajah Pratap finally recognizes her abilities and leans on her. Jaya keeps her dignity and though a neglected, or rather a rejected wife, she does not appear pathetic. There are clear indications that Jaya has a soft corner for that 'blue-eyed Angrez boy' – James Osborne, but both Jaya and Osborne keep a dignified distance. However, one can hardly condone Jaya's weakness in responding to Arun Roy's amorous advances. Is it, one would like to ask, for the western reader?

Raj underscores the importance of doing one's 'dharma'. The Maharajah and the Maharani of Balmer are steeped in this lore and they are intent on performing their duties towards their people. The Raj Guru tells a confused Jaya, 'your dharma is protection, Bai-sa. You cannot escape that destiny.' Jaya feels light and happy when she does her duty toward her people and her country – India – by accepting to be a part of the whole. In the end there is, indeed, the beginning – the beginning of a new era when she files her nomination for the election and the dream of a new and united India becomes a reality.

A River Sutra creates many Indias but it is the perennial India that holds the interest of the writer and the reader. The theme of integration of various religions and philosophies with the geography of the river, which symbolizes the culture of oneness, becomes prominent with each story. It explores the problem of identity through the narrator; he is significant to the story though not its hero, because it is Narmada who is the main motivator and the protagonist. The bureaucrat-narrator's desire is simple: he has fulfilled his worldly obligations and wishes to lead a life of 'real' retirement, but as the narrative advances he logically realizes that retirement is not as unproblematic as he construed it to be. All human experience is subject to speculation and question and there is no end to these. Each episode leads him to an awareness of man's limitations and the inscrutable nature of reality that is beyond human comprehension. The novel thus becomes a record of the bureaucrat's awareness that there can be no renunciation without proper involvement. The perennial flow of the river is like the perennial flow of time. The river becomes a symbol of the eternal time and her minstrel becomes her representative. Hers is a song of love, suggestive of the multi-pronged and multifaceted concept of love. Between Shiva (the Cosmic Ascetic) and his Daughter (River Narmada) on one side, and the narrator and his quest on the other, there is the vast tapestry of life – life in its different settings, life with its many meanings. And this trajectory is representative of existence.

The epigraph to the novel is from Chandidas. It reads: 'Listen, O brother./Man is the greatest truth/Nothing beyond.' The full implication of the novel becomes clear when we go back to the epigraph. It is love in its many forms that leads to the love of man. This is conveyed through the six stories – the story of the Jain monk is not so much of his renunciation as of his yearning to understand love, 'I have loved just one thing in life,' says the monk and lets the bureaucrat narrator brood over the myriad possibilities. The story of Master Mohan and his blind pupil is again of love – love between a teacher and his pupil in the ancient *guru-shishya* tradition. Nitin Bose's love is lust and it is damaging until he sublimates it. Sublimating lust to creativity and study, he gets back his mental peace. But no proposition is as simple as it appears to be on its face value, says Gita Mehta. The case in point is the story of the musician's daughter. Sublimation is thrust upon the musician's daughter before she is internally ready to accept it and she feels miserable. Passionate love is depicted in the story of Rahul Singh and the courtesan's daughter. However, love is not a solution for them because their relationship does not have the sanction of the society and the law. Professor Shankar's story of renouncing the world and again getting involved in it and Uma's story – a reversal of her mentor's – of renouncing the world before it engulfs her, are probably self-explanatory. Finally what matters is love for humanity achieved through comprehending love in its broader sense in terms of human love, or may be through love of nature.

Professor Shankar loves Narmada, not because it is holy but because it is immortal. Its immortality is contained in its power to sustain human record – to be the same when Ved Vyas wrote his *Mahabharata* on its banks or Shankaracharya wrote his *Sutra*, or much later Kipling set his *Jungle Book* in its precincts. Professor Shankar and his team excavating the sites on her banks for archaeological study or the ascetics and pilgrims worshipping her, it is all the same to the River. She flows on, the primordial being, a 'sanctuary' to man.

The theme of *Snakes and Ladders* is again India – not the mystic India of *A River Sutra* or the esoteric India of the Nirvana seekers of *Karma Cola* – but India fifty years after her independence. As different aspects of India reveal themselves to her, the author offers us the snapshots of the nation and the emerging national consciousness. Each short essay becomes a reflection and a refraction of society. This is a postcolonial society which unfortunately perpetuates the colonial and pre-colonial values. The author shows dexterously how we still live in contradictions – a rag-picker, unmindful of his utter poverty takes pride in telling the author that he is a Bhat, the community of bards who once held mystic power over kings; he and the likes of him are wondrously unaware of the 'banish poverty' slogans of the government; there are the educated people who buy a new gadget and worship it before it is installed; and then there is a senior bureaucrat who sitting in his office, expresses his exasperation with the Prime Minister of the country, and has the nerve to affirm the democratic principle, "'she doesn't bloody employ me!' he snarled. 'The people of India employ me'" (13). Such paradoxes, the author believes, make India livable and lovable.

The book is divided in four parts and has in all thirty-five chapters – each showing India's march forward towards progress juxtaposed with the traditional attitudes that still persist and make the country a big paradox. We worship trees but lured by the 'bumper profits' we slaughter them mercilessly; we have the vision to appreciate great filmmakers like Satyajit Ray, but we have the impudence to leave them to die pauper; grand ideas like those of Satyajit Ray's get no financer because such themes do not sell;

Indian elections are the greatest show on the earth but the voters are 'faceless, nameless.' The essays cover a long period from the freedom movement to Indira Gandhi's assassination in 1984 and thence to 1997 when we celebrated fifty years as a sovereign democracy. There are lively, sometimes searing, sometimes acerbic comments on the leaders. In some of her interviews and conversations after the book was published, Mehta admits that she slimmed down the volume considerably to make it precise and to give one woman's vision of her country. The essays are insightful and often witty; she has the unique knack to involve the reader with her anecdotal style that makes the pieces personalized. It is clear enough from the style that she wrote with the western reader in mind. She provides a brief year-wise chronology of events at the end of the book obviously for them and also to make India accessible to the new generation Indians who are not aware of the events of the recent past.

The titles of the four books are in a way hybrid and contain, in a capsule form, so to say, the themes we have been discussing all along. *Karma Cola* is an amalgam of Karma, an Indian concept and cola a western drink. Cola is a sweet fizzy drink that does not contain alcohol but is all the same addictive. Also, the usage quoted in Cambridge International Dictionary, 'All colas taste pretty much the same to me' (Cambridge, 256), is a pointer towards its blandness. *Karma Cola* indicates not only the urge of the phony seekers to understand Karma but also their bland and jaded approach. Karma is a deep philosophy and can be interpreted with myriads of tenets. The very idea that it could be comprehended with hallucinatory drugs is in itself not only ridiculous but also preposterous. From another angle, we could also link the title to the contemporary consumer-oriented philosophy. The questers probably think that Karma could be gulped down like Cola.

Raj is a Hindi word for rule. Accepted in English now, it denotes the period of the British rule in India. In the novel it stand also for the rule/raj of the native rulers. Conversely, it could be construed as an abbreviation of *Rajniti,* which had become defunct in Imperial India. With the Imperial rule exerting pressure on the Rajas and the native rulers dissipating their energies and wealth in self-indulgence there was no 'dharma' and no 'Rajniti'. Jaya is caught between the skewed British rule and the weak Indian rulers. She uses *Rajniti* as a survival strategy but when the two Raj – British and native – end, it is the third one that deprives the erstwhile rulers of their rights and nullify their sacrifices.

Again, *A River Sutra* is a combination of two words – River and Sutra. Sutra in Sanskrit is a form of verse and Shankaracharya's *Narmada Sutra* is a profound tribute to the river, the daughter of Shiva. Human beings must inculcate all those characteristics that Narmada has. She is bliss itself, she is the remover of sins, she can ward off the effects of snake poison and she is the immortal river because on its banks life converges. The bureaucrat narrator is naïve enough to think that escaping into the retreat of the Narmada valley will automatically bring in the fruits of a retired life of renunciation. But just as the river flows miles and miles from its source to its end where it joins the sea, human beings too have to go through life till the final merger. Another interpretation can be that *Sutra* also means thread. Here the river is so prominent that in fact it is the real *sutradhar* of the narrative. One more point may be of interest – the western readers are well aware of the *Kama Sutra* and possibly by using the word 'Sutra' Gita Mehta wanted an Indian tag to attract attention to her work. This idea struck me when I read C.J.S. Wallia's interview in which he begins his interview in conversational tone thus: 'Let me begin with Kama Sutra. Sorry. I was editing an article on Mira Nair's new film, Kama Sutra, just before I came here. I meant to say River Sutra – your novel' (Wallia, 1997: 2).

Coming to *Snakes and Ladders*, the title though in English, has an indigenous allusion. Gita Mehta deliberately chose this title to denote the paradoxes of Indian life. To quote her, 'The traditional Indian game of Snakes and Ladders is played by rolling dice to determine how many squares a player can move his marker up a board starting at square one and finishing at square one hundred. Because of its unpredictability it was one of our favourite games when we were children' (vii). What makes the game interesting is that it has an element of chance, it is suggestive of danger and it means going up and then sliding down to the jeers of the opponents. We, in our fifty years of nationhood (the book was written in 1997) have seen 'a roller coaster ride, the highs so sudden we have become light-headed with exhilaration, the lows too deep to even contemplate solution, as if the game of Snakes and Ladders was invented to illustrate our attempts to move an ancient land towards modern enlightenment without jettisoning from our past that which is valuable or unique' (vii-viii). The epigraph to the novel is from Goethe who had an urge to make a journey to India to see the land in his own way. That the land is unique in itself is again vouchsafed by Mark Twain's words about India to which the book is dedicated, 'To "the sole country under the sun that is endowed with imperishable interest for alien prince and alien peasant, for lettered and ignorant, wise and fool, rich and poor, bond and free, the one land all men desire to see, and having seen once, by even a glimpse, would not give that glimpse for shows of all the rest of the globe combined". Mark Twain 1897.'

Gita Mehta's style and narrative technique is commensurate with the thematic structure of her works. *Karma Cola* has the flippancy of the nomadic life of the seekers. The language has the quality of the 'clash of cymbals and the ringing bells' about it. The mood of the questers – nauseated and frustrated – reflects in their phraseology and disregard for propriety. Use of words like 'mindfucking', 'shit', and many more show their level of breeding. The speed of the jet travel is also evident in the use of terse language, quick sentences and interesting coinages like 'monomania of the west' and 'multimania of the east'. Nothing seems to have escaped the author's keen observation.

In *Raj* the shift of language from the facetious to the serious and upright is noteworthy. When the English-educated young princes like Tikka and Partap speak, their language has the tang of British education. 'Bappa is *foolish* not to send me with them to calm their fears' (114) (emphasis added); Tikka utters these words angrily when his father refuses to send him with the Balmer Lancers to fight on the French front. One can understand the enthusiasm of youth but one cannot excuse the use of derogatory remarks for one's father. There is a quick change over to the proper language and phrases when the Maharajah of Balmer speaks. For example, annoyed at the proposal for Jaya from Sirpur he speaks with authority:

> 'Why is the child being shown that picture? An alliance between Sirpur and Balmer is unthinkable. The Sirpurs are the lapdogs of the British Empire. The ruler is Victoria's godson. He even flaunts her name. Maharajah Victor he calls himself.' Jai Singh's eyes blazed with anger. 'Isn't it enough that the British Raj threatens me with the consequences if I do not send Tikka to England? Must I lose my daughter to an Angrez lackey also?'. (77)

Descriptions of the Balmer household, the zenana and the traditional rituals have an indigenous touch typified by the use of Hindi words. Thus there is the 'solah shringar' training given to Jaya; the reference to 'manwar' ceremony and the ballad of Queen Pushpawati with its typical local colours. The descriptions of the topography both of Balmer and of Sirpur are graphic. I will however, restrict the quotes to only two. About drought-ridden Balmer the author writes:

> Scrub jungle gave way to sand dunes. At sunset, the sudden darkness brought a feverish chill to the empty landscape. The travelers willed their emaciated animals to reach the shelter of villages spaced farther and farther apart before the demon women who had died in childbirth came howling through the night in search of children to replace the stillborn infants they had never sucked. (10)

She describes the wet and green jungle of the Brahmaputra Valley in the Sirpur territory thus:

> As the procession approached the Himalayas, the foliage gained a sinister brightness. The Brahmaputra River, closer to its source in the melting ice lakes of Tibet, flowed with transparent fury down perpendicular waterfalls, and the tribals themselves, with their feathered headdresses and animal-skin loincloths, seemed possessed of a mystic connection with nature absent in the soft creatures who lived on the fertile rice plains around the capital. (285)

The narrative technique of *A River Sutra* follows the 'framed narrative' style which is traditional. The descriptions are rich and though the flow remains steady like the flow of Narmada, the expressions vary with the requirement of the story. Thus, the Jain monk's description of his renunciation ceremony has the glitter of money and the sparkle of diamonds but is exotic and sickening. The stories of Master Mohan and the Musician's daughter have a touch of pathos and the depictions are rhythmic. In the former, however, the presence of the sinister in the dark room where Imrat gives his first and last performance puncture the purity of little Imrat's musical voice. Similarly, the opening sentence of "The Story of the Musician's Daughter", 'It is hard to be the child of genius' (201), appears foreboding. All through the novel, there are a number of descriptive passages that read like Wordworthian diction with too palpable an effect of the English Romantics. This is probably because the author is consciously trying to create a romantic India that is remarkable and uncanny.

Coming to *Snakes and Ladders*, the style and the diction has the brisk movement of the player throwing the dice, climbing up the ladder or sliding down the snake. Let us consider a few sentences: if 'the Indian home has an aesthetic it is chaos, enabling it to accommodate regional influences' (173) and 'perhaps it is because the Indian looks on his home more as a place to live than a work of art. The art, if there is one in India, is supposed to lie in the living' (175). Again in the chapter "Food for Thought" she remarks, 'The Green Revolution had changed India for ever. ... Yet millions of Indian were still hungry, millions of dispossessed villagers were still migrating to the cities' (61). Each chapter starts with an idea that becomes episodic as a number of other ideas or incidents are narrated to develop the basic theme but by the end there is a sudden reversal which is almost like sting-in-the tale ending.

Gita Mehta seems to be in search for a space for herself as a writer, covertly because of her immigrant status but overtly because of her husband's position as the top official in the internationally acclaimed publishing house like Alfred A. Knopf. In her interview with Wendy Smith, Mehta confides that being the wife of a big publisher breeds insecurities, 'imagine: you're working on a book, and Gabriel Garcia Marquez comes for a drink – you think, 'Does the world really need me?' And these nightmare sales for other writers; I hear Sonny say, 'Well, we've sold 1.2 million copies of something and I think, 'Oh my God!' That's why, when I'm really into a book, I go to London; I can't be an appendage to Sonny's work when I'm writing' (Wendy, 1997: 3). She works independently, no doubt, but her books are infused as much by the thought of India as by the Indian Thought, and are interpreted as exemplifying Indian diaspora. A point to note, however, is that neither during her interviews nor in her works does she express the diasporic apprehension of rootlessness, or longing for stability and continuity. All she does is to present India playfully and this has been often criticized as ambivalence and 'imaginatively created India' (Maria, 2001: 2).

The questions that are often raised in hermeneutics these days are, 'Should we interpret literary texts?' and 'Why interpret a text'? Another allied query is how much of the text does a critic take possession of in appropriating meaning to it. It is felt that interpretation and re-interpretations are helpful for communicative reasons as they are instrumental in a reader's quest for new meanings which make him/her aware of the shared meaning of a shared past. Discussing the issue of interpretation Baral points out that since a literary text is an assemblage of various strands it can be understood with the help of 'alternative/plural interpretations of the text in the context of distinct codes, language varieties, cultural plurality, multiplicity of values, and specific ethnic identities, while challenging the dominant ideological and cultural hegemonies' [Baral (b), 2002:12]. According to Hiren Gohain interpretation is a necessary evil because texts have an impact on our lives and they are our heritage of a rich and vibrant human community life. 'Let us approach texts then as historical agents, drawing on tradition, changing it, and changing us in the process, cherishing but not necessarily idolizing them' (Gohain, 2002: 27). As for appropriation, it should not take possession of the text to produce a new text but should follow the principle that appropriation is also 'primarily a letting go'.[3] What we appropriate in and from a text is not the creation or property of another subject, but as Robert Ricoeur observes, 'the projection of a world, the proposal of a mode of being-in-the-world' (Ricoeur quoted in Gohain, 2002: 26). It is a synthesis of the mental perspective of the reader applied to the possibilities intrinsic to the text. Thus, the function of interpretation should be to reveal not fulfill. Ricoeur further points out that possession is a form of taking hold of and hence narcissistic, and as such when appropriation ceases to be a kind of possession, it entails a 'moment of dispossession of the narcissistic ego' implied in possession.[4]

Since a work of literature escapes the meaning its author had intended it to convey, it can be explored as an emerging force having new ideas and insights into contemporary situations. The current pedagogical debate is examining the possibilities for making the study of literature 'socially relevant and culturally significant.' In his introduction to *Humanities and Pedagogy*, Baral points out that as modern culture 'moves from crisis to crisis, the discipline of the humanities becomes important for us notwithstanding the contestations of the fundamental insights they drive home to help us in understanding better the terrible and fascinating enigma of life' [Baral (a), 2002: 14–15]. The strength of a culture, therefore, can be determined from its pedagogic traditions. The cultural process signifies a creative quest for the truth of life; and implicit in interpretation of texts is the proposition to keep the culture vibrant. In order to interpret and understand Gita Mehta's writings, one has to interrogate her texts from the context of her position as a diasporic writer. Does she create a dynamic tradition? Is she able to define her cultural identity vis-à-vis her culture? These are some of the questions that need be addressed.

Gita Mehta's attempt to come back to the cultural folds, to understand the intricacies of her shared past with her community and to transmit part of her vision to the people in her 'second home' has been studied in the following chapters. Home, Dorinne Kondo affirms 'stands for a safe place, where there is no need to explain oneself to outsiders; it stands for community' (Kondo, 1996: 97). That Gita Mehta should feel the need to explicate and explain herself to the west is in itself an acknowledgement of cultural difference felt by a diasporic consciousness. This cultural difference that has become the site of production is regulated by the desire to move in and out of the oppositional cultures, to mythologize the ancient past and to recover and affirm an authentic culture of a lost home; this position is intrinsic to the diasporic condition and also to the postcolonial situation. An argument can be made that Gita Mehta's works foreground the diasporic consciousness with memory and experience affording grounds for constructing agency and registering resistance to the logic of 'othering' by positionality. Re-visioning and mapping this 'identity politics' into a national-cultural space imply a sense of belonging and connectedness. This connectedness is strengthened because of Gita and Sonny Mehta's yearly visits to India when they relax, interact with friends and relatives and imbibe the changed/changing ethos. Gita Mehta's vision of India is not remote as is Jhumpa Lahiri's who admits that hers is a 'tunnel vision'. Not so with Gita Mehta. This provides us the starting point to understand Mehta's work vis-à-vis the ambivalence of a diasporic consciousness in a postcolonial situation and the patterns of affliction in diaspora. By blending the subjective experience with observation and imagination, Gita Mehta creates her narratives out of disparate and heterogeneous material. Diaspora is a reality mediated upon by multiple factors. How these work in the postcolonial/postmodern/diasporic situation will be the focus of the next chapter.

Notes

1. *Raj* was published by Jonathan Cape, London in 1989 and by Penguin, New Delhi in 1993. The edition used here is of 1993. All references are to this edition.
2. On 16 May 1997 C.J.S Wallia interviewed Mehta, which was published in *Indiastar Review of Books*. This is an elaborate conversation in which Gita Mehta talks of her works, the episodes behind some of them, and particularly about her latest book *Snakes and Ladders*. The interviewer's note says: 'This interview took place on 16 May 1997, just before her public reading from *Snakes and Ladders* at the Black Oak Bookstore, in Berkeley, California. In the interview, she came across as a very self-assured, articulate, and charming person. Elegantly sari-clad and wearing a bindi, she spoke with a distinctly Oxbridge accent, developed,

no doubt, during her convent schooling in India and her Cambridge years. Yet, at the end of her reading, which was very well received by the large, admiring audience, she chose to speak to me in classic Hindi.' See http://www.indiastar.com/wallia4.htm.

3 Gohain refers to Robert Ricoeur's essay, "Hermeneutics and the Human Sciences" (1981). He points out that Ricoeur warns us against subjectvising interpretation stating, 'Relinquishment is a fundamental moment of appropriation and distinguishes it from any form of 'taking possession'. Appropriation is also and primarily a letting go.' See Hiren Gohain "On Interpretation: A Necessary Evil" in K.C. Baral ed. *Interpretation of Texts* (New Delhi: Pencraft International, 2002: 15–27).

4. How interpretation leads the further discussion and makes ground for a 'community' of readers has been explained by Hiren Gohain in the paper referred to above. He posits, 'But a literary text is never ever a purely private possession. We not only read, we want to discuss texts, and in discussing we seek common grounds even to disagree. We don't try to talk past one another. It is this sense of community, however difficult or complicated that community can be in today's situation that is lost in the prevailing paradigm. Even Leavis thought that the critic was a reader who could address other readers with the question, That is so, isn't it?'... anticipating the response, 'Yes, but ... .' (24).

Works Cited

Baral, K.C., ed. (a) *Humanities and Pedagogy*. New Delhi: Pencraft International, 2002.

Baral, K.C., ed. (b) *Interpretation of Texts: Text, Meaning and Interpretation*. New Delhi: Pencraft International, 2002.

Gohain, Hiren. "On Interpretation: A Necessary Evil," *Interpretation of Text*. Ed. K.C. Baral. New Delhi: Pencraft International, 2002.

Kondo, Dorinne. "The Narrative Production of 'Home,' Community, and Political Identity in Asian American Theatre." *Displacement, Diaspora, and the Geographies of Identity*. Eds. Smadar Lavie and Ted Swedenburg. Durham: Duke University Press, 1996. pp. 97–118.

Maria, John. "Bookshelf: *Snakes and Ladders* – Gita Mehta." Internet Book Review. See http://www.indiatravelogue.com/book/book1.html.

Mehta, Gita. *A River Sutra*. New Delhi: Penguin, 1993.

—. *Karma Cola*. New Delhi: Penguin, 1993.

—. *Raj*. London: Jonathan Cape, 1989. New Delhi Penguin, 1993

—. *Snakes and Ladders*. London: Random House, 1997.

(All references cited in the text are from these editions and hereafter only page numbers are given in parenthesis throughout the study).

Smith, Wendy. "Gita Mehta: Making India Accessible." *Publisher's Weekly*. May 12, 1997, 53–54.

"Voices from the Gaps." http://voices.cla.umn.edu/authors/ gitamehta.html

Wallia, C.J.S. "*Indiastar* Interview." http://www.indiastar.com/ wallia4.htm

Two

Locating the Diasporic Discourse in Postcolonial/Postmodern Contexts

> It isn't where you're from; it is where you're at.
>
> — Paul Gilroy

> Where does one culture begin and another end when they are housed in the same person?
>
> — Nayantara Sahgal

Opening his discussion on postcolonialism Robert J.C. Young asks: 'Have you ever been the only person of your own colour or ethnicity in a large group or gathering?' and goes on to add 'Do you feel that your own people and country are somehow always positioned outside the mainstream?' These simple questions are powerful pointers towards the psychodynamics of marginality; of a person who never qualifies as the norm, a person who is not authorized to speak but is always spoken for, a person living in a world that belongs to others, that exists for others (Young, 2002: 1). This politics of exclusion by which the dominant voices ensure the 'inside yet outside' position for those who cannot identify with the mainstream culture, applies as much to the postcolonial subject as to the diaspora. Young approaches the issues of gender, ecology, social justice, knowledge and power structure through postcolonial perspective and asserts that though postcolonial theory is not 'a theory in the scientific sense' (6), it gives a set of perspectives about 'the relations between ideas and practices: relations of harmony, relations of conflict, generative relations between different peoples and their cultures. Postcolonialism is about a changing world ...' (7); this changing world is brought about by migration, multinationalism and globalization that have become the defining paradigm for diasporas. Admittedly, the twentieth century diasporas is voluntary and contemporary diasporic writing is the product of a shared culture and shared history, which by implication creates a postcolonial self that questions privilege and power and refuses to acknowledge the superiority of western culture.[1]

For example, Jasbir Jain avers that the postcolonial critics like Spivak, Bhabha and others use western framework to Indian realities with the result that the voices articulating Indian reality are relegated to sideline and they remain either marginal or invisible. Focusing on diasporic writing she laments the tendency to seek patronage of the western audience, which she contends can lead to the 'ossification of cultural contents' (Jain, 2000: 33).[2]

Central to the postcolonial writing is the longing to reclaim an identity and a narrative voice to counter centuries of denial and misrepresentation; central to much of diasporic writing is the longing to retrieve a 'home', albeit symbolically. Both are marked by psychological and ethical dynamics of the notion of nostalgia and reclamation of identity. Nostalgia is not to be understood here as 'home sickness' or 'longing for the past.' It is as Svetlana Boym avers, not always 'about the past; it can be retrospective and protective' (Boym, 2001: xvi), whereby it acquires the characteristic of a futurized past. It is an accommodation with change; a liminal experience on the threshold where the past meets the present. The past is recreated and restored to an imagined pre-colonial or pre-migration time; it is re-interpreted and then it is re-lived elsewhere. It freezes time, fixing a past as we should like it to have been and simultaneously it gives us satisfaction that there still exists a hinterland of 'lost time' where we may seek refuge. Thus, nostalgia leads to the acceptance of change and becomes an abstraction for a 'home,' touched-up, frozen in time, disavowed and yet sentimentally re-configured. The sense of loss and the pain of broken links remain but while one part of the diasporic consciousness looks back, the other constantly anticipates re-plantation in the new culture for survival needs. Together they – the past, the present, and the futurized past – draw on the postcolonial's history, language, culture, and identity.

Critics and theorists, particularly Indian, have serious questions regarding the postcolonial and diasporic representation of home and culture, ethnicity and identity. Mere re-articulation of the past either constructs a utopian version of the homeland or projects a static picture of the society disregarding the changes brought in by forces like globalization and multiculturalism. This is equivalent to replaying the colonial game of viewing the east as romantic: an unfathomable land of myth and mystery, inhabited at best by 'noble savages'. Likewise, if we consider the trend of 'India bashing' we realize that it tantamount to looking at the west for approval, and the writing becomes, what Makarand Paranjape calls 'elegiac' in tone, that does not 'celebrate the homeland but mourns its relentless and innumerable atrocities and tragedies' (Paranjape, 2001: 167).[3] There is no denying the fact that diasporic writing is marked by the yearning for homeland but one cannot overlook either that the diaspora has to strike a balance between his/her survival needs within the diasporic space and his/her psychological need to belong. A subtle inter-relationship exists between the diasporic subject, the homeland and the host country. Yasmin Gooneratne's observation made in the postcolonial context that '(T)he true strength of Indian writing is perceived when writers confront their inheritance boldly and accept its complexity' (Gooneratne, 1980: 36), can be applied to diasporic writing also.

In the area of literary and cultural studies, postcolonialism remains perhaps the most strongly debated term. It could be because it lacks fixed ideological formation or a coherent critical perspective; it can neither be rejected nor accepted. Used as an umbrella term that covers a long and complex history, it gives rise to multifaceted sets of critical debates that further generate debate within the area of 'postcolonial' critical theory, evading the possibility of any specific definition of the term. In several of her essays, Jasbir Jain looks at postcolonialism and postcoloniality from various angles that give the postcolonial discourse a wider perspective. Agreeing that the origin and meaning of the word postcolonial is 'vague,' Jain posits that the concept is deeply rooted in history and cannot be wished away. It has 'provoked a range of definitions and theories ... analysis and critiques,' and has also 'evoked anger and resentment,' but it has opened up spaces for new modalities of expression (Jain, 2000: 12–13). Recent postcolonial discourse has also provided the background for the philosophy of activism that recognizes the dynamic of power of indigenous cultures. Texts born out of the historical reality of domination and enslavement, of migrancy and multiculturalism force 'upon one the reality that geographical and cultural locations matter, that history and memory are important for any formulation of postcolonial theory' (Jain, 2000: 25).

The diasporic theory also addresses the questions of recall, homeland, ancient past, the urge to return and the impossibility of return. In *The Empire Writes Back*, Bill Ashcroft et al. argue that one of the key themes in postcolonial literature 'is the concern with place and displacement'. Dislocation could be due to migration and the resultant sense of loss which is specific to diasporic experience. This explains the diaspora's longing for 'home', the push and pull of their 'in-between' situation, and the creative writer's endeavour to 'create' a notion of home. 'Home' may be an illusory place, a fictional construct built through the myths and fragments of the migrant's imagination, but it is suggestive of the preoccupation of those who have migrated to the modern metropolitan centres from the erstwhile colonies. This also gives the writers sufficient reasons to resist the ambivalence of his/her situation.

Resistance always implies the existence of power and since the notion of power is inherent in the colonial situation, the postcolonial readings of the text often concentrate on the discourse of 'resistance' and 'subversion'. Even the common pattern of postcolonial vocabulary relies on terms like the 'centre' and the 'periphery', the 'dominant' and the 'silenced', 'colonizer-colonized', 'other-self' and the 'hegemony-hybrid'. Interrogating postcolonial theory and the concept of postcolonial literature Arun Mukherjee finds the use of such terms arbitrary; with no rationale in using these and the theory without really investigating the actual ground realities of the so-called postcolonial countries. 'Whatever the motivations of postcolonial critics for constructing this theory, its material effect is the normalization of the unequal curricular space provided to the literature subsumed under the phrase "postcolonial literature"' (Mukherjee, 2000: 15). Mukherjee also counters some of the assumptions of postcolonial theory as problematic.[4] Satendra Nandan, quoting Ashis Nandy, avers that postcolonialism and colonialism are states of consciousness and the experience is imagined and energized through all colonizing narratives. 'My point is that post-colonialism, not unlike colonialism is a state of consciousness, a crucial stage in the continuum of our cultural process and self-awareness .... The belief was that violence and cultural dislocation – that is cultural imperialism – would create a new social consciousness. Instead we got caught in the "hinges of history"' (Nandan, 2000: 50). The important issue particularly for Indian readers of Indian literary texts is to explore the internal colonialism of the traditional order, and the social reality in the context of 'struggles against fundamentalism, casteism and patriarchy'. But this cannot be undertaken within the present postcolonial theory as it has a rigid framework and a critic spends his/her energy in working out how to decode the 'subtle ironies and parodies directed against the departed colonizer' (Mukherjee, 2000: 20).

Such culturally specific issues and the historical truths behind them are ideologically conditioned. It was the progression of many postcolonial writers from modernism to postmodernism, that endorsed the notions of questioning all 'givens': traditions, history and the staid cultural constructs. The writers' search for legends, folklore and folktales which had started with modernism came to be recognized as 'difference' when incorporated into their texts. Postmodernism is a new stage in human history and it looks for new forms of expression. Drawing a line between modernism and postmodernism W. Lawrence Hogue explains that modernism and postmodernism are not essentially different but in literary modernism the writer tends to reject history and looks at high art and mass culture as two antagonistic notions. 'A writer imbued with the modernist spirit will be predisposed toward experiment, if only because he or she needs to make visibly dramatic his or her break from tradition ... wants emancipation from all traditional social roles and traditional modes of servitude because they keep the self stifled and imprisoned ... aspires to save the dignity and autonomy of art and life from the culture of everyday life, from the vulgarities and contaminations of mass culture and from the constraints of traditional culture, which denies individuality' (Hogue, 1996: 75).

Postmodernism closes the gap between mass culture and high culture and makes efforts to show how historical truths are socially and ideologically conditioned. Postmodern literature then is that which consciously exposes 'those narrative strategies, or the process, which would lead to totality, that would advocate an essence, a metaphysics, or a meta-narrative .... The postmodern subject is free from all metaphysical narratives .... The trickster, who exists as a marginal figure ... in histories and cultures is a postmodern subject, with his multiple identities existing without a conflict' (Hogue, 1996:152). On the same analogy let us consider Rahul Singh, the dacoit in Gita Mehta's *A River Sutra* who is given human dimension in the story, thus deconstructing the given ideologies of the traditional society. This is termed de-doxification in which the writing and re-writing of the received mythologies, traditions and culture takes place.

Between postcolonialism and postmodernism where do we place diaspora? Postcolonialism is a politico-cultural concept, while postmodernism is a socio-cultural phenomenon. Postcolonialism is a critical theory; postmodernism is an alternative discourse. It does not explain, it questions; it does not displace, it re-visions. As Linda Hutcheon posits, postmodernism is 'a current cultural phenomenon that exists, has attracted much public debate, and so deserves critical attention' (Hutcheon, 1988: ix). In diasporic consciousness, concepts like the 'centre' and the 'other', 'hybridity' and 'homogeneity', 'displacement' and 'rootedness' are valorized. These terms underscore the significance of location and geography in the creation of the self. In the diasporic discourse, there is constant search for roots through re-vision and re-writing as in the postmodern discourse. There is also a blurring of genre and a foregrounding of inter-textuality. Generally, the diasporic experience is one of migration and migration entails transformation of identity – though it is generally agreed that the present day diaspora is different from the earlier one. As Satendra Nandan points out: in the Indian consciousness, diaspora is 'essentially and vitally one of cultural imagination' (Nandan, 2000: 54); it is not linked to reasons like religious persecution or political or economic or military considerations. The sense of displacement and the range of 'othering' experience changes with time. Lavie and Swedenburg maintain that displacement may be an essential condition of diaspora, but it is not experienced precisely with the same intensity by all; it differs according to time and place, and 'it does not unfold in a uniform fashion. ... There is a range of positionings of Others in relation to the forces of domination and vis-à-vis Others' (Lavie and Swedenburg, 1996: 4). The pattern of responses is generally different but it is possible to detect the point of intersection in the categories of space and time.

Reading resistance to the host culture in contemporary diasporic writing is both problematic and complex: problematic because of the conceptual parameters of the diasporic space, and complex, because the epistemological-psychological nexus tends to reconfigure that space. The assimilative stance that provides the major terms within which most writers of the new diaspora – both male and female – explore the questions of identity, subjectivity and diasporic experience, seems predictably to negotiate the vital questions of exclusivism, location-dislocation, and centre-periphery in favour of the predictable cultural politics of 'exoticism' and acceptance. Since resistance is never an organized action in the diasporic narratives, the individual experiences that go in to record individual acts of resistance can often be construed as part of the person's/narrator's survival strategy and may go unnoticed. Literature, as Rushdie puts it is 'self validating' (Rushdie, 1991: 14) and it gives a convincing platform to writers to highlight and justify their reasons for leaving their homeland. Their reason may be valid or may provide an aesthetic solution but the diaspora mythology of 'home,' culture and return, remains in the consciousness finding expression in the diasporic narratives an imaginative possibility precisely because the dual sense of belonging or half-belonging involves a 'form of accountability to more than one location' (Radhakrishnan, 1996: xiv). As literature mediates between the real and the imaginary, literary texts remain crucial to the formation of diasporic discourse to dis-cover the sites of resistance within the writing.

'Diaspora,' with its inherent sense of dispossession, nostalgia and fluid boundaries, has never been so debated a term as it is in the present postcolonial, postmodern context. If on the one hand, it suggests a kind of discontinuity, a space between two places, it also signifies, on the other, the powerful but unconscious impulse to resist the situation and the equally potent, conscious choice to reconcile, albeit to accept the hyphenated identity. However, in the diasporic experience neither the acceptance of the hyphenated existence nor the disengagement from 'home' with a decision to move forward without looking back is as simple as theorization; it has acute psychological dynamics and endless ethical possibilities. History, memory, melancholia and nostalgia play a significant role in creating a variegated picture. The pain of the loss of the Arcadia – home – impinges upon the memory and produces melancholia; memory brings back the subjective truth whereas history underscores objective reality; and nostalgia working within the framework of the past and the future creates a vision of perfection, endowing the past with a beauty that may not have been there. The cultural vision of perfection bestowed on the past can be re-lived in an imaginary future, but it is not possible to accept it in the present. A paradoxical situation is generated which the diaspora struggles to come to terms with. Therefore, a great deal of critical interest as well as skepticism surrounds the discourse of diaspora and its representation in literature along with its associated formulations such as dislocation and relocation, complicity and resistance, the affirmation of cultural identity and acquiescence to the new transplanted one. Some cultural studies critics have identified three different stages by which a migrant/hyphenated writer passes before he/she achieves the stage of being recognized as de-hyphenated presence.[5]

Diaspora has, in fact, become an inclusive yet extensive new paradigm for the 'exile,' the 'immigrant' and the 'expatriate.' For example, Khaching Tololyan defines diaspora as transnation in character and includes the terms immigrant, expatriate, refugees, guest-workers, exile community, overseas community and ethnic community within the 'semantic domain' of diaspora (Toloyan, 1991: 4–5). Another scholar, Willian Safran (1991), uses the term diaspora for the population who satisfy precise criteria like dispersal from an original centre to two or more peripheral regions and retain a collective memory of the homeland.[6] The concept raises several significant questions in terms of its applicability to the present day reality. Though it still retains its original Greek meaning – 'to scatter' and 'to sow'; and though the basic pattern of location and dislocation inherent in the meaning – dispersal and settlement – remains crucial to it, the contemporary emergence of 'transnationalism' suggests a broadening of its scope. Transnationalism signifies the fostering of social, political and economic relationships among migrants that span several societies. In this sense, the professionals, educationists, scientists and information technologists migrating voluntarily to seek better material prospects, seem to have gained visibility and a coherent identity, even though hybrid. There can be no equation between their condition and the historical-economic determinants of enforced migration of indentures labour during colonialism. While the former are privileged and aware of their status, the latter were engendered by powerlessness, discrimination and deprivation; the former are mobile and often have means to visit and revisit their homeland, the latter lived both physically and psychologically frozen lives with scant or no hope of return. How far is it contiguous then to valorize and romanticize the new Diasporas and their literature? This question is often debated in critical circles.

Taking his cue from Rohinton Mistry's fiction, Makarand Paranjape opines that the new diaspora of Indian English writers, far from being nostalgic for 'home' engages in a kind of its critique. Most writers 'end up demonstrating a self-legitimating logic of leaving the homeland behind and, therefore, at least indirectly, embracing the new diasporic home' (Paranjape, 2001: 167). Harish

Trivedi, too questions the efficacy of using the word 'diasporic' for the Indian postcolonial writers who migrated voluntarily and made a conscious cultural choice. It is misleading, Trivedi asserts forcefully, 'to speak, as is often done, of their chosen location in the coercive and oppressive terms of exile or diaspora, when what actually happened was that these writers voted with their feet – to say nothing of their heart and soul – for the many cultural and material attractions of the West' (Trivedi, 1997: 49). Indeed, many critics like Trivedi, Makarand Paranjape, Jasbir Jain, Meenakshi Mukherjee, Arun Mukherjee and others attest to the fact that the Indian writer is better off than any of the Asian and African writers who suffered forced histories of exile and dislocation. However, these critics also agree that the existence of the diasporic *angst*, and the fear of what Bhabha (1994) calls the 'unhomely moment' cannot be overlooked.[7] Moments of anxiety, along with other tensions, reconfigure the critical geographies and help a reader to define the specific representation of diasporic histories of the authors and their works.

The reading of diaspora often reveals the author's subversive agenda as the narratives both reflect and create ways of seeing and modes of articulation that reinforce dispossession and dislocation and the dichotomy of living astride two cultures. As Salman Rushdie points out:

> It may be that writers in my position, exile or emigrants or expatriate, are haunted by some sense of loss, some urge to reclaim, to look back, even at the risk of being mutated into pillars of salt. But if we do look back, we must also do so in the knowledge – which gives rise to profound uncertainties – that our physical alienation from India almost inevitably means that we will not be capable of reclaiming precisely the thing that was lost; that we will, in short, create fictions, not actual cities or villages, but invisible ones, imaginary homelands, Indias of the mind (Rushdie, 1991: 10).

Literary texts do not simply identify, highlight or redefine the gaps and fissures, the difference and the divergence, the exclusion and the excluding nature of the diaspora, they also militate against the reductive logic of the 'in here', 'out there'[8] labels and the 'otherizing' effect of the diasporic situation. Though the phenomena of expatriation is an almost irreversible state, a condition of 'no return,' both emotionally and psychologically, the expatriate writers try constantly to arrive at some 'self-definition' (Vijayasree, 1996: 225) by maintaining a kind of relationship with the homeland and drawing their creative energy from the original source. Thus an expatriate writer is simply and briefly 'someone who inhabits one place and remembers or projects the reality of another' (Nandan, 1996: 55). In the case of women writers, the diaspora involves double dispossession and despair born out of their exile as well as gendered experience.

Theoretically, women experience diaspora under three conditions – first, when they grow up in a foreign land with their migrant parents; second, by virtue of their marriage when they are uprooted from their parental home and then from their homeland; and third, when they exercise their conscious choice to go to some western metropolitan centre in pursuance of their ambition – higher education or some lucrative job. Whatever the broad categorization, in real life experience they are caught between all the psychological problems of the diaspora, such as dislocation, unbelonging, marginalization, and cultural dissonance that are common also to men, plus a variety of oppressive conditions and discriminatory practices peculiar to gender both inside and outside the community. Add to this the socio-cultural conditioning of both men and women. While men still expect their women folks to remain within the culturally ingrained parameters as some of the characters do in Jhumpa Lahiri's stories, the women are rived by the urge to break free and the psychological constraints that prefigure any such move. The conflict generated by such situations of double bind is traced by many writers. One fine example is Bharati Mukherjee's Dimple in *Wife*. Ravinder Randhawa sums up the diasporic experience in terms of a 'net' wherein one may be trapped.[9] One can imagine the suffocating sense of exclusion when the erstwhile home, where there was familiarity, affection and a sort of commitment becomes an 'imaginative space' and loses its 'hominess'; on the other hand the 'new' home, howsoever comfortable materialistically, never feels like 'home'. The entire situation is like an imprisonment from whence the individual seeks liberation. But this remains at best a fantasy. A writer must negotiate between the essentializing nationalism, the constricting spaces of patriarchal power politics and the cultural ghettoization of the diaspora to evolve appropriate fictional strategy to carve out potent discursive spaces for the articulation of resistance. Since women's texts resist the situation of double-bind, it would be interesting to examine how they offer resistance without antagonizing the host-culture and home-culture, how they adapt their lived reality to their creative experience to arrive at an aesthetic solution.

Gita Mehta's works – two novels, *Raj* (1989, 1993) and *A River Sutra*(1993);one non-fiction-fiction *Karma Cola* (1979); and one collection of short prose pieces *Snakes and Ladders* (1997) – cannot be immediately slotted within the diasporic discourse and yet they are diasporic in many ways. They are innovative in their approach to diaspora, in that instead of weaving the usual patterns of marginalization or the gendered nature of identity politics and ethnicity, they evolve different narrational strategies to convey the notion of 'otherness' through soft irony directed at the peculiarities of both the motherland and the adopted culture in some works, and in others, through the dialectic of self-appraisal. Her works struggle to re-discover the past but the re-visioning is not in the form of longing or in the shape of synthesis; it manifests in the effort to preserve the individual identity of home culture and to show the meaning of 'India'. In *Karma Cola,* Gita Mehta laughs at both the western gullibility and the contemporary Indian pseudo-spirituality; in *A River Sutra*, the focus is on India that *was* and that still *is*, within the contemporary India; in *Raj*, she looks at the native princely India within the Imperial British India; and in *Snakes and Ladders* Mehta tries to redefine the self by returning to the homeland and presents a variegated picture of the many contradictions that prevail in her homeland. The author's relationship with 'home' surfaces subtly as she looks back in awe and wonder, amusement and skepticism at the land of her birth.

In her perceptive paper "The New Parochialism – Homeland in the Writing of the Indian Diaspora," Jasbir Jain draws a broad categorization under which the new diasporic writings of the post-independence period could be studied to understand the authors' relationship to homeland and their interrogation of the dilemma of the diaspora. These are: (i) exotica, (ii) history, (iii) fantasy, (iv) collusion, and (v) use of third space. These paradigms are not mutually 'exclusive or definitive,' but as Jain asserts, 'they do emphasize the fact that the diasporic writer, like all other writers, has constantly to reinvent himself and work out new strategies to relate to his experience' (Jain, 2001: 84). Of Gita Mehta's books, it could be said that *A River Sutra* looks at the homeland from a distance in time and space. It creates myths and an exotic ambience and it can be categorized as 'exotica' as well as 'fantasy.' *Raj* is a re-visioning of history; *Snakes and Ladders* is both a work of collusion and history. It tends to look back and re-construct India as she is; but it also looks at her – i.e., at India – from the author's bemused gaze of a distance onlooker. India's bewildering ethos is both an 'assault on the senses' and 'assault of the senses' (Mehta, 1997: 279). In *Raj,* the author tries to arrive at a self-definition by creating and re-creating the colonial and postcolonial past. In *Karma Cola,* cultural collusion is at play. In all these works, physical return to the 'home' permanently is ruled out but the unfulfilled urge persists at the unconscious level.

The indication of forward movement in all her works gives sufficient clue to assume that the author is not caught between the two opposed worlds but is living in a dynamic world where inter-relationship and intra-relationships among apparently opposing forces produce a satisfactory self-image. In her own words, the experience of living on the three continents is an enriching one. 'There's a tremendous richness to living on three continents. The magic of America is the can-doism, it gives me the belief that anything is possible. Each time I finish a book and think I'll never write another, America makes me think, 'Yeah, I'll have another shot'. London's great virtue is that, as the capital of an empire, its libraries have staggering material on India. And because of the British reticence, it's easy to be alone and write there. My heart is in India – it's home – so when I'm, there I don't write. I just let it all seep through in my prose' (Smith, 1997: 53–54).

What Gita Mehta says about America can well be contrasted with what Bharati Mukherjee lets her Jane/Jasmine say about it. 'This country has so many ways of humiliating, of disappointing. There are no harmless, compassionate ways to remake oneself. We murder who we were so we can rebirth ourselves in the image of dreams' (Bharati Mukherjee, 1990: 29). Or for that matter what Sunetra Gupta's homeless migrant says of London, 'the city of your dreams,' which migrants explore through their subjectivity. Nor does Gita Mehta proclaim like Bharati Mukherjee that she is an 'American' writer. She derives her material from her cultural background and history and articulates both Indian and international sensibility. It is a sensibility which stems from her culture and gives her a kind of imaginative freedom to roam freely in the world at large. This 'organic fusion' can be understood in terms of hybridity. According to Robert Young, hybridity works simultaneously in two ways:

> ... 'organically,' hegemonizing, creating new spaces, structures, scenes, and 'intentionally' diasporizing, intervening as a form of subversion, translation, transformation .... Hybridization as creolization involves fusion, the creation of a new form, which can then be set against the old form, of which it is partly made up. (Young, 1995: 1 and 8)

But, hybridity cannot be and should not be used as a universal concept because writers, whether inside or outside the hybrid space, tend to write from their own individual locations. That has to be recognized by the critic. In case of Gita Mehta's works, hybridity is indicated by the titles that, as Pushpinder Syal opines speak of the cultural duality suggesting the 'cross-cultural encounter in its yoking together' of words like "Cola" or "Sutra" (Syal, 1996:84), and the blending of themes. While Gita Mehta lives in the west, her heart as she reiterates, is in India – a recognizable literary phenomena of diasporic consciousness.

Gita Mehta displays a tendency to glorify India and create an imaginary motherland. This is far more obvious in *A River Sutra* than in her other works. The long descriptive passages and the choice of themes for some of her tales have often been questioned. For example, the story of the courtesan's daughter has rich imagery of the life of yore which can be found in Mirza Ruswa's *The Courtesans of Lucknow*. Mehta's story of the Courtesan's Daughter has all the exotic romance of the life in Havelis that were the store houses of courtesy.

There are passages after passages that elaborate on the significance of courtesans in the royal settings. The author takes pains to convey through the courtesan's words the efficacy of their lives and takes out the social stigma attached to the profession. The courtesan explains that a simple question: how should one pay a compliment to a beautiful woman? has in itself the requirement of good manners befitting a royal personage. You pay tribute to beauty not by telling a woman that she has a pretty face but by implication. 'We required a lighter touch, a phrase that could delight and yet contain a barb to remind us that beauty was a passing thing, and love beyond attainment,' says the courtesan. She further elucidates:

> To give such a compliment is one of the things we taught these princes. But to turn a pretty speech on beauty, a man must be able to perceive beauty. After all, the primary colors are seen by every lout, the ordinary scales heard by every washerwoman who repeats them in her songs while she is beating clothes on the rocks in the river.
>
> But to teach a prince the subtle grading of color or the microtones of melody, to educate a young man's palate so he becomes an epicure, to introduce him to the alchemy of scents – this was the most demanding part of our education. (165)

That probably is not enough; Mehta lets her courtesan weave other impressive images to bring home the fact that these courtesans were not mere dance-girls but were socially useful and highly respected. The courtesan's grandmother was an expert with her dance and music:

> My grandmother wove such magic around those nights. She spoke of being rowed to lake palaces under star-filled sky. Of gossamer nets hanging over beds strewn with jasmine blossoms. Pearls scattered on the sheets. Arched doorways opening onto balconies below which the water lapped softly against the stone foundations. (167)

Similarly, the *Executive's Story* is not a simple one depicting the aberrations of love but it gives us a glimpse of 'what life had been like for the colonial estate managers.' Bose was himself aware of the 'Englishness' of his tea-estate experience, 'I could not stop laughing at the thought that I had entered a British fantasy of India, untouched by the chaos of the last forty years' (116). In the postcolonial setting Bose's life has all the colours of the colonial masters, which remind us of Ashis Nandy's assertion that colonialism does not end with the end of the colonial rule. Nitin Bose's attitude is that of the Pukka Sahib. 'To assure the servants that I was *pukka* as any other sahib, I began issuing orders in an unnaturally military way. They lost the looks of insecurity brought on by my display of levity, as I supervised the unloading of my luggage. My barked orders, my courtesy underlined by firmness, my eye for detail, drew a portrait of my persona for them to circulate on the estate' (116). In another echo of colonial times, Bose writes an article on the customs of the tribals which his uncle asks him to submit to the *Asia Review* for publication (147). Not only this, even pre-colonial tribal practices are upheld in this section of the novel as is evidenced by the immersion of the idol by Nitin Bose and his getting cured after that.

Another exotica is created in the story of the musician's ugly daughter with music and musical notes replete in the total atmosphere. 'Men are fools,' the musician would say as he walked with his daughter in the jungle. 'They think only humans respond to beauty. But a feeding deer will drop its food to listen to music, and a king cobra sway its head in pleasure. Listen. Do you hear that peacock's cry? It is the first tone of the scale of *sa*' (204). The chapter has a lively mixture of musical notes and the blending of colours, of birds and animals imparting lessons in music and of the power of the veena to lead one to salvation. 'The Vedas say that by playing the veena with the correct rhythm, keeping its notes and its characters intact, a man can hear that sound and attain salvation' (207).

It may be noted here that though Mehta is trying to impart the subtle nuances of the culture through her stories, she somehow seems to be speaking from the periphery. The sound grounding in culture which Shashi Deshpande displays in her *Small Remedies* which has the inset story of Savitribai Indorekar, the scion of Hindustani music, is missing here. Not that Gita Mehta lacks knowledge. Her information is authentic but somehow it appears done up for foreign readers. It is generated because of her diasporic situation in which she tends to look at the land and look at it from distance of time and space. It could be because she reflects on the issue of identity when confronted with otherness (as is evidenced in the episode that led to writing *Karma Cola*) and the process of reflection-evocation, using the prop of memory, helps in visualizing the beauty and richness in retrospect.

Coming to the question of a grounding in culture, again Mehta lacks the sense of belonging to any particular place. Her works are set in India; they speak for and of India, her culture, her mythology, her rich traditions – sometimes with irony, sometimes with seriousness and often times with a longing to demystify the stereotype picture that the west usually associate with India. But where is that feel of the locale? Where is the scent and the sound of the land? Let us take a passage from Sura P. Rath's description of his childhood countryside:

> Born sometime around the mid-twentieth-century after the Indian National independence, after the declaration of the republic status of the country, I can embrace my postcolonial identity as an Indian. In addition, my early education and training in the indigenous cultural texts, such as the Bhagabata, the Puranas, the Gita – much of it recited to me at four in the dew-damp mornings in the harvest seasons supposedly to please the gods but more practically perhaps to ward off early morning theft from the barn next door – all make my experience authentic and real. There was little or nothing imagined about my 'imaginary community'; the soil, the sand, the cow dung all were real. The text was as much in the book as it was on the stone steps of the village pond, where vermillion covered rectangular stone claimed its divine status as a goddess and received morning and evening worship. The text was there on the mud walls where the most complex mythic images were meticulously drawn in circles and triangles with Jhoti (pureed rice), where gods smiled in their cosmic glee. (Rath, 2005: 95–96)

Such intimately personal descriptions cannot be cited in Gita Mehta's texts. In *Snakes and Ladders* Mehta looks back wistfully at her country and tries to evoke an atmosphere with myriads of indigenous sounds and smells that make India, but somehow it remains at the level of 'seeing', not 'feeling'. It is India seen, as if, through binoculars and video cameras which capture colours but not the essence. Here are a few snippets from the last chapter of *Snakes and Ladders:*

> The scent of parched earth in the monsoon rains
> when peacocks fan their tails to dance.
> The green sweep of parakeets crossing the sunset.
>
> The popping of water lilies, the snarling of pi-dogs,
> the koyal bird crying for rain.
>
> The white horizon of the holy Himalayas.
> The shriek of the train whistle, coal-dust on wooden
> seats, a river crossing at night.
>
> Glass bangles sold by lantern light, fragile colour
> fracturing the dark
>
> The stench of the Indian bazaar – flowers, incense,
> over-flowing gutters, petrol, dust, sticky sweets.

Let us compare these with V.S. Naipaul's intensity of feelings at the end of his journey. It cannot be overlooked that *An Area of Darkness* presents the disillusionment and frustration of the author as he sees his India – decayed, dirty, incompetent and corrupt, but as the time for departure arrives the pain of leaving the country comes to the fore with surprising sentimentality. It is not the country of glossy travel books but a country with its human side:

> Afternoon now and the train's shadow racing beside us. Sunset, evening, night; station after dimly-lit station. It was an Indian railway journey, but everything that had before seemed pointless was now threatened and seemed worth cherishing; and as in the mild sunshine of a winter morning we drew near to green Bengal, which I had longed to see, my mood towards India and her people became soft. I had taken so much for granted. There among the

> Bengali passengers, who had come on, was a man who wore a long woolen scarf and a brown tweed jacket above his Bengali dhoti. The casual elegance of his dress was matched by his fine features and relaxed posture. Out of all its squalor and human decay, its eruptions at butchery, India produced so many people of grace and beauty, ruled by elaborate courtesy. Producing too much of life, it denied the value of life; yet it permitted a unique human development to so many. Nowhere were people so heightened, rounded and individualistic; nowhere did they offer themselves fully and with such assurance. To know Indians was to take a delight in people as people; every encounter was an adventure. I did not want India to sink: the mere thought was painful. (Naipaul, 1964: 256–57)

It could be argued that Mehta is writing about the India of 1997 in relation to the rapid social and political changes that have followed postmodernism and globalization, while Naipaul was looking at India of 1962–1964, closely following decolonization. Whatever be the rationale, it is obvious that Gita Mehta does not portray family, group, community or society in her writings and her diaspora exposes the fluidity of homelessness.

Despite the fact that Mehta is not morose and her books emit the *joi de vivre,* one finds a kind of emptiness, a kind of recurring sense of loss, which is not obvious but which is there all the same. One has to give her credit for presenting India's attractions and for projecting an Indian world view; also she is not self-defeating nor does she present a self-berating rhetoric of protest. How do we then discover her diasporic leanings? For Gita Mehta, 'home' is 'India' but there is no particular 'home' with hearth and the traditional/modern nexus that we find in many of the Indian urban homes even today. Writers like Shashi Deshpande, R.K. Narayan, Raja Rao and many others, despite their urban or diasporic milieu present a family space to think of, to return to. On the contrary, in Gita Mehta there is a sense of constant movement. In *Snakes and Ladders,* she gives a brief autobiographical account without ever mentioning her home. Her mother gets her labour pain while she is dancing in the club, is taken to hospital, and Gita is born; her parents are constantly on the move from jail to jail; and the children are sent to a hostel. Everything is in a fluid state. Understandably, it was because of the times – freedom struggle, the necessity to hide from the British clutches to manipulate the struggle further. Such a situation is portrayed in Anita Desai's *Where Shall We Go this Summer?* One of the reasons why Sita, the protagonist suffers is often assigned to the unpredictable situation in which she and her siblings grow as their freedom fighter father moves about and is unable to give home to the children.[10] In Gita Mehta's works there are no such psychological implications but the tendency is to keep things volatile. In fact, she does not even give the names of her illustrious parent, not even of her uncle who was sent to the Cellular jail at the age of fourteen. After the first chapter the essays are on people, leaders, places but the perspective of a traveler or rather a tourist remains all through.

In *A River Sutra*, the main narrator is nameless and homeless; the only thing we know about him is that he was a bureaucrat and after his retirement he came to the Narmada Guest House for peace and tranquillity. In *Karma Cola*, the seekers are of course, faceless wanderers. Jaya, in *Raj*, is twice displaced – as a result of her marriage into a far off kingdom and second, because of her estranged husband who is almost always absent. Being uprooted from the familiar surroundings of Balmer in the northwest to Sirpur in the northeast is a kind of internal diaspora. Beside language problem there is every possibility of cultural alienation. Mehta never tells us this though we as readers wonder how Jaya could be communicating with the Maharani – Pratap's grandmother and the servants. As if this were not enough, Jaya has to undergo the traumatic experience of being uprooted from her culture when Maharajah Pratap insists that Jaya needs to be 'civilized' and employs Lady Modi to teach Jaya the 'sophisticated' ways of the western culture.

Such Europeanization of culture shown in the postcolonial texts – set in the colonial period – underscores the significance of the 'historical fact' of European colonization (Ashcroft et al., 1995: 2). That colonialism has seeped down the colonial psyche and particularly in the collective unconscious of the people is interwoven in many situations in Mehta's works: such as the attitude of Nitin

Bose or the princes – Pratap, Tikka and Victor – or the duality in modern Indian psyche as evidenced in *Snakes and Ladders*. Ashcroft and others opine that postcolonial texts have a "complex and hybridized formation" and cannot be read exclusively with either the traditional angle or from a western perspective. Discussing the works of R.K. Narayan Ashcroft et al. posit:

> Within the syncretic reality of a post-colonial society it is impossible to return to an idealized pure pre-colonial cultural condition … . The post-colonial text is always a complex and hybridized formation. It is inadequate to read it either as a reconstruction of pure traditional values or as simply foreign and intrusive. The reconstruction of 'pure' cultural values is always conducted within a radically altered dynamic of power relations. (Ashcroft et al., 1989: 109–110)

As a postcolonial, diasporic writer, Gita Mehta reveals an overt attempt to assume the 'centralist' position, but ironically she gets caught within the dialectical structure and struggles with the traditional representation based on the indigenous roots, on the one hand, and the archetypal Orientalist discourse on the other – which presents the Indian society as corrupt, stagnant and infantile – and then makes interesting reversal to achieve a sense of self and a coherent nationality and identity. This probably can be understood with reference to what A.K. Ramanujan terms the 'context-sensitive' way of Indian thinking. 'No Indian text comes without a context, a frame …' says Ramanujan. He further adds that 'Texts may be historically dateless, anonymous; but their contexts, uses, efficacies, are explicit' (Ramanujan, 1990: 39). This context sensitive approach is all-pervading and is deeply rooted in our culture, religion and philosophy as also in our way of life. In the present epoch of postmodernism, postcolonialism and transnationalism the western context-free approach is also accommodated with the traditional context-sensitive approach of our thought and behaviour.[11] Gita Mehta's works with their fine incursions into both negotiate her position between two cultures. Since diaspora is directly related to the physical and cultural uprooting, a diasporic writer is in a vulnerable position but even then he/she has a vantage point from which to look at the culture and the 'home'. The process of writing is a means for Mehta to articulate her role as the spokesperson of the two diverse cultures whereby she problematizes the question of cultural identity. How she manages it, we shall see in her first venture *Karma Cola*.

Notes

1. See also Homi Bhabha, *The Location of Culture* (New York: Routledge, 1994). Bhabha asserts that the demography of the new internationalism is the 'history of postcolonial migration, the narratives of cultural and political diaspora' (4), of displacement, of the poetics of exile. He feels that the new discourses of cross-cultural consciousness are significant connective tissues in the present postcolonial situation.
2. See Jasbir Jain, "Postcoloniality, Literature and Politics," in *Contesting Postcolonialism*, ed. Jasbir Jain and Veena Singh (Jaipur: Rawat Publications, 2000). See also Meenakshi Mukherjee, "Interrogating Postcolonialism," pp. 3–12; Arun Mukherjee, "Postcolonialism: Some Uneasy Conjectures," pp. 13–20 and Satendra Nandan, "The Diasporic Consciousness: From Biswas to Biswasghat," pp. 49–66. All in Harish Trivedi and Meenakshi Mukherjee, ed. *Interrogating Post-colonialism: Theory, Text and Context* (Shimla: IIAS, 2000).
3. Discussing Rohinton Mistry's two novels, *Such a Long Journey* and *A Fine Balance* as diasporic texts, Paranjape observes that in novels such as these, the writers bid 'a farewell to India' and though they draw the raw material from the land, they seem to be more than eager to accept the host country. See Makarand Paranjape, "One Foot in Canada and a Couple of Toes in India: Diaspora and Homeland in South Asian Canadian Experience." *In-Diaspora*. ed. Makarand Paranjape (New Delhi: Indialog, 2001).
4. In several of her papers written in the decades of the 1990s, Arun P. Mukherjee critiques the postcolonial discourse for showing scant respect to national and cultural differences. She summarizes the highlights of these papers as follows:
   (i) The theory claims that the major theme of literatures from postcolonial societies is discursive resistance to the now absent colonizer.
   (ii) It unproblematically assumes that the writers who write back to the centre are representing the people of their society authentically.

(iii) The theory downplays the difference between the settler colonial and those colonized in their home territories, using the term 'colonized' for both of them. I feel that it trivializes the experiences of those who suffered genocide and pauperization under colonial rule, not to mention cultural deprivation.

(iv) In its use of terminology like 'the oppressed', 'the colonized people', and 'the indigenous' to describe postcolonial societies, the theory suppresses internal hierarchies and divisions in these societies. It does great disservice to the minorities in these societies by deflecting attention away from their oppression by using a unitary vocabulary which, as Rey Chow suggests, confers the 'subaltern' status on the entire postcolonial world, discarding the fact that it is ridden with hierarchies. See Arun Mukherjee, "Postcolonialism: Some Uneasy Conjecture," in *Interrogating Post-colonialism*. eds. Harish Trivedi and Meenakshi Mukherjee (Shimla: IIAS, 2000).

In Gita Mehta's works the problem of hierarchical structure, the pauperization, and the colonial high-handedness appears at various stages which will be taken up during discussion of the texts.

5. Daniel Aaron gives the three phases thus: in the first stage, the writer wants the reader to know his cultural identity and uses ethnic features in his texts to set straight the negative attributes associated with the group; in the second phase, the writer is not ready to appease the dominant group and re-inventing his/her ethnicity, the writer adopts a new tactic – it is the strategy of essentialism to counter the dominant group's essentialism; the third phase is almost of assimilation: he/she adopts the language and culture of the dominant culture, and feels a part of that society. It can be interpreted as the writer's ability to transcend narrow boundaries of nationalism and look at the self in the light of transnational paradigms. See Daniel Aaron, "The Hyphenated Writer and American Letters." *Smith Alumanae Quarterly* (July 1964, 213-17)

6. According to William Safran's criteria, the term diaspora also displays, apart from memory of the homeland, partial alienation from the host society; aspiration to return to an ancestral homeland; commitment to the maintenance or restoration of that homeland; and derivation of collective consciousness and solidarity from a relationship with the homeland. See William Safran, "Diaspora in Modern Societies: Myths of Homeland and Return" in *Diaspora: A Journal of Transnational Studies*, 1 (1) 1991: 83–99.

7. In his *The Location of Culture* Homi Bhabha points out that feeling/fear of being 'unhomed' does not signify being homeless. The notion is lodged

in the concept of 'unhomely moment' that creeps on a diasporic consciousness. To be unhomed 'is not to be homeless, nor can the "unhomely" be easily accommodated in that familiar division of social life into private and public spheres. The unhomely moment ... creeps up on you stealthily as your shadow ...' (9).

8. See Bharati Mukherjee, *Jasmine* (New York: Viking Penguin, 1989: 21). 'Out there' and 'In-here' are the trope that Mrs. Ripplemeyer uses. These suggest difference and distance as well as the binary nature of cultural identity.
9. Ravinder Randhawa describes the diaspora within Britain in terms of a 'net' in a paper she read at Queen Mary and Westfield College in 1996. As qtd. in Susheila Nasta's *Home Truths: Fictions of the South Asian Diaspora in Britain* (London: Palgrave, 2002), 206 and 277 (n. 105).
10. See Usha Bande's discussion in *The Novels of Anita Desai*. New Delhi: Prestige, 1988 and *Writing Resistance: A Comparative Study of the Selected Novels by Women Writers*. Shimla: Indian Institute of Advanced Study 2006. In the former, Bande deals with Sita from psychological angle trying to understand her uprootedness, and in the latter she takes up her resistant attitude to highlight Sita's problem in the context of the feminist revisionist strategy. See also "Is Sita Mad?" *Indian Literature* (Sahitya Academi), 139 (September–October 1990): 179–184.
11. A.K. Ramanujan makes an interesting observation regarding context-sensitive and context-free approaches in his paper "Is There an Indian Way of Thinking?: An Informal Essay." According to him the entire fabric of Indian thought is contextual to such an extent that each statement or idea is related to some specific context having properties and effects, with microcosm and macrocosm contained within the same body of thought. The Western way of thinking is context-free but with the advent of modernization, there is free interplay between context-sensitive and context-free approaches with the result that there is free borrowing from India to the West, or wise versa. Of the many examples he gives, I quote here only one: 'In music, the ragas can now be heard at all hours and seasons. Once the Venkatesasuprabhatam, the wake-up chant for the Lord of Tirupati, could be heard only in Tirupati at a certain hour in the morning. Since M.S. Subbulakshmi in her devotion cut a record of the chants, it wakes up not only the Lord, but anyone who tunes in to All India Radio in faraway places'(56). See *India Through Categories*, ed. McKim Marriott (New Delhi: Sage, 1990).

Works Cited

Aaron, Daniel. "The Hyphenate Writer and American Letters." *Smith Alumnae Quarterly,* July 1964, pp. 213–17.

Ashcroft, Bill, Gareth Griffths and Helen Tiffin, eds. *The Empire Writes Back: Theory and Practice in Post-Colonial Literature.* London: Routledge, 1989.

—. eds. *The Post-Colonial Studies Reader.* New York: Routledge, 1995

Bande, Usha. *The Novels of Anita Desai.* New Delhi: Prestige, 1988

—. "Is Sita Mad?" *Indian Literature,* New Delhi: Sahitya Akademi, 139 Sept–Oct 1990: 179–184.

—. *Writing Resistance: A Comparative Study of the Selected Novels by Women Writers.* Shimla: Indian Institute of Advanced Study 2006.

Bhabha, Homi. *The Location of Culture.* New York: Routledge, 1994.

Boym, Svetlana. *The Future of Nostalgia.* New York: Basic Books, 2001.

Gooneratne, Yasmin. *Diverse Inheritance.* Adelaide: Centre for Research in the New Literatures in English, 1980.

Hogue, W. Lawrence. *Race, Modernity, Postmodernity: A Look at the History and the Literature of People of Color Since the 1960s.* Albany: State Univ. of New York, 1996.

Hutcheon, Linda. *A Poetics of Postmodernism: History, Theory and Fiction.* New York and London: Routledge, 1988.

Internet: http://www.geocities.com/clintonbennett/Lectures/GitaMehta.htm.

Jain, Jasbir. "Postcoloniality, Literature and Politics." *Contesting Postcolonialism.* Eds. Jasbir Jain and Veena Singh. Jaipur: Rawat, 2000.

—. "The New Parochialism: Homeland in the Writing of the Indian Diaspora." *In-Diaspora.* Ed. Makarand Paranjape. New Delhi: Indialog 2001, 79–92.

Lavie, Smadar and Ted Swedenburg., eds. *Displacement, Diaspora, and the Geographies of Identities.* Durham Duke Univ. Press, 1996.

Mukherjee, Arun. "Interrogating Postcolonialism: Some Uneasy Conjectures". *Interrogating Post-Colonialism.* Eds. Harish Trivedi and Meenakshi Mukherjee. Shimla: IIAS, 2000.

Mukherjee, Bharati. *Jasmine* 1989. Rpt. New York: Viking/ Penguin, 1990: 21.

Naipaul, V.S. *An Area of Darkness.* London: Andre Deutsch Ltd. 1964.

Nandan, Satendra. "The Diasporic Consciousness: From Biswas to Biswasghat." *Interrogating Post-Colonialism*. Eds. Harish Trivedi and Meenakshi Mukherjee. Shimla: IIAS, 2000.

Nasta, Susheila. *Home Truths: Fictions of the South Asian Diaspora in Britain*. London: Palgrave, 2002

Paranjape, Makarand. "One Foot in Canada and a Couple of Toes in India: Diaspora and Homeland in South Asian Canadian Experience." *In-Diaspora*. Ed. Makarand Paranjape. New Delhi: Indialog, 2001.

Radhakrishnan, R. *Diasporic Mediation: Between Home and Location*. Minneapolis, MN: University of Minnesota Press, 1996.

Ramanujan A.K. "Is There an Indian Way of Thinking?: An Informal Essay." *India Through Categories*. Ed. McKim Marriott. New Delhi: Sage, 1990.

Rath, Sura, P. "Home(s) Abroad: Diasporic Identities in Third Spaces." *Theory and Praxis*. Eds. Prafulla C. Kar, Kailash C. Baral and Sura P. Rath. Delhi: Pencraft International, 2003

Rushdie, Salman. *Imaginary Homelands*. London: Granta/Viking, 1991.

Safran, William. "Diaspora in Modern Societies: Myths of Homeland and Return" *Diaspora: A Journal of Transnational Studies*, 1 (1), 1991: 83–99.

Smith, Wendy. "Gita Mehta: Making India Accessible." *Publisher's Weekly*, May 12, 1997 pp. 53–54. (Internet http://www.PeopleVirginia.edu/-pm 9k/59/tales.gitapub.html)

Syal, Pushpinder. "The Threads of Narratives: Gita Mehta's *A River Sutra*" *The Postmodern Indian English Novel*. Ed. Viney Kirpal. Bombay: Allied Publishers, 1996.

Tololyan, Khaching. *Diaspora: A Journal of Transnational Studies*, 1 (1), 1991: 4–5.

Trivedi. Harish. "India and Post-colonial Discourse," *Critical Theory: Western and Indian*. Ed. P.C. Kar. New Delhi: Pencraft International, 1997

Vijayasree, C. "The Politics and Poetics of Expatriation: The Indian Version(s)." *Interrogating Post-colonialism*. Eds. Harish Trivedi and Meenakshi Mukherjee, Shimla: IIAS 1996

Young, Robert J.C. *Colonial Desire: Hybridity in Theory, Culture and Race*. London: Routledge, 1995.

Young, Robert J.C. *Postcolonialism: A Very Short Introduction*. Oxford: Oxford Univ. Press, 2002.

Three

Karma Cola : A Cross-Cultural Feast

> 'Perhaps these expatriates are the Moors,' I thought, 'And I am one of them, after all, arriving here in search of something that matters to nobody but myself and staying, perhaps to die.'
>
> — Salman Rushdie
> (*The Moor's Last Sigh*)

In the opening paragraph of her "Introduction" to the 1993 edition of *Karma Cola*, Gita Mehta recalls a letter she had received from a young American woman recounting her traumatic experiences in India with drug-peddling, lecherous gurus. She concludes her letter thus: 'after reading your book I realized I should never have trusted Gurus who wore Adidas running shoes' (ix–x). The reference to 'Adidas' shoes, a global mercantile item, brings out the connotation of consumerism, and simultaneously the image of commodification of spirituality. A few pages later in the book, one German seeker comments that there should be 'quality control on gurus. A lot of my friends have gone mad in India' (18). 'Quality Control' is also a referent to commodities and signifies the harm that substandard quality does to the consumer. That was in the late 1960s and early 1970s when hordes of young westerners disillusioned by the rampant materialism in their native lands started reaching India to escape the boredom and monotony of their consumerism-oriented life, and unwittingly commodified India and her culture. The unscrupulous elements in India took undue advantage of their naivety and brought the country into focus for wrong reasons. Gita Mehta explores this situation and brings out a lively yet hard-hitting book that takes to task the 'instant nirvana' enthusiasts and their 'instant, fake gurus'.

Published in 1979, *Karma Cola* – Gita Mehta's first work – carries with it the ominous implication that it is dangerous when philosophy is masqueraded as pseudo-spirituality and bought and sold by mediocre sellers to mediocre buyers. The infantile desire of the buyers to seek self-realization through the crude bands of black-mailers has been banal. Both the seekers and their gurus tarnished the image of the country abroad. In recreating the stories of the bizarre exploitation and the resultant trauma with remarkable irony and sarcasm, *Karma Cola* demonstrates convincingly how cheap publicity and vulgar patronization have staked Indian culture in the bazaar for sale; and that justifies the sub-title, "Marketing the Mystic East". The book is the outcome of Gita Mehta's annoyance – as we have discussed in the chapter 1 – a righteous annoyance at the triteness of an observation, emanating from scanty knowledge of Indian thought-system, that *karma* (emphasis added) can be explained by anybody, anywhere and to anyone. Mehta channelized that anger into subtle humour and exposed the shallowness inherent in the entire scenario when 'thousand and thousands of them, clashing cymbals, ringing bells, playing flutes, wearing bright colours and weird clothes, singing, dancing and speaking in tongues' (5) arrived and there was 'chaos' with nobody knowing what the other stood for.

The emergence of the Hippies[1] in the USA, closely followed by the Beatles[2] and the Rolling Stones,[3] was responsible for the influx of the seekers from the west. These were young men and women identifiable by the use of drugs, shabby lifestyle and irreverence to authority. Initially, these three movements had positive agenda. The Hippies were alienated youth who began their crusade for peace and love in the mid-1960s; the Beatles were a music group that established a Rock style of their own; and the Rolling Stones were also a branch of Rock music that had separated from the parent body. These groups had strong identification with the 'teen' generation; they were against the old order and advocated change; they stood for simplicity and brotherhood. But what started with a socio-cultural perspective degenerated into a contaminated ontological condition obsessed with Nirvana through karma through drugs. Soon, karma lost its original philosophic-spiritual signification and came to be seen as a panacea for everything and anything. In theory, they defined karma in terms of mental vibrations that could lead to self-realization; in practice it acquired the magical quality as a by-word for any casual occurrence – chance, co-incidence, happy indication, omen and/or any flux. Gita Mehta shows with a tongue-in-cheek style the mockery they made of this highly profound term:

> "I can't visit London, anymore. The Karma there is too heavy for me" says the Iranian hairdresser.
>
> "I crashed my car last night. I have bad Karma," says the Mexican student.
>
> "That dude's dangerous. He has heavy Karma," says the Harlem drug dealer.
>
> "Craps – it's a low Karma game," explains the American gambler's girlfriend.
>
> "My daughter is called Rani," says the German mother, "the night she was born in Goa my friend and his lady had a daughter in Los Angeles and they called her Rani. We have such *close* Karma". (100)

The Indian culture and spiritual thought became a negotiable construct and Karma/Nirvana became a big joke. It is this crux of the situation thriving on self-deception, exploitation and mutual incomprehension that impelled Gita Mehta to use it for her mock-ironic book.

It is commonly believed that *Karma Cola* is about the influx of the 'Nirvana-seekers' of the 1960s–1970s – the Hippies, the Beatles and the Rolling Stones – who invaded the East in search of peace, gave in to drug-addiction and ended up in asylums. This would probably be a simplistic view of a work that handles a significant issue from different angles. A close reading of the first few pages suggests that the Hippies have gone but their place is taken by far more serious barterers who are marketing India at a higher rate and with more dangerous speed.

> The hippies are gone. This is all supposed to be over. Under my mango tree I indulge in an orgy of sober reflection.
>
> Can it be, I enquire of a parrot who has just evacuated on my head, that this is just the beginning? Do these fantasies go beyond the marketplace, beyond your simple buying and selling of shoddy goods?
>
> The parrot is swinging upside down on a mango branch in an exaggerated carefree manner.
>
> Consider the possibility, I elaborate, that this business should be traced not to the bazaar but to the brothel.
>
> A half-eaten mango drops on my lap. (12)

Sociologists agree that no influx of the nature of the Hippie Movement can fade away without leaving its effect on the socio-cultural matrix. As Gita Mehta's imaginary conversation with the parrot suggests, and the social history of the period also substantiates, the Hippies and the other young rebels messed up the environment of the pristine places like Goa and Kullu-Manali and the religious towns like Haridwar and Benaras, making them dens of drug-smuggling and such other anti-social rackets that became a headache for the administration and the locals.

The first person narratives of many of the ex-Hippies who had the good fortune to escape drugged-deaths and who later wrote their experiences are revealing. Cleo Odzer's *Goa Freaks: My Hippie Years in India* is one of the poignant accounts of how these young men and women wasted themselves. Cleo, a model from New York heard of the Hippie community living a glamorous life of rebellion and excitement on the Goa beaches, came to India drawn by the supposed adventure, joined the tightly knit community and became a hard core drug addict and smuggler. She returned to the USA in 1980, underwent a rehabilitation program and got back to normal life, completing her Doctorate in Anthropology and working for de-addiction centres. But Cleo went back to Goa again, gave in to her old habit and died in 2002. The book is an eye-opening record of official connivance and the social apathy of the residents who tolerated the freaks because the foreigners brought money. The locals knew that smuggling, thefts and other unethical activities were going on right under their noses but greed proved stronger than values. Even after the Hippies left or many of them died 'mysterious deaths,' beaches like Anjuna and Calanguti maintained the flavour of the Hippie days – the Wednesday Flea Market is still there, the drug-kings have become moneyed landowners and the small traditional bungalows nestling in the green paddy fields are now big hotels hosting the international holiday-makers.

Gita Mehta covers the period of almost two decades in *Karma Cola*. It opens with a quick look at the Hippie den when a Brazilian and a Frenchman invite the narrator to their 'bug-infested hotel room' saying, 'Come tonight. Moon is full. Karma is right for looking at jewels' (3). The bewilderment of the author who finds no clue as to what the Brazilian meant by 'Karma' and 'jewels' generates humour which is the mainstay of the work. The Hippies in their 'stoned incomprehension' did not know what they were looking for; and we – Indians – did not understand how to march forward in the twentieth century with rapid speed till the Hippie movement waned and its place was taken over by the big players. The arena is now set for those who are spending thousands of dollars to hold conferences, conduct camps, and market tourism. The first chapter, entitled "Reinventing the Wheel" gives a quick glimpse of the change over from the hallucination of the drugged visitors to the more realistic and calculated moves of the new global approach. From chapter two onwards the book reexamines the fantasies, the disillusionments and the accompanying pain. Mehta reaches the conclusion that the messing up of western utopia and the eastern mysticism have created a situation of no-return; and she applauds the 'confident ones' on both sides who have gone from 'zero to hero' – this is how and where India's mathematical 'zero' matches western materialistic 'hero' (193).

Each snippet tells a new story or experience; in their flippancy and quick-flow these snippets are commensurate with the lifestyle of the seekers – vigorous yet hallucinatory. The language is clipped, with short sentences, and is rhythmic like their clanging cymbals and chiming bells. Sentences like 'shuttle religion. Shuttle fantasy. And at what price? your reason? your religion? your health?' (18) convey maximum meaning in minimum words. The irreverence for order and authority is brought out through phrases and words such as 'shit', 'mind fucking', 'bloody' and many more. Somehow, they fit the trend-setting Rolling Stones and the unconventional lifestyle of the Hippies and the Beatles and go well with the speaker's personality without making a reader wince at the use of slang. Such expressions, though undignified and profane otherwise, display either the sense of humour of these social drop-outs or their irritation. Let us take an example. Narrating his experience with a 'holy man,' an American designer puts it thus:

> "I stopped laughing for a month", says the American designer, who has whirled with dervishes in Turkey.
>
> "That old man with his nice white beard turned on me and said, 'Be careful how you laugh. You become what you laugh at.'" "Scared the shit out of me". (20)

The author shows marvellous skill at using various figures of speech to enhance the effect of her language that is meant to produce humour, like alliterations: 'meaninglessly meaningful' or 'meaningfully meaningless'; repetitions such as 'Mind control. Market control'; euphemism: 'The only thing is, I may have to stay stoned forever, see. My professional reputation depends on it' (123); antithesis: 'It is here [in India] a noisy, dirty silence. So many millions being born, living, dying, without fuss. This I appreciate. So little fuss. We Swiss are supposed to like order. Well this is order' ... (75); and oxymoron, hyperbole, pun and exaggeration even in titles such as 'Om is where the Art is' for 'Home is where the heart is' or 'behind the Urine Curtain'. The narrators of the various incidents are nameless like the hordes of nameless, faceless mass crowding the eastern countries – India, Nepal, Afghanistan and Pakistan. Interspersed between the episodes is factual information which helps in moving the story forward. This information is provided by the narrator-observer who is always moving with the seekers like the roving eye of the camera. That the narrator is a female (and by implication the writer) is made implicit by the epithets like 'madam' or 'sister' that the shop-keepers or the gurus or their disciples address the narrator with.

Karma Cola, is a slim book that looks at a major problem with grotesquely comic style. By the time a reader keeps the book down, he/she realizes that the author has, in fact, not trivialized the issue; instead she has tackled the problem from a wider and deeper angle, though she has camouflaged her intensity in a satirical vein. The result is that as one reads on, the canvas gets wider and we realize that the author has in actuality told many tales of suffering, blundering, deceit and bewilderment. Against the western expatriates' experience of India is situated the Indians' experience of the expatriates. The conflicting demands of 'this-worldly' and the 'other-worldly'; the myth of the mystic east and the materialistic west; and the antithetical temperament of the Occidental and Oriental identity, all come under her scanner, giving a new direction to the theme of 'East-West encounter,' to use a cliché.

The east-west encounter that Gita Mehta is interested in is not the usual stereotype colonial/postcolonial tussle between the two at socio-cultural level, or the abstract constructs like the 'esoteric' east and the 'materialistic' west. She refuses to glorify any one block; instead she shows the damage done to individuals and the cultures because of half-baked knowledge, misconceptions and misinterpretations; and the resultant chaos:

> The seduction lay in the chaos. They thought they were simple. We thought they were neon. They thought we wave profound. We knew we were provincial. Everybody thought everybody else was ridiculously exotic and everybody got it wrong. (5)

The incoherence of those who profess to have profound knowledge of Oriental philosophy and also the superficial reconciliation of skepticism and mysticism is stressed by hilarious incidents like the one at the World Conference on the Future of Mankind. An earnest American student's question if science is not leading us into 'the possibility of total self-annihilation', brings forth one of the vaguest answers that can mean anything or nothing or everything. The Speaker, a meteorologist, answers the American student's question thus:

> 'Don't live in the shadow of death, young man', he warned. 'Let us say there is a nuclear holocaust. What will it do? I shall tell you what it will do. It will cleanse the world!'
>
> Don't you understand? We are going toward a post-nuclear, post-Armageddon *Golden Age*!' (17)

As if that were not inane enough, Gita Mehta draws us further into the charade. 'The American student nodded sagely and sat down, grasping the moral significance of nuclear war for the fist time.' Her final blow to the superficiality of both – the eastern speaker and the western seeker – comes with the last line, 'And India acquired another willing convert to the philosophy of the meaningfully meaningless' (17). This is, indeed, an eloquent means of revealing the dichotomy arising from the ridiculous circumstances. Both for contextual reasons of accessing and assessing the problem through a literary work and also to comprehend the cultural osmosis leading to the evolution of new syncretic culture, *Karma Cola* is of special value.

In keeping with the fast emerging trends of globalization, this syncretic culture takes over the karma-awareness that the Hippies popularized. Driven by interests different to those of the Hippies and others, the up-market hoteliers and various other organizations and associations get busy in 'marketing' India through conferences and seminars. The World Conference on the Future of Mankind is organized in Vigyan Bhavan. The venue gives it a seal of authenticity and 'Establishment seriousness'; the same venue has another conference in the afternoon on tourism prospects. This is hosted by the Pacific Area Travel Association and their agenda contains, among other topics, 'the problem of selling India to the world' (12). A couple of kilometres from there, Swami Muktananda is busy in his seven-week seminar on Kundalini trying to transmit his shakti to his devotees, 'a respectably international and populous gathering who sit cross-legged and patient through discourse on meditation' longing for 'the Swami's shakti – the direct transmission of cosmic energy from guru to devotee' (12). The overall picture is of consuming and getting consumed. Deborah Root terms our contemporary culture as 'cannibal culture' in which the question of 'difference' has mellowed considerably. She further opines that in our 'cannibal age of mass appropriation', the 'Otherness' is not considered inaccessible nor is it mute incomprehension of the other. On the contrary, by the time the latest 'ethnic' product reaches the latest consumer, the so called 'difference' is already half-consumed (Root, 1996).[4] Studying the impact of the consumer culture on India, Graham Huggan points out in his essay "Consuming India" that in the present era of consumerism, India is fast emerging as an 'exhibition' item, a global mercantile tool, with its own 'consuming multitudes' finding 'themselves and their country, turned into the objects of others' consumption' (Huggan, 2001: 255). This has been well brought out by Gita Mehta's tongue-in-cheek descriptions of the aims of the various international conferences.

The seminars and conferences so organized to sell 'fabulous India' have formidably high-sounding titles: 'Truth, Justice and Spirituality', 'Moral Values and the Future of Mankind', 'Meditation and Dedication' and many more. A few more pages and we learn that even the Maharishi who has an ashram in Switzerland, is planning a high-profile conference of scientists and spiritualists. All these conferences have high-brow intellectual participation. Thousands of delegates assemble in Delhi from all over the world, 'supreme court judges, heads of philosophy departments, journalists, film stars, income-tax officials, nuclear physicists, cabinet ministers, meteorologists and maharajahs ... all these people from all over the world and from every conceivable background were discussing meaning of karma and the significance of moral action' (13). But their deliberations are ridiculously shallow and their ideas are vague. The author looks at the scenario in bewildered amusement and wonders if these 'fantasies' would ever go beyond the market-place? Her question is answered by the parrot swinging cheerfully up side down on a mango branch, first by evacuating on her head and then dropping a half-eater mango on her lap (12) as if symbolically pointing out the naivety of her optimism and the frivolity of the buying and selling game. The arithmetic of these seminars and conferences is simple – you sell, we buy; we sell, you buy. We have 'Karma', you have 'Cola'. If we have the metaphysical soft drink (Karma) to offer, you have dollars. Swami Muktananda is selling his shakti, the World Conference is vending karma, and the hoteliers are marketing India. Indian cultural troupe hawking folk songs and folk performances in colourful costumes has further put the culture on sale, and above all the Indian matinee idol is bartering his own Gods through *Hare Krishna, Hare Ram*, 'the biggest box office receipt' (19). This is almost a bazaar scenario and can well be called 'conspicuous consumption,' a term popularized by Thorstein Veblem in his *Theory of Leisure Class* (1989). 'Conspicuous consumption' stands for demonstrative use of goods and services with a view to asserting one's wealth and power' (George, 1998: 122).[5] In *Karma Cola*, the east seems to assert its cultural and spiritual power and the west, its dollar-power, both using each others' services in an atmosphere charged with superficiality.

If the superficiality of approach of the western seekers is irritating, the ambiguity and greed of the Orient is baffling. Bordering on the irrational, Indian ambivalence is mind boggling. Gita Mehta elaborates it sarcastically: the Indians have 'spent a couple of thousand years cultivating the transcendence of reason, another couple of thousand years on the denial of reason, and even more millennia on accepting reason but rejecting its authenticity' (18). The dichotomy is apparent in their tolerance for parallel trends. For example, a film like *Hare Rama, Hare Krishna* does not occasion 'mass religious indignation' (20), and in the name of culture, vulnerable aspects like the snake-charmers, jugglers and puppeteers are displayed as cultural mercantile items.

The eastern scene thus falls embarrassingly short of western expectations but then the western ideologies get diffused in the eastern incoherence. Everything – eastern and western – appears flagrantly anachronistic. The interplay of eastern tradition and western techniques creates a new ideological challenge as the children of the free lifestyle couples grow without nationality or home, the gurus get pro-active, karma gets modified into the Rock title songs, and the hallucination induced by drugs is termed mystical experience.

Mystical experience is one of bliss; a pure joy of having gained spiritual insight into things; of having apprehended the infinite and eternal through the finite and temporal; of achieving oneness with Divine spirit. William Wordsworth elucidates it as that "blessed mood' in which we 'see into the life of things' (Tintern Abbey: 37–45).[6] A simple Sanskrit adjective to understand this state is *Satchidanand* (Sat+Chit+anand), often satirized as "Always Happy" (when translated in its mundane sense). Since there are perceived similarities between mystic visions and the heightened awareness produced by hallucinogens, the mystical experience has been seen in an unwholesome light in the west. The tendency to conceive the east as mysterious and exotic has had its perils. Not only the current groups of 'Nirvana' seekers, but even poets and writers have exaggerated its esoteric quality and its dream-like magic. Coleridge's "Kubla Khan", Thomas Moore's *Lalla Rookh*, and Byron's *Don Juan* interpreted the east in terms of its magnificence and romance. Thomas De Quincey's nightmares of 'oriental imagery and mythological tortures' are an example of a westerner's highly representative vision of the east. He writes of being sacrificed, stared at, and grinned at by monkeys. He is disturbed by the 'ancient, monumental, cruel and elaborate religions of Hindostan' and he dubs Asia, in general as 'the seat of awful images and associations' (De Quincey, 1890: 441–443).

Such opium-induced fears, Coleridge's fantasia "Kubla Khan" (again induced by opium) and the imaginary land of colours and romance portrayed by Thomas Moore's *Lalla Rookh* heighten the expectations of the western travelers. Victor Jacquemont,[7] the French traveller to Kashmir in 1830–31 was so frustrated at not finding the Kashmir of *Lalla Rookh*[8] that he called Moore 'a liar to boot'. Jacquemont had brought *Lalla Rookh* specially to read in Kashmir, but what he saw in reality belied the picture. Brigid Keenan, who travelled in Kashmir in around 1988–89 writes that though a great deal has been written about Kashmir since Thomas Moore's book came out, the picture of Kashmir presented in *Lalla Rookh* has held the fancy of the westerners. 'Moore's rosy picture has somehow endured all the battering it has received and, without realizing it, even today's visitors to Kashmir (who are more unlikely to have read his poem) probably have their expectations heightened and coloured by the flowery imagination of this Irishman who never went there at all' (Keenan, 1989: 95). A number of factors have given rise to the various myths associated with the Orient and as John Steadman records, myths still continue:

> To Western eyes, the East is still the home of marvels, and many Occidentals will still believe almost any romantic tale about it – the Indian rope trick; Shangri-la; rishis who are as old and wise as the Taoist Immortals and still haunt the Himalayan ranges; Tibetan Lamas who fly on kites, undergo initiation ceremonies for 'opening the third eye', and project themselves in space or time at will. More than one volume of deliberate fantasy has passed for literal truth.
>
> We still live in a mythopoeic age. But we still want a Euhemerus to distinguish fact from fiction and history from myth. (Steadman, 1969: 38)

That the myth persists is affirmed by the dazed Nirvana enthusiasts in *Karma Cola*. In Part IV, meaningfully entitled "Tricks and Treats", Gita Mehta pokes three-pronged fun – at the guru who raises a man from the dead, at his mystified American disciple, and at the incompetence of government officials. 'The man, although an American, had lived in India for some time and was therefore only intermittently subject to those attacks of uneasiness that overcome foreigners in the presence of the supernatural' (47). The official machinery's efficiency also comes under her mild attack. Since the morgue officials could not find the body, but were 'full of goodwill' for the cause, they 'offered to produce another still for the happy event' (50). Finally, it is the Master who locates the correct body. The American is so 'fuzzy on the details of the miracle' that he cannot recount the great event of raising the man from the dead with any coherence. For him, the real 'miracle was when the Master found that body' (50). In fact, says Gita Mehta, 'the streets of India are lined with miracles' (46).

It is, indeed a miracle that though in modern times western machine and eastern mysticism have come closer 'for the advancement of man' (51), the concepts of 'the other-worldliness' of the east and 'this-worldliness' of the west still hold strong. Discussing the process of metamorphosis of Asia into a new society, Steadman elaborates:

> 'Asia', declared an Anglo-Indian writer 'is not going to be civilized after the methods of the West. There is too much Asia and she is too old'. This prognosis was fast becoming obsolete when Kipling made it, and it is flagrantly anachronistic today. For Asia, we all recognize, is rapidly transforming herself. From Japan to Ceylon, her historic civilizations are undergoing a sea change, and it is precisely by, through and because of the 'methods of the West' that they are doing so. This interplay of Eastern traditions and Western techniques is, indeed, one of the most striking features of the modern Orient. The twains *are* meeting, and the signs of this fusion are evident throughout the East. (Steadman, 1969: 298)

On several occasions in the course of her narration, Gita Mehta explodes the notion of Indian 'other-worldliness', for she is sure that 'the mystic east, given half a chance, could teach the west a thing or two about materialism' (x). The gurus, the 'Gods', the sadhus – people who are supposed to be above material greed – are all out to dupe the unsuspecting seekers. They not only demand 'fees' for services rendered but also extract exorbitant amounts from them. And the so-called 'rational' westerners fall 'a prey to men who were demanding not only complete and unquestioning obedience to their commands, but also extracted payment for that privilege' (45–46). The author mocks at both – the seekers, weakened by their 'magnificent obsession', and their gurus dazed by the lure of Mammon:

> The price of abject servility could vary from paying a percentage of your income to handing over your whole stash. No rebates. No refunds. No questions. An outstanding example of Taxation Without Representation. Surely such a takeover owed its success to a general debility in the host body. (46)

In psychological parlance the authority of the Indian gurus and the servility of the western seekers are both indicative of the 'having' mode of existence. Eric Fromm defines the 'having mode' as a way of life 'centred in property and greed and an inordinate desire to possess.' The gurus are greedy for material gains; the disciples are greedy for 'quick nirvana'. Thus those who exercise authority – the gurus, and the objects of authority – the disciples, are both corroded by the 'having' orientation. Eric Fromm explains the difference between 'having' authority and 'being' authority:

> Our understanding of authority in the two modes depends on our recognizing that 'authority' is a broad term with two entirely different meanings: it can be either 'rational' or 'irrational' authority. Rational authority is based on competence, and it helps the person who leans on it to grow. Irrational authority is based on power and serves to exploit the person subjected to it. (Fromm, 1976: 25)

'Competence of authority' signifies the leaders' skill, wisdom and experience. Since 'being' authority is growth-oriented, the guru or the leader radiates authority and does not require giving orders or threatening; the 'having' authority creates an artificial image and in order to assert itself, it has to take recourse to tricks or threats to ensure obedience. Most of the gurus to whom the western seekers turn are not integrated personalities. Far from having any spiritual insight, they do not even possess the moral training and the elegant simplicity implicit in the native tradition. They are, in fact, 'con-men' who almost force the unsuspecting westerners into believing the Maya-Karma masquerade and induce them to part with their possessions.

Gita Mehta directs her attention to the 'monomania of the west' and the 'multimania of the east' to show how painful it is for those from the former set of thinking to understand the latter. Since we, Indians look at the world as 'Maya', we have the advantage of having 'the profound consolation of knowing that everything and every perception is a con, and worse, a self-induced con, a view enshrined in the Hindu concept of Maya' (35). The visitors do not have this advantage and baffled by the inherent contradictions they fall an easy prey to the guru's tricks. Here, the intended pun on the words 'con' and 'Maya' performs a dual function – it states a significant fact of our metaphysical thought and also pokes fun at its present corrupt form. The 'con-men' (tricky gurus) induce the visitors into believing that the world is an illusion (Maya) and hence it is imperative to renounce everything to attain 'nirvana'. The Maya (money) from their purses finds a way into the coffers of the gurus. The hapless seekers, divested of their cash, living in miserable poverty and filth, unable to return to their homeland, either live in humiliation or die humiliating deaths due to dysentery or drugs.

Of the many cases of penury, madness and death, some are narrated by the author with undercurrent of humour and bathos. One young American thought himself to be on a 'nude sadhu trip' and under the effect of hallucination ran up and down in a Pan American Airways plane stripped of all his clothes. It took two pursers to control the frenzied boy and get him dressed. As the doctor-in-charge of the situation recounts, such cases of obsession are many; but ironically, the doctor's attitude is one of complicity, 'these are harmless people who want a little attention. But more than that, they want reassurance that they are still human beings from other human beings' (87). In another instance the omnipresent narrator spots a 'starving English girl', sitting outside a hotel in Benaras, sketching in public to interest passers-by to buy her sketches. Later, it is discovered that her 'great-grandfather was a viceroy' of India. Her companion hits her hard on learning that she has sold one of her sketches and turns in fury on the narrator who is present there, 'You people used to lick her shoes. Now you buy her rotten pictures so you can buy her company. Get out! Get out before I throw you out! You're slaves, all of you, filthy beggars ...' (73). Yet another case is that of a French young woman who stays with her baby girl in the jungle behind Delhi University. The villagers think she is 'an incarnation of the Goddess. Others think she is a witch. Or insane' (127). She is suspected of having murdered her guru-husband and her son born of him. She entertains a mad hope she will replace the 'Mother' at Pandicherri Ashram. Living in filth, infested with lice, she reminiscences the time when she 'discovered' her guru through his reflection in the running water of the Ganga at Haridwar. Soon, they lived together and brought forth children.

At this juncture, let us reflect on three questions: first, how do these gurus manage to intimidate the so-called 'rational' westerners; second, what is the attitude of the gurus towards their disciples; and third, how deep is the motivation of the seekers to attain the desired spiritual goal? We try to look at the issues in reverse order. The seekers come to the east in search of 'instant kicks'. The gurus/sadhus have casual attitude towards them and consider them 'good catch' to be manipulated for material gains. These gurus manage to subdue them into submission – both physical and material – by using ostensibly esoteric tactics of being vague, ambivalent or just by maintaining an inscrutable silence. This generates an atmosphere of duplicity, superficiality and incomprehensibity on both sides. It is Kalyug, the era of jet-speed; if the seekers want Nirvana in an instant, there are gurus ready with 'instant' salvation tips. As one of the gurus confided to a correspondent of *Time* magazine, 'My followers have no time. So I give them instant salvation. I turn them into neo-sanyasis' (102).

The irony of the entire rigmarole is that concepts like sanyasa, meditation, karma, salvation, nirvana; the precepts of the *Gita* and the *Upanishads*; the teachings of the great sages; and the symbolic significance of Shiva-linga, Kali drinking blood, or Durga on her tiger, have been reduced to infantile vacuity. The author clarifies the Indian position with due gravity (without using her shafts of humour): 'A sanyasi in India is halfway to being a saint, a man who has renounced the world to seek the truth, a renunciation that is social as well as physical. His vows are not significantly different from those who join monasteries in the West – dedication to poverty, chastity and if the sanyasi is a teacher, obedience' (103). Similarly, when Lord Krishna spoke of meditation, self-knowledge, and infinite bliss, his emphasis was on disinterested action. In the Hindu system of thought the divine can be realized through the study of theology (Jnana-Yoga), or through rigid mind-control (Raja-Yoga); through right action (Karma-Yoga); or through love and devotion (Bhakti-Yoga). But ironically, the western seekers interpreted love as lust, meditation as oblivion induced by hallucinogens, sanyasa as living in filth, Shiva-linga as sex-symbol and karma as everything. Gita Mehta feels piqued that a highly philosophical doctrine like karma should be so distorted:

> Karma is now felt as a sort of vibration and Krishna is a doe-eyed pinup. As options proliferate all over the globe, the ability to understand the nature of necessity appears to be diminishing and bondage means something else again. So the terminology has accommodated itself to the needs of those who use it. (100)

A telling example of how the new converts to Hinduism started marketing our gods is provided intermittently in *Karma Cola*. When the western enthusiasts started pouring in, their 'first wave' country-cousins, who were already dyed in the lore of the healing-powers of India and who 'glowed with vegetarian good health', not only became the new-comers' guides but also sold them their knowledge:

> The soft sell pulled them in. Hard grafts kept them there. The new society immediately acquired its Vaishyas to trade on increased expectations of their colleagues. The traders offered cut-price tours to India with names spanning all seven chakras of human possibility. They patched together the broken ivory bangles of Hindu widows with silver ornaments and sold them to the travelers. They discovered the yoni and the lingam shapes of the mortar and pestle, and soon everyone was grinding sex into their spices. They handed on the names of holy men and hospices and sold the clothes appropriate to every occasion. (68)

The traders and buyers here are westerners. Soon, the newcomers are inducted into the ashrams. Now, the marketers and consumers are Indian gurus and their western disciples and vice-versa. The Hindu gods become the 'cool' ones, witnessing non-chalantly the 'Bhaktas' heating dope at the brightly burning clay wick-lump; nirvana, which in its original sense offers identity with the Absolute Being, is sold at a price; and at Bom Jesus Cathedral a woman bites off the big toe of St. Xavier's body to ascertain that the body is real. Thus, whether it is the Hindu faith or Buddhist philosophy or Christian heritage, everything is over-simplified into a single marketing formula, characterized by reaffirmation of miracles. And one of the miracles is the unquestioned acceptance of the fact that if a westerner becomes 'Hindu minded' and dies, the probable cause of his death could be his

'Hindu-mindedness' (164), as the police officer surmises in the case of the Dutch millionaire's death. Gita Mehta's acerbic observation about the marketing strategies for spiritualities has some grain of truth in it:

> It would appear that when East meets West all you get is the neo-Sanyasi, the instant Nirvana. Coming at the problem from separate directions, both parties have chanced upon the same conclusion, namely, that the most effective weapon against irony is to reduce everything to the banal. You have the Karma, we'll take the Coca-Cola, a metaphysical soft drink for a physical one. (103)

Keeping aside satire and sarcasm for a while, we look at the attitude of the west towards the eastern spirituality before the onslaught of the twentieth century seekers. Though the East-West dichotomy has always been there, the wholesale imitation of the east and the wholesale rejection of the west or vice-versa was less obvious at least at the intellectual levels. There was a judicious and selective compromise between the two views, despite diversities, and a desire to know the other. As John Steadman points out, 'among the disciples of Eastern spirituality one must number more than a few Western intellectuals' (Steadman, 1969: 100). Aldous Huxley, Paul Valery, Max Mueller and many others tried to understand the east, her culture, art and architecture, her religion and spirituality. Gita Mehta calls them the 'Brahmins of Western intellectual thought' who paved the way. 'Aldous Huxley had struggled with Vedanta and dared to expand his mind. William Butler Yeats, while collaborating on a translation of *The Upanishads* had found "in that east something ancestral in ourselves, something we must bring into the light". These were the thoughts of the highest caste, the scholar, deliberating on language, meaning and despair' (67).The contribution of these scholars to the eastern as well as western thought was immense. John Steadman also elaborates that thinkers such as these tried to transcend the East-West barriers and added insight to the existing thought.

> Some sought to transcend the limits of sectarianism by adding the insights of the Orient to those of the West. Some, like Aldous

> Huxley, were looking for a *prisca theologia*, a perennial philosophy. Some, like Paul Valery and (to some degree) Martin Heidegger, admired the negative methodology of certain Eastern philosophies and their concern with Non-being. Some, like Dr. C.G. Jung, found their approach to the unconscious significant for European depth psychology. Some found in Buddhism a congenial reconciliation of skepticism and mysticism that enabled them to stress the value of religious experience without committing themselves to religious dogmas. Some found in the impersonal, undifferentiated Absolute of some of the Indian religions a substitute for the personal divinities in whom they could no longer believe. These, in effect, tried to bypass the religious crisis of the West – the long, unresolved conflict between reason and dogmatic faith – by positing an ultimate spiritual reality which transcended logical demonstration and religious dogmas alike, which could not be grasped through words or apprehended through concepts, and about which nothing could be positively affirmed or denied. (Steadman, 1969: 100)

The Beatles, Rolling Stones and the Hippies faced approximately the same conflict – the conflict of the unresolved religious, social and cultural crisis; the conflict between reason and unreason, consumerism and faith. But, the problem with them was that they wanted to escape than to resolve the crisis. Instead of searching for answers, they searched for instant solutions, some kind of getaway to evade the problem. Many nirvana seekers also admit: 'The fact is I didn't really come here to get here. I sort of drifted here to get away from there' (64); 'Just I was tired of dollars, dinars, telephones, telex,' says Swiss banker turned sadhu; 'the simple answer to the whole movement is that we come here to get unwired. Where else *is* there to go?' (78). An Italian countess, come to get the mantra from the Maharishi, confesses, 'I am old and lonely. I have need of the peace ... Shanti' (107); the French girl living in the jungle near Delhi University reached India via Turkey, 'It all began with my mother in France. She was *La vrai bourgeoise*, always worried about the neighbours. She cared more about them than about me, so I ran away' (129). Others are equally candid when they say that they wanted 'to escape from that terrible world where everyone is mind-fucking everyone else;' 'we left home to get away from that shit' and so on. In short, these young ones are the victims of ennui, nausea and boredom born out of materialism. There is no seriousness of purpose, no scholarly inquisitiveness.

The hollow approach of the seekers is matched by the shallowness of the gurus and sadhus eager to make neo-sanyasis out of them. Each ashram has its specific program chalked out for its inmates. Here is Maharishi with his seat in Switzerland offering Transcendental Meditation courses. To his disciples he gives special individual mantras for peace, Shanti, with a name tag; and if a particular mantra does not work, he shrewdly replaces it. But to the high-brow scientists, he explains atom and particle theory enshrined in our doctrines and warns them to 'ring the bell for EUREKA!' (109). In another ashram, the concentration is on laughter, while in yet another, body control and mind control is taught through violence. The approach of the gurus towards the western seekers is dismissive. As the matriarch of one ashram admits: 'These people want toys. They are fascinated by sex and violence;' so 'Bhagwan gives them games and riddles. He tells them to beat each other, make love, do whatever comes into their heads' (38). If someone gets a broken limb or becomes mad, he/she is sent to the local hospital, where the nurses 'give them pills' and thus the ashram steers clear of them. The Ma tells the narrator casually that those who do not get well in hospital are treated differently. 'Oh, them. We sedate them, put them on a plane and send them back to their own countries' (39). Thus shattered in body and spirit, ailing and insane, the seekers either languish in India or end up in some asylum in their home country.

The gurus give a bad reflection of Indian spirituality, and Indian society. Not that India lacks real spiritual men, real gurus who can lead the disciple on the path of Enlightenment, and who have had western followers. Men like Aurobindo, Swami Vivekananda, Swami Yoganand and many others were highly revered for their knowledge and understanding of spiritual precepts. But the sadhus and holy men who sprung up with the new wave were shamans controlling the gullible seekers by their tricks. The stratagem they follow to hold them under their awe can be summed up as: ambivalence, double-talk, obscure statements, angry outbursts or silence.

In higher spiritual practices of the eastern tradition, silence is one of the methods to impart knowledge of the Absolute. The Absolute is beyond words, He can be experienced mystically or can be realized intuitively, but cannot be talked about. According to one Mahayana legend, once when Buddha was asked the secret of nirvana, 'he refused to reply in words; he merely looked at a golden flower and smiled' (Steadman, 1969: 74). This contemplative silence is followed in Hinduism too. In *Karma Cola*, Gita Mehta pokes fun at the gurus who maintain a tight-lipped silence or answer a question with a counter question, 'What is the Answer?' or 'What is the question?' (70). The guru, in fact, is too shallow to understand the question or give a convincing answer but his 'international clientele refuse to believe this, so they take his politesse for profundity' (70); and in some cases if the guru answers at all he produces some banal remedy. Thus by making 'spiritual' knowledge inaccessible to their Western disciples, the gurus insulate themselves. 'In a tradition where the question asks itself and the answer replies itself and all that remains is to establish the identity of the asker, clearly the Occidental is going to experience serious difficulty in eliciting any information at all, be it spiritual, physical or just the fastest way to get to the next town' (71).

Chinese cryptic poetry and Japanese Haiku (particularly of Basho) enshrine deep spiritual truths in unintelligible, short phrases that look unconnected. For example, one Chinese verse reads thus:

> This breeze/So fresh
> That moon/So bright
> At first/Come cheap
> This stream/So near
> That peak/So far
> As one/Run deep.

In this poem what is felt and heard is set against what is seen; what is near is set against what is far. Yet underlying the contrast is the sense of unity. Gita Mehta takes her cue from such esoteric religious practices and makes fun of the gurus who confuse their credulous disciples by their circumspection. The Maharishi's long conversation is so circuitous that it is beyond the grasp of the two scientists. 'Come, gentlemen. Let us join hands. It is Kalyug. The Age of Darkness. We have no time to wait thirty or forty years for scientists to find the right words. The moral issues are already clear' (109). This is an ambiguous statement that may bring forth several questions – what are the moral issues? Why can't we wait for thirty-forty years? What is the Maharishi going to discover? Likewise, the conversation between the American scriptwriter and the sadhu about sexual control is again an example of misdirection and deviation. 'Learn this from India if you learn nothing else, my son. The flesh is the only battlefield. Wars are won by the soul. The mature man seeks to understand his nature until he understands Nature' (59). The height of comic effect is achieved when the American, back in Los Angles, 'cites his experience as the sort of miracle you can come across in India' (59).

The author pokes fun at the strategy of those gurus who force new names on their disciples, those who repeatedly say the meaningless 'it's beautiful' and also those who only giggle or smile and make a mockery of everything. In one ashram a child is named Buddha. 'God calls him the Buddha .... He's a very high soul' (28) elaborate his disciples. This little Buddha wants 'guns and soldiers' as toys. Hearing his demand the narrator goes into peals of laughter as it appears too contradictory for this 'high soul' to demand weapons of destruction. But the real ludicrous is yet to come – when her uncontrollable laughter calms down, the excited disciples utter a pointless, 'Isn't that just beautiful?' One does not know whether the child's demand is *beautiful* or their laughter is.

The new names assigned to the devotees obliterate their identity but do not change the individual in any significant way:

> Here's a good one.
> You be Buddha, the Enlightened One.
> You are Abhimanyu, who knew how to enter the circle, but not how to leave.
> You are the just king, Yuddhistra.
> You are Saraswati, Goddess of Learning.
> Nobody is Joanie anymore. (35)

Such tactics completely intimidate the seekers into believing in their transformation and also reposing faith in the power of their gurus. It takes another decade and a half before they stream out of the ashrams disillusioned and angry. But, at the height of the wave, everything that the gurus say or do, appears 'spiritual'. Soon the wave becomes part of the Indian towns and cities where the Hippies concentrate. A large segment of Indian population feels overwhelmed by them.

Public reaction to the visitors is influenced by their self-interest. By and large, the Indian mentality is of *laize faire*; something to the effect that says: 'as long as they do not harm me personally, I just connive at them.' Gita Mehta records the initial shock wave in Goa at the libertine ways of the Hippies. The shock gave way to indignation and anger when the citizens discovered that their beaches had become open-air brothels. But political torpor, administrative apathy and public helplessness just let the Hippies be. The 'authorities took the line of least resistance'. The schoolgirls were instructed to take another route to their convent and it was felt that since the 'hippies weren't actually harming anyone' (19), the authorities should not create a 'national scandal' by dislodging them. Mehta quips, 'Goa now has two unique attractions. The beach, for the tourist who wants cheap thrills, and the Cathedral, for the tourist of a religious bent' (91).

The public in general took all Europeans as promiscuous and of easy morals – Hippies or no Hippies, any white-skinned woman was an object of 'desire'. The experience of a highly educated scholar woman at Khajuraho is an eloquent example to substantiate this fact (87–88). In Anita Desai's *Journey to Ithaca* too, Sophie traveling alone has horrendous experience when lecherous men thought her easily available.

Sometimes even the ordinary people like the sweeper woman showed deeper understanding of the situation. She was far more rational than the irrational seekers. The Sweeper woman felt sorry for the victims of guru's tricks when she saw a young girl imagining that she was happily 'bathing in his [the guru's] energy'. Asked if she [the sweeper woman] believed in the guru, her simple reply was: 'No, sister. I don't believe in the guru. He is playing games with these people. Look at this girl. Has he given her peace or has he just made her desire stronger? I tell you, sister. These days I have only one god. The Municipal Corporation' (148). On the other hand, the shopkeepers near the ashrams who call the seekers mad or foolish, are happy with them because the Hippies give them business. The government machinery is as somnolent as ever and it only wakes up when there is some crime, but nothing seems to come out of their investigations. The Indian girl from a 'good family' charged of murdering the Dutch millionaire or the French girl charged of poisoning her guru-husband and her son go free as the allegations are not proved. The Anand Marg killings have the hand of a strong mafia and no one dares touch the issue or expose the crime – neither the media nor the police.

The Hippie movement that started with their innocuous search for peace involves all the continents and cultures, the people from the grassroots to the highest political dignitaries; and also the C.I.A., K.G.B., and the Interpol. It is an accepted fact that when a movement becomes widespread, its socio-cultural aspects, its international significance and its plus and minus points interest the litterateurs. The Hippie movement started drawing attention of writers, poets, dramatists and even film-makers.

Western seekers coming to the east in search of self-realization is not a new theme in literature and writers have dealt with it from different angles – the profundity of eastern thought, the obscurity of Indian mysticism, the mind-boggling doctrines of its philosophical schools, the far-reaching implications of its archetypal spirituality. Add to this the concept of pilgrimages in search of 'other things' as Kipling's Kim does. Kim's guru, the old lama, is his companion all through his pilgrimage who helps him attain a therapeutic vision in the end. In Herman Hesse's *Siddhartha* and Somerset Maugham's *A Razor's Edge*, the heroes reach India in search of redemption and after initial conflicts, physical and psychological problems, and resistance generated due to the diametrically opposed world-views of eastern and western metaphysics, they finally feel at peace with themselves. In A *Razor's Edge*, Larry moves about Benaras and other places, gathers experience and at some point of time and space gets self-revelation. Hesse's *Siddhartha*, after a long conflict within stands on the bank of the river with Vasudeva and suddenly sees the light, the aura of which reflects in his face. He attains serenity of knowledge. This is the serenity of one who is not confronted with conflicts of desires, and who has found harmony with the stream of life. Siddhartha has surrendered himself to life and he belongs to the unity of all things. The gurus in these earlier works are not the 'con-men' of *Karma Cola*; they show the way and after doing their duty they may or may not remain part of the plot. In later novels, however, particularly after the Hippie influx of the 1960s, the seriousness of tone gives way either to the satirical element or nausea. Ruth Jhabvala's *A New Dominion* (1972) and *Heat and Dust*, (1975), and Anita Desai's *A Journey to Ithaca* (1995) explore the Indian gurus and their benign/demonic power over the western seekers with the use of irony and satire.

A New Dominion exposes a dubious guru, called Swamiji, who exercises hypnotic power over the Western characters – Lee, Margaret, Evie and Raymond. The Swamiji runs a Universal Society for Spiritual Regeneration of Modern World, like Gita Mehta's Maharishi, and wants to spread his message in the world, as the Maharishi too plans through his conference of top scientists of the world. The Swamiji's method is to expand the mind by 'breaking' it. He breaks them so irreparably that the characters are emotional and physical wrecks, reduced to 'nothing'. Living in hunger, filth and uncertainties, Margaret dies of jaundices, Lee loses her sense of direction and Evie becomes a tragic-comic figure feeling free after leaving the Swami but pursued by her obsessive hatred for him. Lee's experience with the Swamiji is one of nausea, terror and helplessness, 'He was saying, "How stupid you are, what a stupid little fool"; he said it in quite an affectionate way but that was only the beginning. He soon stopped being affectionate. He said terrible things and he did terrible things .... *He* was the only person there. He was terrible, terrifying' (Jhabvala, 1972: 163). In *Heat and Dust* again there are seekers – the narrator, who despite her 'rationality' and professed purpose of visiting India, allows herself to be 'used' by her lover and gets pregnant; and Chid, who though sexually virile is spiritually shallow. As Major Minnies warns, the westerners should keep their 'distance from Indians' because one may love India but she always 'remains an opponent, even sometimes an enemy, to be guarded and if necessary fought against from without and, especially, from within: from within one's own being' (Jhabvala, 1975: 170–71).

Anita Desai places two European characters in India – Matteo from Italy and Sophie from Germany and shows their physical journey from Italy to India and their spiritual journey within India. What they lose or gain at the end of their odyssey is subject of another debate, but it could be mentioned here that the concepts of 'making and breaking' the followers, the esoteric practices of the gurus, their ambiguous statements leave the seekers clueless. The narrative takes us through hunger, filth, poverty, hopelessness and directionlessness of the Hippie camps and the dubious ashrams. There is no final resolution, only a dulled peace as Matteo leaves for the Himalayas and Sophie sands puzzled and stunned at the end of the novel looking at her husband walk towards an unknown destination. The long epigraph to the novel affirms 'that the most significant and satisfying experience is the journey itself; may be it is beset with difficulties, but it is worth the trouble .... Ithaca cannot give external 'riches' to the questers but it can certainly vouchsafe inner direction. The analogy fits India well enough' (Bande, 2003: 19–20). But India cannot be taken for granted; one has to be ready to garner the experience with positive attitude.

This brings us to two significant points, 'what India does to the foreigners' and 'why'? I would like to repeat and reproduce a few significant lines from the poem on Ithaca:

> Always keep Ithaca fixed in your mind.
> To arrive there is your ultimate goal.
> But do not hurry the voyage at all.
>
> Ithaca has given you a beautiful voyage.
>
> And if you have found her poor, Ithaca has not defrauded you.
> With such great wisdom you have gained with so much experience.
> You must surely have understood by then what Ithacas means.

(Epigraph to *Journey to Ithaca*)

The tone here is positive and clear. If a seeker-voyager fails to find the desired treasure, the imperfection is his, not Ithaca's (by implication, not India's). I take this view though I am aware that some critics do not subscribe to the view that Ithaca implies India.

In *Heat and Dust*, the narrator analysis the influence of India on the basis of Major Minnies' monograph entitled "On the Influence of India on the European Consciousness and Character."

> India always ... finds out the weak spot and presses on it .... For Dr. Saunders it is something, or someone, rotten, for the Major this weak spot is to be found in the most sensitive, often the finest people .... It is there that India seeks them out and pulls them over into ... other dimension ... another elements, one in which the European is not accustomed to live, so that by immersion in it he becomes debilitated or even destroyed. (Jhabvala, 1975: 170–171)

Thus, if Europeans/westerners seek to immerse in it and feel debilitated or despaired is it India's fault? The problem arises because of the overwhelming spiritual aura associated with India, which is exaggerated because of the popular misconception about eastern spirituality and western materialism.

Gita Mehta also seems to hold this view. She dexterously weaves situations alternately in such a manner that one cannot fully exonerate the gurus or accuse them. In one conversation the Swiss banker remarks that the Germans are frightening because they 'go to the mountains, the Himalayas, The Abode of Snow' and 'try to be Supermen'. This is 'what India does to them' (74). A clear indication of devastating insanity, perhaps! Not the gurus but their own mental state is responsible for such an aberration. In another incident, one guru while teaching the concept of free love and exhorting his disciples to release their pent up desires by any method available said that 'they must love him as a father, a mother, a brother, a lover, a husband, to reach knowledge of his Godhead' (149). One American woman disciple took him too literally and 'burst into his room one night screaming, "Take me, Lover! I'm yours"'. The guru had a hard time guarding himself from the frenzy.

This does not mean that all gurus and sadhus are irreproachable and impeccable. Most of them use words having double-meaning and their actions or decisions are equivocal. One guru interprets his teaching thus:

> "There is no sin but self-loathing. The Self is God. If you loathe your body you loathe yourself. Go towards your body, go toward your desire, and then go *past* them. The death of desire is the birth of Atman". (149)

In normal metaphysical setting, these words carry authentic connotation and their essence cannot be doubted but with the foreign disciples who are keen to act out their sexual fantasies, his words acquire a different tinge. Most of the gurus do not want Indians in their ashrams because of obvious reasons. The ashrams are the hubs of esoteric sexual rites, Tantirc love practices and sexual orgies. What the foreigners accept as a matter of religious practice, the 'horny' Indians may resist. So, they find it convenient to keep Indians at a distance, sometimes they allow those Indians only 'to bask in the warmth of the ashram's sexual liberation' who 'have a vested interest in maintaining the discretion' (150). This ensures that the ashram's secrets remain guarded and the police are kept at a bay.

Whether the police are really hoodwinked or not, is yet another matter. The criminals go scot-free because of inaction on the part of the law-enforcing authorities and also because of the strong following they build for themselves. A journalist wonders 'what sort of chemistry' Shobbraj possesses to attract women despite his terrible crimes. 'Not just our women. There was a girl here from *Paris Match*, a supposedly hard-bitten French journalist. Even she ended up with a serious crush on this madman' (170). There are other stories too – a Tantrik's ritual murders in Rishikesh, the hero-worshipping youngsters in Goa who find 'The Man' quite imposing though he is an acknowledged smuggler. I remember here Shakespeare's *Julius Caesar*, when Cassius opines that Caesar is great because 'we are underlings'; on the same analogy, these smugglers and killers and cheats are worshipped because of the weakness of the system – the individuals, the society, the administration and the politicians.

Unfortunately, politics, administration, society and religion, have intruded into the movement that started with the ennui of the western youth who wanted to find a release from the tedium of their societies into the more religiously-oriented, almost primitive societies of the east. Over the decades, the nature of the influx of foreigners has changed. What started with Hippies, Beatles and the Rolling Stones was picked up by the marketing giants. The consumer greed on both sides gave it a boost and soon the Karma-wave involved crime, political intrigues, and the entry of Interpol, K.G.B., C.I.A. and what not. Cleo Odzer recounts her first hand experiences with crime in her book *Goa Freaks: My Hippie Years in India*. She was involved in smuggling, drug abuse, and even the passport racket.[9]

There came a time when these 'disenchanted' seekers left the shores of India and went back broken in health and spirit, unable to adjust to their own society. Most of them complained that the gurus were partial or that there was politics in the ashram, or he/she was tired of doing the dirty jobs. But it would be naïve to believe that the problem ended with their departure. The eastern Nirvana and the western Utopia soon joined hands in other matters and we all got confused further:

> For us to reprogram ourselves, for us to fully grasp that life is not about doing time but about making time, means that we have to dump most of our philosophical perceptions overboard and accept the imperative of history, hoping we will not become exiles in our own land. (192)

Mehta closes her work with a toast to those who fear and also to those who are beyond fear and hence cannot hear; but in that there is subdued warning: it is not for puny man to understand 'Infinity', and by implication to comprehend India. 'India says, Trade you the void for the Zero, and the Western optimist says, Sure, is that all it takes to be Enlightened? India does not remind optimists that she conceptualized the Zero in order to make infinity tolerable. Imagine a universe without mathematical definition. Or put another way, look on the immeasurable' (185). Do we hear a faint echo of patriotic fervour here? Or is it Gita Mehta's biting humour *encore*?

Karma Cola is classified as a work of non-fiction, but it reads almost like a novel. The author intrudes upon each scene; the persona sees things and gleans first-hand knowledge of the various situations. Her intervention gives authenticity to facts and saves the book from being a mere documentation of the Hippie movement in the country and its impact on the socio-cultural matrix. Without blaming or favouring any block – eastern or western – she records her observations with accuracy and punching remarks. As Laxmi Parasuram points out, 'The form she has chosen gives her ample opportunities to come out with biting remarks and this is mostly done through the figure of a roving observer who is always present on the scene. This observer, gifted with a panoramic vision both of space and time, scans vast areas of history with a rare insight and enables us to figure out the chaotic trends' (Parasuram, 1991: 237). We may also add that besides 'panoramic vision', the narrator has quick wit and the ability to poke fun. The non-fiction form and the presence of the narrator help her to be free to cover a vast territory. With the seekers, she travels to places with jet-speed – Haridwar, Benaras, Delhi, Chennai, Pune, Bombay (Mumbai), Calcutta (Kolkata), Goa and even New York and Switzerland. Since the work is not bound by the necessities/niceties of plot, characters or story, the observer-narrator enjoys the facility to flit past events and people without pausing unduly for further effect. This creates fast forward movement and an impression of journey. The titles chosen for the chapters are eloquent and have a touch of humour: "Karma Crackers", "Be Bop", "Vox Pox". Each snippet ends with an epigrammatic observation or remark – 'More of that old black magic. Mind control, Market control. Out of control' (169); 'Interpol may yet catch up with her ... . If they do, ... then depending on which culture she's currently coming from, That's either Karma. Or it's showbiz' (140); 'God's cool,' he stated with simple finality. 'How true', said my escort and we left' (97). 'Sacred knowledge in the hands of fools destroys' (28).

Karma Cola covers a period of almost two decades from mid-1960s to the end of 1970s. We, looking at it from the vantage point of distance in time can feel the onslaught of consumerism linked with what Simon During called the 'global popular', on Indian culture (During, 1995: 343). Marketing 'magnificent India' is no longer a new concept now. The cross-cultural transactions, the transformation of Indian culture on the western lines and the tension between an old traditional approach and the new outlook are shifting the society from an insular to a global one. At this point, one tends to agree with Gita Mehta that since the 'rock and roll' is being performed by the east and the west together, it is possible that a time may come when we obliterate our identities and 'if the Indian wants to learn about India he will have to consult the west, and if the west wants to remember how they were they will have to come to us' (192). The dilemma of those who still fumble with 'home' and 'om' can best be understood in terms of Paul Scott: 'I thought that the whole bloody affair of *us* in India had reached a flash point. It was bound to because it was based on a violation' (Scott, 1968: 427).

Notes

1. The Hippie movement began in the United States in 1960s and spread to other countries by mid-sixties and declined in 1970s. The term Hippie or Hippy was coined in California in 1966–67 when alienated youth began propounding a philosophy of peace and love. These were mostly young men and women who dropped out of society and developed their own subculture often called counter-culture. Originally, hippies were part of a youth movement composed mostly of teenagers and young adults between the ages of 15 and 25 years who rejected the established institutions, opposed middle-class values, rejected political and social orthodoxy and criticised nuclear weapons and the Vietnam War. In fact, the hippies inherited the tradition of cultural dissent from the Bohemians and the Beatniks and considered the dominant culture as a corrupt, monolithic entity that exercised undue power over them, which they called as 'Big Brother' or 'The Man'.

   In its early stages the movement was a positive one in that it discouraged materialism and propagated universal brotherhood; Hippies became known as flower children and their influence as flower power. Their philosophy came to be epitomized by the Beatles' song "All You Need is Love." The Hippie culture influenced the Beatles and the Rolling Stones and together their influence spread worldwide through a fusion of rock music, and folk music. The Hippie ethos also found expression in literature, films, dramatic arts and visual and performing arts. Hippies popularized a new life style exalting marijuana and LSD as instruments of pleasure, colourful clothes, beads, bells, long hair and shabby dressing up in peasant blouses and non-Western clothing. Some other aspects of their lifestyle were sexual libertarianism, communal living characterized by free and open love relationships, and extensive travel. These aspects quickly superceded the original philosophy of the movement. Violence and widespread drug abuse became the hallmarks of hippiedom. Today, the term denotes one who is generally uncouth and does not fit into society. (Condensed from T.J.S. George, compiled. *The Enquire Dictionary*. New Delhi: Harper Collins, 1988 and *Wikipedia* Internet entries).

2. The Beatles were a music group that became leaders in the pop revolution of the 1960s. John Lennon, Paul McCartney, George Harrison and Ring Starr, were the four British youngsters who began the Beatles movement. Their first music performance was in Liverpool after which they soon evolved a Rock style of their own. Although these four were highly gifted songwriters who had innovative spirit and originality, their lifestyle was considered outrageous. They kept long hair, followed shabby dressing-up, had an irreverence for authority and advocated drugs. In 1967, the Beatles met Maharishi Mahesh Yogi at Hilton, London. They were influenced by the Yogi's philosophy and attended a weekend 'initiation' conference at Bangor in North Wales. The Maharishi gave each one of them a personal mantra. The Beatles were at the height of their creativity during their stay at Maharishi's Ashram in India. Their songs recorded for *The White Album* and *Abbey Road* became a rage of the time. Since they had a strong identification with the teenagers they became popular with the westernized youth all over the world. Their contribution to society and music was recognized by the British government when it gave them the MBE award. Ironically, the situation became embarrassing as the award represented establishment while the Beatles were anti-establishment. The Beatles lasted only for a decade and the movement disintegrated in the late 1970.
3. Like the Beatles, the Rolling Stones were a globally popular rock group which sprung up in England in 1960s. The band was formed by Brian Jones in 1962 and was later led by singer Mick Jaggar and guitarist Keith Richards. They were bolder and harsher than the Beatles both in their musical style and their use of drugs. Their songs known as *Blues, R&B* and *Rock n' Roll* remained a craze for over thirty years. Like the Beatles and the Hippies, these too influenced the younger generation world over and came to be recognized as a socio-cultural force. After their 1969 tour of the USA, they almost mesmerized the society and were recognized as the greatest Rock and Roll Band in the World. These youngsters were identified with shabby dressing-up, drugs and unconventional lifestyles (Condensed from *Wikipedia* internet entries and *The Enquire Dictionary*).

4. The discussion here has been summed up from Root's book *Cannibal Culture: Art, Appreciation, and the Commodification of Difference* (Boulder: WestView Press, 1996).
5. The term Conspicuous Consumption was first used by Thorstein Veblen, a Norwegian-American economist and sociologist in his work *The Theory of Leisure Class* (1899). The term stands for the use of goods and services with a view to asserting one's wealth and power and is associated with the *nouveau riche*, a new class that emerged in the nineteenth century capitalist societies. Conspicuous consumption is an essential feature of the consumer society. It denotes the acquisition and display of expensive items to attract attention to one's wealth. Those who go for ostentatious consumption usually equate it with social status and are driven by the notion that one must not only consume in excess of one's needs but must be seen to do so. (*The Enquire Dictionary*, p.122).
6. William Wordsworth in his 'Lines Composed a Few Miles above Tintern Abbey' describes mystical experience as:

   That blessed mood, in which the burthen of the mystery,
   In which the heavy and the weary weight,
   Of all this unintelligible world,
   Is lightened. We are laid asleep In body,
   and become a living soul:
   While with an eye made quiet by the power
   Of harmony, and the deep power of joy,
   We see into the life of things. (Lines 37–45)
7. Victor Jacquemont was a French traveller who was sent by the French Government 'to investigate the natural history of India in all its branches and collect material' for the Museum. Born in Paris in 1801, Victor had an inborn flair for natural history and scientific investigation. He was appointed in the Museum of Natural History and from thence was sent to India. Jacquemont visited many parts of India including the Himalayas. He wrote home letters which were later translated into English and published as *Letters from India: Describing A Journey in The British Dominions of India, Tibet, Lahore and Cashmere during the Years 1828, 1829, 1830, 1831*. Though these letters, written to his family and close friends, were not meant for public reading, their publication helped later travellers to know the unexplored parts of India.
8. Thomas Moore's *Lalla Rookh* is considered the bestselling epic poem which is often termed a kind of Arabian Nights romance for its exquisite description of the topography – through which the Princess's caravan passes from Delhi to Kashmir – and the antiquarian character of the east.

It is a fictional account of the journey to Kashmir undertaken by Lalla Rookh, the beautiful daughter of Aurangzeb the Moghul Emperor. Lalla Rookh means 'Tulip Cheek'. She is betrothed to Aliris, Sultan of Lesser Bucharia. On her journey to the valley of Cashmere, where the wedding is supposed to take place, she is entertained by a young Persian poet named Feramorz, who relates the four poetical tales of romance. The young Princess falls in love with the poet but culture and propriety prevents her from revealing her heart to her family. Saddened that the journey would soon be ending, Lalla Rookh becomes thin and pale. However, on her wedding day she discovers that her betrothed the king of Bucharia is none else but her lover, the young poet. *Lalla Rookh* became the rage of the reading public as much for its dreamy tale as for its heady combination of romance, exoticism and oriental fantasy. It inspired the romantic imaginations of readers and artists alike. The book was so popular with the nineteenth century readers, particularly the travellers to India that it ran into many editions during Moore's lifetime.

9. In *Goa Freaks,* Cleo Odzer narrates her years with the Hippies and her experiences as a smuggler and a dope addict. She opened a den at Anjuna beach which was called Anjuna Drugoona Saloona. According to her, the drug trade had a huge chain and was very well organized. Though the police had all the clues of her activities they did not take any action. She comments that by comparison the police in Thailand and other South Asian countries were strict and vigilant on drugs, nudity and other crimes. Odzer's work shows the ridiculously tolerant attitude of the average Goans and the apathy of the administration. The Goans argued that the Hippies were welcome because they brought Goans affluence; however, some of the citizens felt that these visitors should respect the social mores, which of course they failed to.

Works Cited

Bande, Usha. *Cultural Spaces and Diaspora: Journey Metaphor in Indian Women's Writing*. Shimla: Indian Institute of Advanced Study, 2003.

De Quincey, Thomas. *The Collected Writings of Thomas De Quincey*. 14 vols. Ed. David Masson. Edinburgh: A&C Black, 1889–1890.

During, Simon. "Postmodernism and Post-colonialism Today." *Textual Practice* 1 (1), 1987. Rpt. in *The Post-colonial Studies Reader*. Eds. Bill Ashcroft et al. London/New York: Routledge, 1995.

Desai, Anita. *Journey to Ithaca*. New Delhi: Minerva, 1995.

Fromm, Eric. *To Have and To Be.* New York: Bantam Books (A Division of Harper & Row), 1976.

George, T.J.S. Compiled. *The Enquire Dictionary.* New Delhi: Harper Collins, 1988.

Huggan, Graham "Consuming India" *Post-Independence Voices in South Asian Writings.* Eds. Malashri Lal et al. New Delhi: Doaba Publications, 2001.

Jacquemont, Victor. *Letters from India: Describing A Journey in the British Dominions of India, Tibet, Lahore and Cashmere, During the Years 1828, 1829, 1830, 1831.* London, 1934.

Jhabvala, Ruth P. *A New Dominion.* 1972. Rpt, London:Granada, 1983.

—. *Heat and Dust.* London: John Murray, 1975.

Keenan, Brigid. *Travels in Kashmir.* New Delhi: Permanent Black, 1989.

Odzer, Cleo. *Goa Freaks: My Hippie Years in India.* New York: Foxrock Book, 1995.

Parasuram, Laxmi. "*Karma Cola*: Another Version of East-West Encounter." R.K. Dhawan. Ed. *Indian Women Novelists.* Vol.5. New Delhi: Prestige, 1991.

Root, Deborah. *Cannibal Culture: Art, Appreciation, and the Commodification of Difference.* Boulder: WestView Press, 1996.

Scott, Paul. *The Jewel in the Crown.* 1966; rpt. London: Granada, 1980.

Steadman, John M. *The Myth of Asia.* London: Macmillan, 1969.

Four

Raj: Between Rajniti and Kootniti

> I feel freedom's embrace in a thousand bonds of delight
>
> — Rabindranath Tagore

"On a cold January morning when Jaya was five years old, her father insisted she accompany him into the jungle. The Maharani objected. The Maharajah overruled her" (*Raj*, 1993: 1).

With these three, short, scintillating sentences, Gita Mehta opens *Raj* and captivates the reader. These three sentences are crucial to understand the socio-cultural-historical pattern of the novel because they imply that: (i) the novel is going to be about some Maharajah; (ii) Jaya is likely to be at its centre; and (iii) the work may question patriarchal power structure. In that *Raj* opens up the possibilities to be read as a historical narrative, a colonial/postcolonial novel, and a feminist text. We reach at this resolution of signification not because it has essential historical signifiers or because it reconstructs a 'native' past or critiques the suppression of women's voices. This would be an essentialist view of a work that presents cultural, historical and political implications with acute understanding and perceptive assertions. The pervasive influence of the colonial cultural and political realities on the Indian 'native' rulers is an all-too-well-known phenomenon. Likewise, the invisibility of women, the power-wielding impulse of traditional patriarchal society and the dichotomy between the public and the private self-image of the culture have become dominant themes of contemporary women's discourse. As for diasporic woman's writing, it tends to look at these issues from their vantage point of distance in time and space.

There is no denying the fact that colonial discourse is 'an apparatus of power' (Bhabha, 1992: 293),[1] and that it tends to impose its own culture on indigenous one, thus distorting native history. According to a Chilean poet-composer, 'The cultural invasion is like a leafy tree which prevents us from seeing our own sun, sky and stars. Therefore, in order to be able to see the sky above our heads our task is to cut this tree off at the roots' (Jara, 1984: 121).[2] Obviously, it is not possible to cut the tree at its roots but it is possible to negotiate a dialogue with history through revaluation of the local past. While problematizing the notion of history at personal and national levels and juxtaposing it with a traditional sense of history vis-à-vis its relationship to existing power systems, *Raj* offers itself to multiple critical positions. Gita Mehta is restructuring here the historical data and ordering it to a design, plot and sequence. The process requires re-visioning and re-writing the past 'to make a story,' situate it within the socio-cultural context and discover meaning and a sense of belonging in her own history. This is a postcolonial position in which the author is granting equivalence and importance to what the 'centre' once called 'margin', and what colonialism called 'native' and hence 'the other'. As a postcolonial writer, writing in a decolonized period, the author has undertaken to re-inscribe her country's past.

In *Raj*, Gita Mehta draws our attention to one of the most distressing experiences of cultural violence of colonialism. The fifty years that she depicts – 1897 to 1947 – was historically a period in which the country was fortified by an undeclared but obvious entanglement with imperialism and the native India that existed within the British India was as troubled and the rulers were as hapless and hopeless in the strangle-hold of the British power politics as the masses in the Imperial British India. Fear psychosis had gripped the nation including the native kingdoms. Pandit Nehru describes the anxiety-ridden sections of the entire society before the emergence of Gandhi on the political scene thus: 'The peasantry were servile and fear-ridden; the industrial workers were no better. The middle classes, the intelligentsia, who might have been beacon-lights in the enveloping darkness, were themselves submerged in this all-pervading gloom .... There was no adjustment to social purpose, no satisfaction of doing something worthwhile, even though suffering came in its trail ...' (Nehru, 1946: 310). The Rajas and the Maharajahs were no better off. That the Maharajah of Balmer – Jaya's father in the novel – was a frightened man is conveyed by the last line of the 'Prologue': 'Not until she became a ruler herself did she [Jaya] comprehend that the Maharajah [of Balmer] taught his children the tradition of courage when he was himself a frightened man' (5). Fear continues to haunt the rulers till the end of the novel – first it was the fear of displeasing the British and thus of being black-listed or disinherited on smallest pretexts; then there was also the fear of the nationalists spreading their message of freedom among the people in the native States; then came the most important and sensitive issue of merger with the Indian Union. Gita Mehta quotes Sardar Patel's insightful words to form the epigraph to Chapter 71, the last one of the novel, 'The capacity for mischief and trouble on the part of the rulers ... is far greater than could be imagined. Let us place ourselves in their position and then assess the value of their sacrifices' (456).[3]

For the rulers accession to the Union meant not only complete liquidation of their kingdoms but also obliteration of identity, which they construed as personal defeat and humiliation. To cite one example from literature, the Maharajah of Begwad in Manohar Malgonkar's *The Princes*, scared of an affront to his regal dignity should merger become a reality lets himself be attacked by a tiger during a hunting expedition and thus commits suicide. For him it is a better proposition to die a valiant death than to submit meekly. Jaya, on the contrary, is quick to read the signs of time and decides to join the Union. It does not mean that she had no qualms; after all, as a Regent, it was her duty to protect her 'son's kingdom' and safeguard his interest. Like other rulers she too was not willing to hand over her legacy, the oldest kingdom of Sirpur. But she realized that it was futile to fight a losing battle. The Raj Guru's words come to her rescue, '"What is the first principle of Rajniti, Bai-Sa?" and her reply, "the people",' and she gears herself up to give voice to her people as their elected representative.

The novel maps and dramatizes within the fabric of its narrative the important events of the national freedom movement. But unfortunately, freedom comes with an unhappy note. Partition is not the issue in this novel; but communal frenzy that led to inhuman brutalities is. Even the remote [fictional] state of Sirpur in the north-east is scorched by partition violence. Jaya's young son and the Prime Minister of Sirpur State, Sir Akbar are killed by the violent mob of fanatics 'demanding to know why a Hindu king was traveling with a Muslim' (446). The irony is that this incident takes place much before partition is to be finalized and Jaya shudders to think 'What would happen when the British Empire's boundary lines for the two new nations became public knowledge' (448). Within this framework Gita Mehta weaves the story of Jaya. The public domain – both at the national level and the state level – was beset with anxiety, fear, death and desolation; the private domain of Jaya was no better, it was full of uncertainties, deaths and dejection. The author has interwoven the political and the personal so intricately that the work goes much beyond the scope of being a historical record of our freedom struggle or a racy account of the grandeur and frivolity of the exuberant princes. *Raj* presents a deeper perspective on colonialism, feminism and historicity when read in the context of postcolonialism and postmodernism.

How does one read the novel from its multiple critical positions? This question is best answered if we approach it as a woman's saga of success. What distinguishes *Raj* from some other works dealing with the princes is exactly this angle, i.e., the woman's angle which gives it a new dimension. There are a number of works on the erstwhile native kingdoms, notable among them being E.M. Forster's *The Hill of Devi* (1933), Mulk Raj Anand's *The Private Life of an Indian Prince* (1953), Manohar Malgonkar's *The Princes*, (1963), Kamala Markandaya's *The Golden Honeycomb*, (1977), and Nayantara Sahgal's *Mistaken Identity*. Of these, the first three are by male authors and the focus in on the male world of the

Maharajas; women have but peripheral existence in these. In Kamala Markandaya's novel women play an active role though it is Prince Rabi's story. Nayantara Sahgal in *Mistaken Identity* is wholly preoccupied with her male protagonist Bhushan because it is the story of his vindication. Gita Mehta presents Jaya's story – a princess thrown into the fray by a relentless fate that snatches away her brother, father, husband and son, and leaves her to face the realities alone – realities of political situations and personal misfortunes. Jaya carries herself with dignity and accepts the challenges with fortitude.

This is the quality of *Raj* that critics appreciated almost unanimously. *Raj* is a saga, says Anima Amin 'not only of a country's struggle for independence but of a woman's battle to claim her rights both as an individual and as the head of a State' (Amin, 1999: 156). Calling it 'a success story that reads almost like failure', N.K. Jain avers that 'Jaya responds to change in her personal and political life with surprising openness and resilience and manages to hold her own in the male-dominated world' (Jain, 1998: 208). Another critic opines that when Jaya moved to the centre of power from the periphery of the political/patriarchal structure she 'handled the slippery political situations ... with great tact and skill,' drawing her strength from the tenets of Indian culture (Sarojini, 2006: 93). As a woman, Jaya is a pleasant mixture of tenderness and strength; as a ruler she displays acumen and courage. After all, her father's foresight in training her to face 'fear' with boldness and his efforts to induct her into 'Rajniti' do not go in vain. He used to tell his children – Tikka and Jaya – 'Rulers are men and men are always frightened. A man cannot govern unless he confronts his own fear' (5). In Manohar Malgonkar's *The Princes*, Maharajah of Begwad exhorts his son Abhay Raj, 'It is most important not to squeal, to show hurt. Be a man, my son' (Malgonkar, 1963: 33). These words do not refer to the male or the female; they allude to the human psyche.

It would be of interest here to see how *Raj* compares with some of the earlier novels on the theme of the Indian princes. Kamala Markandaya's *The Golden Honeycomb* deals with a long period in the life of one kingdom – Devapur and its three rulers, whereas *Raj* tells the history of two separate kingdoms – Balmer in Rajasthan and Sirpur in the north-east, joined by one protagonist – Jaya. *Raj* handles the political situation in the country from the angle of the rulers and does not concentrate much on the fiery period of the freedom struggle from outside the kingdoms although there are allusions to the nationalists of all beliefs – those who subscribed to Gandhiji's non-violence and those who did not, and also to the period when the country was seething with anger and resentment against the British and was enthused with patriotism. In fact, these events intrude into the narrative via the rulers and through those like Mrs. Roy or Arun Roy who frequent their kingdoms. On the contrary, in Nayantara Sahgal's *Mistaken Identity* and Kamala Markandaya's *The Golden Honeycomb,* the protagonists are made a part of the nationalist movement despite their royal backgrounds. Rabi feels one with the commoners when he is saved and nursed to health by Jaya, a mill-worker. Bhushan sees human goodness during his jail years and learns to look at the common man with respect.

This may be taken as a hint of the approach of democracy. Or this may also be the 'big story' of modern India as Makarand Paranjape points out. This story is the story of our growth as a nation and like all big stories it has many key themes such as unity in diversity, our multiplicity, our response to the postcolonial situation, partition, independence, and many more. Some of these issues are taken up in *Raj* directly or indirectly – directly when the native rulers are affected by them, like the colonial attitude of British Imperialism, westernization, independence, democracy and communalism; and indirectly, by the treatment the novel gives to nationalism, partition, and socialism. We come across these through Jaya's story of growth which is also the story of India's growth.

Predictably, Jaya's development has different dimensions – as a daughter, princess, wife, mother, friend, ruler and above all a woman, but somehow the novel is disillusioning at the level of development of human relativity. Human relationships – person to person and person to society are two major concerns of a creative writer and Shashi Deshpande, Anita Desai, Kamala Markandaya and many others consider interpersonal relationships of great significance in a work of fiction, the failure of which lands the characters in trouble and give a writer canvas to portray or solve those troubles. In one of her interviews Shashi Deshpande asserts, 'Human relationship is what a writer is involved with. Person to person and person to society relationship – these are the two primary concerns of a creative writer and, to me the former is of immense importance. My preoccupation is with interpersonal relationships and human condition (Deshpande, 1994: II).

This failure of *Raj* to build bridges across persons and situations may be because of the setting of the novel and the anxiety of the author to highlight aspects like the political tensions, the distance and difference in social situation of rulers and the common man, and many more external factors. Even Sahgal's *Mistaken Identity* has this limitation. On the contrary, Markandaya's novel is a 'fine mixture of historical realities and fictional setting. It shows [her] subtle art in handling the characters and situations and reveals her deep insight into human relationships (Bande, 2004: 107). Moreover, women play a significant role in moulding Rabi and though they are not given centre-stage, they have strength of character enough to draw Santha Krishnaswamy's attention who opines that in portraying her strong characters and able women, Kamala Markandaya 'opens up newer, mature frontiers by stressing the importance of filial and conjugal life' (Krishnaswamy, 1984: 229). All these novels record personal histories but they are also political novels with the history of colonial India. Written in the postcolonial era, they transfer some of the contemporary epithets to the earlier times and leave us wondering if the authors are not seeing the past in the light of the present. Whatever be the case, it cannot be denied that *Raj* gives us a new perspective to understand the history of our princely kingdoms and principalities from a woman's point of view.

Raj is a third person narrative presented through Jaya's consciousness. The omniscient narrator picks up the threads of the then existing political/historical conditions and guides us through Jaya's life from her birth, approximately in 1901 to the time she fills in her papers for elections. When the privy purses were abolished in 1971, we imagine that Jaya could be around seventy but we do not get to know her reaction because the "Afterward" merely documents the event and does not make it a part of the story. In the novel the heroine is both a mute observer and an active participant in the events that surround her – a mute observer of the happenings over which she has no control, be they political whereby the princes were stripped of their power, or human whereby her husband and the other princes invited their own downfall by their excesses and vagaries; she is an active participant in life-situations when she foresees the coming crisis and acts with dexterity to forestall the conflicts or troubles that were latent in the existing politico-cultural order of the times. She accepts change with a modicum of flexibility without being self-destructive like Mulk Raj Anand's Maharaja Ashok Kumar or revengeful like Malgonkar's Abhay Raj. This in itself is an indication of the strength she is invested with.

Through this deftly controlled and ingenuously patterned narrative, the author has re-written a significant period of India's colonial history. As a postcolonial writer, Mehta has the advantage to look back and recapture the past with a renewed vision; she can interrogate the imperialist history and situate the historical in the socio-cultural-political space. When a fiction writer attempts to comprehend his/her past and undertakes to reconstruct the historical events in fictional form, the 'portrayal of history becomes a project of understanding the present' (Mukherjee, 1992: 8). The project, in fact, is also to keep alive the historical memory and this desire is generated not so much from the wish to narrate the collective history that has been lived through but more so from the need of the knowledge of what had not been lived through. The past justifies the present. In the case of a diasporic writer the urgent need is not to lose the past because along with this loss goes the loss of space. 'Write' says a Spanish author, 'in order to remember', and remembering has a positive dimension because it reconstructs and wards off discontinuity. Moreover, by recovering history, one becomes a part of that history. Probably, this is a revivalist attempt to assert continuity. Once, talking about the significance of past to the present, A.K. Ramanujan asserted in an interview that one cannot isolate the past from the present because both are connected:

> Because you cannot entirely live in the past, neither can you live entirely in the present, because we are not like that. We are both these things. Either the individual past or historical or cultural past. It is with us, it is what gives us richness of what you call it – the richness of understanding. And the richness of expression. (quoted in King, 1987: 279)[4]

History, coloniality and the diasporic experience lends Gita Mehta a rich domain to revise and reconstruct the past; in the process she charts out a fictional world for the female identity to be incorporated in it. According to Juliet Gardiner, history and literature both require a negotiation of 'observation, memory and imagination'. Gardiner further clarifies that the 'historical reality is a special case of fiction as speech is a special case of writing ... and nature a special case of culture' (Gardiner, 1988: 12). It is often argued that a woman gives feminine perspective to history. So, how do we read when women write history? Is it from the angle of feminization? But then, will it not be a limited purview? These questions have been answered convincingly by Jasbir Jain in "Post-colonial Realities: Women Writing History". She posits that feminization of history does not connote any derogatory sense, rather it signifies that in writing history women give 'centre-stage' to the marginalized and try to free history from hegemonic control. This brings it closer to the actual happenings. Jain also explains that in the postcolonial situation, writing historical narrative denotes an attempt to interrogate the past, seek explanation and 'to reclaim an autonomous identity' (Jain, 1996: 161). What she says is relevant to our reading of *Raj* and hence I quote her further:

> The term feminization is not being used to indicate a personal, feminine response to history, but as an attempt to free history from purely masculine pursuits, from hegemonic structures, from an ideological thrust, and to bring it closer to the actual happening which work in several diverse directions and cannot easily be accounted for by a cause-and-effect explanation. It also seeks to subvert the conventional idea of feminization as passive reproduction of knowledge. Feminization here implies a new awareness of power relationships, a surfacing of the hitherto marginalized voices and a widening of historical imagination. (Jain, 1996: 162)

The salient points of this discussion can be summed up thus: Feminization of history means (i) giving voice to the marginalized; (ii) freeing history from ideology; (iii) taking it out of hegemonic control; (iv) generating a new awareness of power relationships; and (v) understanding the social dislocation of social relationships.

Commensurate with the above assertion, *Raj* concentrates on the history of Balmer and Sirpur (the native States) and Imperial British India, and the struggle for freedom from the point of view of a marginalized female – Jaya (we call her marginalized because though belonging to the ruling family, she is still the 'other' in the male dominated set-up). The four books – Balmer, Sirpur, Maharani and Regent – are also the four stages, metaphorically, of Jaya's life. Born and brought up in Balmer, the young princess is trained to be a 'ruler' as also a woman. The training that her father envisaged for her stands her in good stead when fate wills it that she should rule over her kingdom of Sirpur. As a Maharani and later as a Regent, she administers her people with caring touch. Raj Guru's words always stay with her, 'your dharma is protection, Bai-sa. You cannot escape your destiny' (454) and she does everything with public good in view. With scant faith in Arun Roy were he to be elected from Sirpur, she broods, 'If Arun Roy was elected from Sirpur, what would happen to the kingdom's different tribes and religions? Would he speak for them? Would he give a sympathetic ear to their concerns against the greed of the majority'? (460). Jaya is concerned for the marginalized of her state. To them she wants to give voice in the new political set-up. Even her attitude to the *Praja Mandal* activists is one of understanding and sympathy. This etches out more prominently when we read it vis-à-vis Malgonkar's *The Princes*, in which the Maharajah and after him Prince Abhay Raj are unable to accept the *Praja Mandal* in their kingdom. Even the author (Malgonkar) seems to have secret sympathy for the rulers. He paints Kanak Chand as a dubious character, with whom the readers too cannot empathize, and thus Malgonkar successfully avoids giving 'centre-stage' to the marginalized.

Two recurring signs that endorse women's strength and rulers' duties are the balled-singers singing of the valiant Queen Pushpavati and the Raj Guru elaborating the principles of Rajniti, respectively. Queen Pushpavati is acclaimed as 'the greatest queen in India, famed for her prowess with the sword.' The ballad-singers appear on all important occasions in the kingdom and sing the praises of the legendary queen. The Ballad runs thus:

> Two thousand years ago the great Queen Pushpavati was all that remained of the sons of the Sun.
>
> Her father, her brothers, her husband, all her great line lay slaughtered in the City of the Hundred Temples.
>
> Queen Pushpavati The greatest queen in India Famed for her prowess with a sword Who could draw a bow almost as well as a man Who rode at the side of her husband in pursuit of the cheetah This warrior queen was now a widow .... (13 and 455)

The ballad goes on to tell the long story of how the land came to be called Rajputana because of the valiant queen and her son, and their lineage.

The analogy befits Jaya who has lost all the male members and yet who has to nurture her kingdom like a mother and protect it like a patriarch. The Raj Guru anoints her with a blood-mark on her forehead, and reminds her to protect her people. Major Vir Singh's observation is meaningful at this point, 'I see that the man who anointed your father a ruling king has now anointed you a democrat, Bai-sa' (454). The passage of time and the changing perspective of the nation are revealed when one compares the two situations. Long back, in 1897, it was the birth of Tikka, heir to the kingdom that was announced with the booming of thirty-nine cannons; now, in 1949, the birth of a democrat (Jaya) is announced by an elephant trumpeting from the distant corrals. The Raj Guru is keen that Jaya should use the knowledge he had invested in her, the knowledge that the first principle of Rajniti is the welfare of the people:

> 'What is the opening lesson of Rajniti, Bai-sa?' 'First there is the praja, the people', she whispered. The Raj Guru nodded in satisfaction. 'I once told your father, as I am telling you now, this ancient land is old in the ways of government. It has witnessed the councils of nobles, and fiats of emperors, the whims of kings, the reigns of priest, the tolerance of great republics. Things go wrong

only when men forget the first principle of government. The people'. (453–54)

The understanding and acceptance of traditional Indian principles of governance heralds a new beginning for Jaya. Interestingly, at the end of the novel Arun Roy and John Osborne argue each claiming credit for having taught democracy to the rulers. Osborne remarks as Jaya signs the election papers, 'Congratulations, Bai-sa. It was the dream of the British Empire to teach the princes of India about democracy.' Arun Roy counters him, 'What did the British Empire know about democracy? ... we have taught the Indian rulers that lesson' (461). Jaya is amused at their naivety in putting across their tall claims and taking credit for something that has always been the part of Indian polity and jurisprudence. Remembering Raj Guru's words Jaya laughs loud and clear, and her laughter merges 'with the silver waters of the river' (461).

The 'laughter' is an indication that there is no sense of loss or rancor in Jaya. Just as her joy rolls 'across the Sirpur Law Courts and the narrow lanes of the bazaar' to join the river, her kingdom has joined the Indian Union for greater good. The novel ends on a happy and optimistic note, but the author is not quite sanguine about it. In the "Afterward" she expresses her disappointment at the abolition of privy purses; we do not know if Jaya too would have reacted as the author does but if Gita Mehta's words are to be taken as an indication, it was a betrayal, a breach of faith. May be the rulers were not in favour of merger; may be their contribution to the freedom struggle was negligible (they had their reasons) but they did sacrifice their identity by agreeing to merger. Sardar Patel understood this and he assured them security. Gita Mehta draws our attention to these facts:

> "Disbanding their armed forces, the Indian rulers merged voluntarily with a nation that did not even have a constitution. In return, the Union of India agreed to pay the rulers privy purses to assist in the discharge of their financial obligations". (462)

In recognition of their sacrifice, the government had reaffirmed the agreement between the Indian Union and the kingdoms. At that time, Deputy Prime Minister had said, 'Our obligation is to ensure that the guarantees given by us are fully implemented. Our failure to do so would be a breach of faith' (462). Ironically, what began on a democratic note comes crashing down and by 1971 it is substituted with a re-enactment of colonial diplomacy and power politics of imperialism.

Democracy has different connotations to different people in the novel. To high-profile leaders like Gandhi, Sardar Patel and others, it means a great national achievement with a vision for a bright future; to the native rulers it brings in fear and anger of an uncertain future; the unscrupulous leaders like Arun Roy (or Kanak Chand in *The Princes*) look at democracy as an opportunity for self-aggrandizement and to the common masses to whom it is supposed to give 'voice' it has scant utility. The words of the senior ballad-singer whose troupe has again appeared to sing of Queen Pushpavati are meaningful:

> 'Now we have heard that we are all kings. We have been told our voices will carry the same weight as the voice of our anointed ruler.'
>
> 'Such news has made us happy. But know this.' 'No ruler's voice has ever carried the same weight as ours. Our voices tell of generations that have risen and fallen like the shifting sand dunes of this harsh land.'
>
> 'Without us, deeds and lives would have long since been blown away, like dust in a desert storm, and proud men would not have been humbled by the greatness that has preceded them'. (455)

In the traditional set-up the bards have given meaning and continuity to the kings and kingdoms. They are the preserver of records; they are our oral historians who forge the connecting link between the past and the present. When they are told that they have a 'voice' in a democratic set-up, they do not understand its significance; they do not know what to do with this new power. Probably they have a point here if we take into consideration the fate of the poor in independent India even after more than half a century. Let us digress a little here. In *Snakes and Ladders*, Gita Mehta encounters a young rag-picker who proudly tells the author that he was a 'Bhat ... the community of bards who once held mythic power over Kings' (*Snakes and Ladders*: 37). This is what has happened to our democracy, Gita Mehta laments. However, she is not the only one to force our attention to experiences that are a repetition of the colonial dictum of oppression. Naipaul is filled with a personal sense of defeat and humiliation in *An Area of Darkness* and in his other works at the shattered dreams of democracy. Thus, in the political and economic dislocation practiced during the postcolonial period do we see the reversal to colonial ideology. The colonial episteme is maintained by a reiteration and repetition of the historical specificity, which has generated skepticism.

The rhetoric of the novel suggests that the impact of imperial and colonial ideology on the native rulers was essentially crippling. The British political doctrine of difference and inequality, of cultural and economic exploitation and the deployment of diplomacy based on the principle of fidelity to the British produced complicity that confused the native rulers, created ambivalence and rendered them impotent, inert toy rulers. The aim of the Imperial strategy was to transform the princes and their traditional culture in order to establish a new one based on the concept of 'superiority of the western culture'. That the princes fall a prey to the designs is reiterated through the examples of Tikka, Prince Victor and Pratap. Those rulers who show unwillingness to send their sons to England for education, are threatened with dire consequences; those who like the Sirpur princes are given to sensuous life are admonished. Either way they are trapped by the dominant ideology of the Imperial power.

Edward Said's definition of imperialism and colonialism may be of some relevance here. 'Imperialism' he says is 'the practice, the theory, and the attitudes of a dominating metropolitan centre ruling a distant territory; 'colonialism', which is almost always a consequence of imperialism is the implanting of settlements on distant territory' (Said, 1994: 8). Both imperialism and colonialism thrive on the notions of superiority and inferiority and are 'impelled by impressive ideological formations' that assert that certain countries or people are 'subject races' and require domination. The Indian native rulers were subjugated tactfully by both imperialist tendency of the British and their colonialist approach to implant their norms. Maharajah of Balmer was almost forced to send Tikka to England for higher education. As Kuki-bai reveals to Jaya, the British do not trust the Maharajah. 'Sometimes your father has no choice. Many years ago, Balmer needed money during a terrible famine and your father went to the Tsar of Russia for help. Now he is no longer trusted by the British Raj. The new Viceroy says that if Tikka is to remain heir to the Balmer throne he must go to England' (71).

The Maharajah is enraged at this injunction of the British. He expresses his anger and fear in words having a clear ring of revolt against the British policy of subduing the rulers. It also shows the fear of the alien education and atmosphere on his young son. The novelist saves Tikka from ruining himself like the Sirpur princes – Victor and Pratap, because of his early death but there are instances in the novel to prove that Tikka too was getting distant from the traditions of his land. English education exposes him to writers like Kipling, Burke, Baden-Powell and Macaulay. They give him vision which he is too young to put to practical use. He understands that the British look down upon us as "natives" and they practice discrimination on the colour of skin, yet he plays to their tune. The west, particularly England, symbolizes progress with 'the underground railway that ran beneath the city of London', the factories manufacturing car and acroplanes, and the explorers racing to the two poles (57–58). On the contrary, life in Balmer is primitive:

> Tikka did not know how it had happened, but the Captain's presence diminished Balmer. With a deepening sense of disloyalty, he regarded his father as a ruler blind to the advances of the real world outside the orders of his kingdom. He avoided his mother, embarrassed that he now saw her as a woman steeped in the superstitions of the harem. He despised himself for despising his parents and desperately wanted the Angrez tutor to acknowledge that he was not like them. (58)

What Macaulay had foreseen was coming true. These were the 'mimic' men who talked in the 'master's' tongue but were not his equal; who could see the weakness of their own culture but had neither the will nor the means to rectify it. This is what Fanon calls the 'perverted logic' of colonialism:

> Colonialism is not satisfied merely with holding a people in its grip and emptying the native's head of all form and content. By a kind of perverted logic, it turns to the past of the oppressed people, and distorts, disfigures and destroys it. This work of devaluing pre-colonial history takes on a dialectical significance today. (Fanon, 1982: 169)

The British Government had contrived many ingenuous and subtle schemes to keep control over the ruling princes.[5] Schemes like gun-salutes, decorations, and conferment of honour pleased the rulers but conversely these generated rivalries among them, each vying to have an upper hand over the other. This in turn gave rise to sycophancy, cringing and fawning before the Englishmen. If somehow a ruler offended the British masters, he had to face the humiliation of being degraded by several seats in the Darbar. Consequently, the Rajas and Maharajas spent their energies and money in futile attempts to keep the English humoured and thus neglected their people. With nothing to do for/in their kingdoms most of them whiled away time and money in useless pursuits and landed in misery. Diwan Jarmani Dass's book *Maharaja* is a revealing account of the debauchery, dissipation and drunkenness of the Indian rulers during the pre-merger period. As the Diwan of Patiala and Kapurthala Jarmani Dass had seen 'deepest low of inhuman lust and their wild eccentricities'. This was almost all over India except perhaps a few kingdoms where the rulers were upright. Gita Mehta depicts the Maharajah of Balmer as one of the ideal kings. To take some other instances from literature, we have towards the low-side Maharaja Ashok of Mulk Raj Anand; Bawaji II and Bawajiraj III in Kamala Markandaya's *The Golden Honeycomb*, and Bhushan's father (the self-styled "king" of Vijaygarh) in Sahgal's *Mistaken Identity*.

The condition of Sirpur was no better. With Victor squandering money on the American actress and Prince Pratap entangled in the Esmee Moore affair the State was constantly under threat of being disinherited. It was Jaya's ingenuity that saves Sirpur. Later, when Pratap was to be officially coroneted, it became a gala event particularly because of the Viceroy's decision to attend the ceremony, 'a singular honour, bestowed in recognition of the Sirpur ruling family's unwavering loyalty to the British Empire' (284). All the rulers flocked to Sirpur to pay obeisance to the Viceroy. This was height of sycophancy and degradation. Not only in the novel but in real life situations the rulers made themselves ridiculous when they vied with each other in 'canvassing for honours and decorations from the king Emperor and used all means to secure them' (Jarmani Dass, 1970: 312). The Political Department and the Viceroy took advantage of the situation created by the 'whims and idiosyncrasies' of these rulers.

Caught between the imperialist colonialist forces on one hand and the traditions of governance on the other, scrupulous Maharajahs like Jai Singh felt furious at the impossible situation they were in – they were suspected if they adopted welfare measures for their people, they were warned if they wanted their sons to study in India, and they were subjected to discrimination in England. On one occasion Maharajah Jai Singh resents the British prejudice even in as innocuous an activity as cricket which should have nothing to do with politics. He makes his resentment known to Captain Osborne in no uncertain terms, 'you told my son cricket illustrated the British ideal of fair play, Captain-Sahib. Why is my son not in the school team when he is better cricketer than his fellow students?' (87). Captain Osborne gives a lame excuse saying that it could be because of the school boys who are often cruel to their classmates. At this the Maharajah throws facts at his face, 'Unfortunately, my son's exclusion was not brought about by the cruelty of children but by school rules which prohibit a native from equal participation in school activities. Rules that are similar to the practices of the Empire, wouldn't you say?' (87).[6] On another occasion Maharajah Jai Singh is present when the Raj Guru is teaching Jaya the tenets of *Rajniti – Saam, Daan, Dand* and *Bhed* and in utter dejection he parodies the original meaning thus:

> *Saam*, I tend my people, putting their survival above the vanities of an empire, and I was called seditious. *Daan*, I provided for the state, and my only son was taken hostage by the Angrez. *Dand*, how can I be just when I cannot give sanctuary to those who fight injustice in the British Raj or try a man who has the ear of the

> Angrez? What then remains of monarchy but *bhed*? Intrigue, flattery, imitation – the weakest arm of monarchy. This is what it means to be an Indian king in the British Empire. (91)

In his despair the Maharajah bursts out in anger at the British tactics of usurping native kingdoms – Udaipur's mints are in British possession; the Maharajah of Baroda has been warned and instructed to ban Mazzini's books; Balmer is forced to send his son to England; in Manipur and Rewa things are threatening; in the south, thrones tremble because their kings dare to be progressive. In fact, all over India rulers are in a state of fear as their ancient lines are replaced by lackeys (91–92).

The Maharajah breaks the toy soldiers in the Billiard Room. 'Why waste time playing games of war?' he says when the rajahs and the maharajahs are just pawns in British hand. That they are pawns is reiterated often in the novel. Speaking to Maharajah Dungra in London, Jai Singh remarks, 'The proudest warriors in the world have become toy soldiers to decorate British parades' (21). Even in Malgonkar's *The Princes*, the Maharajah of Begwad always talks proudly of his Lancers and Cavaliers, 'the Bedars have always been soldiers,' he reasserts but in his heart he knows how powerless the rulers are in the hands of the British. That the native kings were living in a make-believe world is vouchsafed by naïve remarks like those of the Maharani of Balmer, ' "Go to London, Durbar. You are the voice of the people's assembly. Victoria must listen to you. India's Empress cannot ignore India's suffering" ' (16); or when the Viceroy consented to attend Prince Pratap's coronation to formally recognize Maharajah Pratap's 'ruling powers' (284). It is ridiculous how the entire machinery – the Viceroy and the Sirpur ruler – is out to show the power of the Rajas and the Maharajas on a grand scale when in reality the rulers are puppets with strings in British hands.

Gita Mehta brings out the futility and ridiculousness of elaborate ceremonies like the coronation of Prince Pratap. The ludicrous is subtly put across thus: on the day of the religious ceremony the Dowager Maharani points to 'a square object covered with red silk and whispers, 'The Sirpur gaddi'. In fact, the so-called 'gaddi' was so disintegrated and fragmented (like the rulers themselves), that it was just an apology for the throne. Two other incidents require mention. One, after the ceremony the Raj Guru presents the Sirpur sword to the new Maharajah, '"This sword is the final power of the sovereign, the symbol of justice. But there is no justice without dharma, and the dharma of a king is the righteous service to his people"' (282). How hollow are the words like dharma, justice and power! What significance can they have when the rulers are prostrating before the British throne? These facts impinge on the reader with impunity. The second incident relates to the exposition of dharma:

> Take heed, O sovereign. First, there is the People.
> May you be zealous in performing your duties.
> May you give in just measure.
> May you be humble in the presence of the wise.
> May you be learned. May your presence have dignity.
> May your zeal be tempered by humanity.
> May your union with the people be as the union between the Goddess and the Ascetic. (283)

These ancient tenets practiced across the land, in this case from Balmer (west) to Sirpur (east) are myths, far from the lived reality. With the vantage point of her postcolonial situation, the author subverts such passive regurgitation of rituals.

The rulers are no longer free to administer justice, nor are they potent enough to rule their people with 'dignity'. In fact, by the curious logic of the colonial psychology, they are frightened: as much of loosing their traditions, as of being victims of colonial violence. Ashis Nandy calls it the psychological fear of falling a victim to 'a culture in which the ruled are constantly tempted to fight their rulers within the psychological limits set by the latter' (Nandy, 1983: 3). The native rulers are in a situation of double bind: on the one side is the imperial power (their rulers), on the other, the awakened segments of the public like the Newspaper men, the reformists and the Nationalists (the ruled). Fear stalks Maharajah Sirpur too and it recoils on their marital life. Jaya understands her husband's fear psychosis, 'more Maharajah Pratap prostrated himself before the British Empire, the more he hated his wife as the symbol of that empire's power over his private life ...' (288). The British were following Machiavellian tactics in liquidating the rulers. They would advance them loans and encourage them to spend it as they wished but soon they would extract the price; it may be in any form – allegation of excesses, threat of disinheritance or submission. They would play court intrigues by backing up rival claimants to the throne or create belts of friendly powers to counter each other. As a child Jaya could not understand her father's fears, but now she is able to gauge her husband's fright, because he had been a willing victim of colonial designs, and Jaya herself is insecure as if standing on slippery grounds.

Paradoxically, Tiny Dungra addresses Jaya as 'the fearless Princess'. But we know how fear pervades her life – fear and the agony of a rejected wife; fear for the safety of her husband and her son (when they are ill); fear that the Imperial power, knowing Pratap's excesses and moral laxity may grab Sirpur, fear that the Nationalist sentiments may sweep through her kingdom. Despite this, Jaya does not appear helpless; somehow she carries herself with decorum and tries to solve the problems with political acumen and personal strength. Neither as the 'colonized' ruler nor as the 'colonized' woman in patriarchal power structure does she appear weak. Ashis Nandy may approve of her portrayal because he does not accept the colonized as 'the gullible, hopeless victim of colonialism caught in the hinges of history' (Nandy, 1983: xv). It is in human nature to fight our individual battle for survival, each in his/her own way. The various Rajas and Maharajas (in real life situations as well as in the novel), have evolved survival strategies like sycophancy, silence, helping the Nationalists on the sly and so on. Some of them, like Maharajah Jai Singh toe willy-nilly the line set for them by the British. Maharajah Jai Singh is not happy is clear from his answer to Dungra's question as to what he thought of the imperial masters: 'What does it matter what I think Hukam? I have no army to give weight to may views' (21). Nevertheless, they all knew that there was no way out but to evolve some tactic so as to survive. Years after this conversation, Jaya decides to play Polo with the Prince of Wales to impress him and to save the kingdom (Of course, she has other motives too, which we shall take up later). Even Lady Modi is taken by surprise at this change, '"Well, darling – to go straight from Purdah to a Polo game in front of the Prince of Wales! .... You are about to become a legend"' (223). Jaya becomes almost a legend; the Prince of Wales thinks her goal was the best in the game (225); she gains Dowager Maharani's approval; and her husband's confidence – a far more significant achievement for a purdah woman.

Prince Pratap is happy that he has finally got consent from the Prince of Wales to travel abroad. 'He wouldn't have done that if you had been hidden in the Purdah Palace, covered with henna,' he tells Jaya and adds, 'Since you seem to have received the royal seal of approval, I suppose it's safe to display you in Calcutta ...'. As if his callous remarks, reducing her to an object of display are not enough, he makes his intention clear, 'now, I'm going to enjoy myself at last' and he hurriedly leaves her for more voluptuous pleasures. She is distraught. Her condition can be symbolically understood as she hears the 'mournful melodies of the flutes' coming from the river side. But the novelist does not want her protagonist to be mournful and depressed. Jaya must recognize her inner strength. And the Sirpur Prime Minster's meaningful parting words underscore the importance of her own power. She could wield power over her husband, if not at emotional level, at least at the level of more practical issues of material gains. 'A polo mallet can sometimes be as useful as a dagger. You have studied Rajniti, even if Prince Pratap has not. Such knowledge would give a wife great power over her husband if she used it intelligently, hukam' (227). It is then that Jaya decides to turn the key in her favour.

Here we come to the most significant question of the discussion – Jaya as a woman. Admittedly, Gita Mehta is not a feminist writer, nor does she claim to portray women's problems. Despite this it is a woman-centred narrative. Jaya has all the problems that a woman may have – a callous, uncaring husband, insecurity, loss of all male members of the family and a restrictive social order. Add to this an early marriage to the man in absentia whom she could never love and who in turn never accepted her. Jaya's condition as a woman can be surmised by the letter published in *The Bombay Chronicle*, a copy of which Mrs Roy sends her. The letter writer's agony is hers too. The letter chronicles the anguish of a rejected wife. It opens with self-justification and a tone of self-flaggration. 'It will seem strange that a person from my class should seek the help of the public – and that through the agency of a daily paper; but there are limits to human patience and suffering' (237) and after recounting her problem the letter-writer points out, 'We are treated like chattels. We are taught to be slaves. Our duty is merely to satisfy the whims of our masters. We are deprived of our self-respect. Our existence is a mere cipher.' She further asserts, 'I want my status to be regularly defined. I want to fight for the many voiceless women who are being ill-treated … . We have no rights. I want my rights' (238). The anonymous letter writer appears to be a Maharani and incidentally, Jaya's troubles and sufferings are identical to what the letter says.

Although we sympathize with the anonymous Maharani, our interest here is to explore how Jaya manages to guard her self-esteem without making her anguish public. Gita Mehta invests Jaya with opportunities and qualities that very few women of her time could dream of having. Thanks to her father's political acumen and social awareness, she is trained on par with Tikka. Her exposure to outdoor training, her interactions with Mrs Roy and her interest in Tikka's activities give her visibility and boldness. Jaya comes across three kinds of women in her childhood home: British women like Mrs Osborne, the educated Indian woman, Mrs Roy and the traditional women – her mother and the harem ladies/servants. Of these, Mrs Osborne charms her but Jaya understands instinctively that she cannot be emulated. Mrs Roy has strong views about nationalism, freedom and democracy that baffle Jaya. Her efforts to enlighten herself on these issues are forestalled because as a female child in a traditional set-up she has social constraints. Soon, the laws of the royal household are clamped on her and she is relegated to the female quarters. However, these formative influences stay with her and help her when faced with trying situations.

The author provides a convincing view of the restrictive but all the same colourful life in the Zenana. The women's sly and meaningful jokes, their giggles, Kuki-bai's tales and the excitement of learning 'Solah Shringar', make the atmosphere lively. By the time the princess is ten, Kuki-bai thinks she is 'already a woman.' With the arrival of marriage proposal from Sirpur, Jaya's childhood ends. Soon Jaya realizes 'with an aching sense of loss that she had ceased to be a child' (77). She is subjected to the do's and don't's of a patriarchal power structure. Even Tikka, just sixteen, clamps his rules on her: do not speak to the Angrez boy, only speak to the servants, not the ladies, do not ask too many questions and so on. Then, there are the rules of the royal household to be obeyed. As Amina Amin points out 'Mehta creates a circle of oppressive forces which impinge on the lives of women like Maharani Jai Singh and Jaya Singh reducing them to pawns in the socio-political game their men-folk play' (Amin, 1999: 155). Despite this, Jaya feels secure inside the walls of the Fort. The political atmosphere outside the Zenana is so charged with imperialist policies and the native politics countering each other that Jaya feels 'safe only inside the carved walls of the Zenana, fearful that if she stepped outside the world of women, she would be swept away by the restlessness blowing through the ancient fort like the hot winds that warned of desert sand storm' (62). This is indicative of the home/world dichotomy that was to become an important paradigm of national movement, and women's issue.

It is striking how Gita Mehta records the changed climate in which rationalization and reform come into conflict with the ideology of traditional norms. Three forces run parallel in the novel showing three points of view that define the social and cultural principles for locating the woman's position in the existing colonialists/nationalist set-up. Maharajah Jai Singh is genuinely interested in reforms and is the catalyst for change; people like Raja Man Singh are the representatives of the dominant view upholding women's subordination to traditional norms; and third, the typical imperialists/colonialists like Prince Pratap of Sirpur perpetuate an ambivalent attitude toward change as per their self-interest.

Critiquing the socio-cultural aspects of the women's question through the nineteenth century and early twentieth century, Partha Chatterjee avers that 'nationalism did in fact provide an answer to the new social and cultural problems concerning the position of women in 'modern' society, and that this answer was posited not on an identity but on a difference with the perceived forms of cultural modernity in the West .... The relative unimportance of the women's question in the last decades of the nineteenth century is to be explained not by the fact that it had been censored out of the reform agenda or overtaken by the more pressing and emotive issues of political struggle. The reason lies in nationalism's success in situating the 'women's question' in an inner domain of sovereignty, far removed from the arena of political context with the colonial state. This inner domain of national culture was constituted in the light of the discovery of tradition' (Chatterjee, 1994: 117).

Both Jaya and the Balmer Maharani are governed by the 'inner domain' of the traditional culture. The Maharani is not only conditioned by the traditions but she has also internalized those norms. She cannot and does not go beyond the accepted. Jaya is tender and raw, she could have adapted herself to the requirement of the emerging 'new' culture but the traditions hold fast and Jaya is pushed into the laws of the Purdah despite her father's disclaimer that 'his daughter was not to be raised in Purdah' (44). For a few years Jaya's early training has a pleasant combination of outdoor activities as per her father's desire and the traditional lessons as per her mother's wishes. From music lessons to Rangoli classes and thereon to the training of managing the royal household with the Maharani, Jaya goes in the afternoon to English lessons, riding, shooting and polo as also lessons in Rajniti with the Raj Guru. This ends soon, however, when the Maharani decides to take her training into her own hands in a bid to make her a woman. Jaya is twelve and the Maharani is apprehensive that the training her father was giving her would cut her off from her roots. 'Who will marry such an overeducated girl? Her in-laws will resent her. Her husband will be insulted when she flaunts her learning in front of him' (94).[7] Incidentally, instead of losing her identity in the women's domain, Jaya develops a balanced personality – she has all the virtues that the culture envisages for women plus self-assertion, decision making and the ability to form a new identity for herself which the colonial politics required. This does not mean, however, that the women's question is solved in the novel. That would be too simplistic to assume. Jaya as a woman has many more dimensions which we can understand only after we see the Maharani's position vis-à-vis her husband and the existing norms of the Rajput royalty.

Maharajah Jai Singh is forward-looking and progressive, and above all he is portrayed as genuinely interested in public welfare. When the draught of 1898 turned severe, with no rains consecutively for three years, the Maharajah wanted his wife to come out of the purdah and travel with him across the kingdom to assist in famine relief as some other Maharanis were doing (31). The Maharani of Balmer is stunned to hear his decree, 'you must break purdah,' followed by his assertion, 'Savage times require savage measures!' (31). She is almost paralysed because this would 'destroy a thousand years of tradition' (31). She is at cross-roads – if she removes her veil, she would be 'like the eunuchs – neither a woman within the protection of women, nor a man in the world of men' (33); but if she refuses, she would be disobeying her husband and 'shame the ruler before his subject.' Removing the veil in a tradition-bound set-up is easy said than done. It has its repercussions. The Maharajah's argument is hypothetically sound – since the 'praja' calls him 'Bappa' (father), she is by implication their mother. Her dharma is protection of her children. Such idealism, however, clashes unwittingly with traditions. Her 'naked face' horrifies the men who stare at their Maharani in disbelief and then lower their eyes in shame. On her return from her tour, she is treated as an outcaste. Her entry into the zenana is forbidden because she has sinned against the eleven-hundred-year-old history. The Purohits declare that as a polluted woman who has interacted with the commoners, she has lost her purity and her entry without purification would pollute the entire zenana. Their argument is steeped further in patriarchal power politics – the Maharajah cannot be polluted by anything he does because he is the anointed of the gods, whereas the Maharani is 'only his wife' and she carries pollution on her person. Here the words 'only his wife' denote the subaltern position given to women.

Such hypocritical codes of patriarchal morality oppress women, irrespective of their status in the society or the royal household. Be they the concubines or the Maharanis or the women in the harem, their lot is to satisfy man's lust, uphold his status and just obey his command. What happens to Jaya is also not much different from what may happen to any women – princess or commoner. Despite her progressive father's strong reservations Jaya's personal interest has to be sacrificed for the interest of the kingdom. She is 'given' in marriage to the 'sword' of a man she almost hated. Though trained as a boy in valour, she is not empowered to protest and she has to accept her marriage in silence. Her first reaction to Pratap's photograph was sharp – on seeing the 'heavy lidded eyes and bored smile' on his portrait, Jaya's 'stomach contracted, regurgitating the sweetmeat, bitter with bile, back into her stomach' (137). This bitterness stays with Jaya all along. As the Sati-Mata had predicted, her life was not going to be smooth, 'Go towards your fear, child. Only then can you find courage to endure the life that stretches before you, exiled from your sex' (126). When the ascetic had called her 'the barren one', the Maharani was upset. But here 'barren' meant that she will be devoid of the joys of marriage. Jaya faces her 'fears' with fortitude and achieves her freedom from the confining limits of patriarchy which makes her, in a way, a historical figure – historical, not because she is a part of the royal history of Balmer and Sirpur and of the colonial history of India, but because she is like the women in the nationalist struggle of her times who appropriated both the feminine values and the masculine qualities. Gita Mehta seems to suggest that emancipation lies in women's ability to reach at a synthesis of the 'inner' and the 'outer' world, the spiritual and the material worlds – something that her mother, the Maharani of Balmer, had achieved.

Going back to Jaya's mother, we see the pathos of her situation. Soon after the Maharajah's death, she is discarded as polluted by her widowhood and hence declared unclean and unfortunate. The heartlessness of the patriarchal society is revealed when Raja Man

Singh annexes her kingdom and dismisses her almost contemptuously:

> This woman's association with the House of Balmer has ended. She has neither husband nor son to keep her in old age. What shall we give the widow? ... It is written in our ancient scriptures that we owe the widow nothing – not the food from our cooking vessels nor the water from our wells. (162)

Such humiliation piled on a Maharani whom they called 'mother' acknowledges the hegemonic attitudes. The exiled Maharani stays in the Dungra kingdom in an ashram, engages in social welfare activities and later joins Gandhiji's Salt March. This is how she achieves her Sati Mata status. In a way the novel here affirms the important role the nationalists played in giving visibility and voice to women and helped in generating consciousness. The Maharani's journey from the inner sanctum of her palace to Gandhiji's Ashram and thence to Salt March is her physical journey from the inner to the outer world; but from another angle, it is her journey from the material to the spiritual domain. Describing the dichotomy generated during the nineteenth century nationalist discourse between the western and eastern views and between the outer and the inner, Partha Chatterjee explains that the outer was considered the material domain which lies outside us and hence is 'a mere external that influences us, conditions us, and forces us to adjust to it. Ultimately it is unimportant. The spiritual which lies within, is our true self; it is that which is genuinely essential' (Chatterjee, 1994: 120). Although outwardly the Maharani has gone from *Ghar* to *Bahir*, she has in effect surrendered the material for the spiritual. She is a saint whom they all called Sati Mata (235).

Contrary to Sati Mata's (Maharani's) journey, Jaya's journey from Balmer (almost the western end of India) across the vast country to Sirpur (the northeastern end) can be termed as diaspora within the country. Conversely, her journey from girlhood to wifehood and onward to womanhood is her journey of self-affirmation. Book Two, entitled "Sirpur" is a saga of her diasporic self – rootless, lonely and uncertain. Her entry into the kingdom of Sirpur after her marriage is almost pathetic: sitting with her (absent) husband's sword 'across her knees', she looks out at the ancient, alien land with its variegated vignettes of life totally different from the familiar scenes of Balmer. Life in the Purdah Palace is equally new and foreign. 'To keep herself sane in the strange limbo of being a bride but not a wife,' Jaya would often look up the photographs of Prince Pratap. Time hangs heavy in his absence but little does Jaya know that after his return it will be worse. He comes home two yeas after the wedding and promptly rejects his wife, '"I'm afraid you won't do, Princess. You really won't do at all"' (189). He orders her to remove all her traditional decorations, 'wash all that nonsense off your hands and feet. And change out of these Christmas decorations.' The fatal blow to her dignity as a woman comes when he makes clear the nature of their relationship, 'Ours is strictly a marriage of convenience, Jaya Devi. Should a necessity for children ever arise, I am sure we can both rise to our duty, but until then ...' (190). Thus crushing all her dreams, he frees himself of his responsibilities as a husband and pursues his dissipated way of life. Pratap's attitude reveals two points: the corroding effect of the English education on the culture and the traditional male attitude to women.

The Rajas and Maharajas having several wives, a large harem and any number of girl friends was an accepted fact. *Raj* mentions the dancing girls the Maharaja of Patiala kept and the number of his wives and mistresses. What angers and frustrates Jaya is Pratap's peremptory dismissal of his wedded wife. 'The empire has instructed me to stay in India. If I am permitted to travel abroad again, I shall have to be accompanied by a wife. That's why I agreed to our marriage. So here we are, Jaya Devi. You cannot eat quail or wear a sari. You know no languages. Yet through you I must outmaneuver the Empire which forced me into this marriage' (191). Jaya is ashamed and indignant but she cannot counter him. The irony of the situation is that Jaya with a sound knowledge of four languages and excellent English was of no use to her husband. In the image of a 'good' wife, Jaya had even tried in Pratap's long absence to learn the local Sirpur language to please him. All this is of no avail. The man is callous, selfish and blind to his wife's needs.

Jaya accepts the harsh verdicts of her husband with befitting poise and leads her 'barren' existence alone, but she is not meant by the author to slide into oblivion. Gita Mehta gives Jaya the visibility she could not have attained as Pratap's wife but which she gains by her personal abilities. She learns to defeat him in his own game by quickly learning to be 'chic' and 'elegant' in the western style under Lady Modi's guidance; soon she is his companion in clubs and at dinners; she plays polo; goes hunting; travels with him to England; and takes decisions where the ruler himself fumbles. But, all this has a flip side too when we consider how woman is held a pawn to guard her husband's honour. Long back it was her mother, the Maharani of Balmer, who had come out of her veil to help her husband in relief work and to save his honour; now her daughter, Jaya, tears aside her veil to help her husband hoodwink the British into believing that he is an 'improved' man and hence fit for the throne. Whatever the motive, it is the woman who is made to compromise her beliefs.

The strength of the Indian woman lies, traditions aver, in her supposed superiority and spiritual strength. To guard it, women were required to keep the inner sanctum away from outside gaze. In the colonial period this invisibility became a subject of much speculation and since the colonizer could not and did not understand the enigma called Indian woman, they developed different perspectives. There is some truth in what Lady Modi tells Jaya, 'Darling, it is precisely because you are raised in Purdah that such tales are credible to the British. Even Rudyard Kipling wrote that royal women from the Himalayan kingdoms are sold into prostitution. You see, the British never meet you. The Empire has no access to you or power over your lives' (197). During the nationalist movement, the Indian leaders recognized the need to educate the woman so that she would 'have some idea of the world outside the home, into which she could even venture as long as it did not threaten her femininity' (Chatterjee, 1994: 130). Gita Mehta does not portray Jaya as a gendered stereotype but as a female agent, with a voice and a will. Thus by breaking the impasse generated by her situation, the author clearly displays the contemporary postcolonial strategy to inscribe female subjecthood. Jaya is given her space. She is invested with the power to bargain and she bargains hard; gets herself titled as the Regent should anything happen to Pratap and is saved from the humiliation her mother had suffered. On another occasion she extracts a promise from Pratap that if she played polo with the Prince of Wales she would be exempted from the dance during the dinner. She feels empowered by her assertion. This answers our question raised earlier regarding the motive behind her insistence to play polo.

Gita Mehta wrote *Raj* in the decade of the 1980s and it was published in 1989. The author, therefore, has all the advantages of hindsight. She exploits her postcolonial situation and gives Jaya the centre-stage, gives her abilities and intelligence, whereby she gains visibility. As a woman in the traditional culture, Jaya is the marginalized and her husband, the patriarch is the centre, but by the reverse logic of the postcolonial text, it is Jaya who wields real power. Even then, Jaya is the sufferer. Kumkum Sangari points out in one of her essays that it is problematic to construct the history of female agency because of the difficulty of 'owning' a voice. 'It calls for a reconstruction of the complexity and historically changing definition of female agency – as it is attributed to women and as it is enacted by women – alongside transitions in notions of female selfhood and individuation' (Sangari, 2002: 36).

Denial of her right to be a wife is an unbearable agony for Jaya. There are occasions when she loses her self control and weeps. Her pain reveals the wound of becoming a victim of Pratap's inebriated nocturnal assaults (287), of being an object of his consumption, instead of his companion in tenderness. Hurt is always there: first it is the rejection, then as a mother she is denied the right to feed her baby. She is angry at Pratap's decree that she should not breast feed her child. Having 'robbed her of the dignity of being a wife' he was now 'stealing away the rights of maternity' (298). Jaya makes it known by her expression, though not by her speech, that his order was unjust. Arun Roy's mock-sympathetic words move her to self-pity, 'Poor Bai-sa. So many roles to perform, and not one of them allows you to be a woman. But perhaps you do not yet know what it is to be a woman' (383). Self-pity leads her to self-assertion and in a weak moment she falls a prey as much to Arun Roy's designs as to her own desires. This betrays fundamental contradictions in her self-image but it occasions a critique of the hegemonic control over the female body which she rejects. This may be construed as her march from the self-sacrificing Indian woman to the self-assertive 'new' woman; or we may give her a long rope and justify her natural human desire or we may interpret it as her vengeance on her callous husband who used her to satisfy his own lust without ever caring for the demands of her body.

The postcolonial/postmodern critics of *Raj* tend to understand her at human level, and do not doubt her virtue. N.K. Jain explains that Jaya's relations with Arun Roy do not diminish her nor is it inconsistent with her self-image as a true *sati*. 'The event is significant because it shows that Jaya is no ascetic and because it brings her the long denied sexual fulfillment and also because it wipes away the humiliation she had suffered at the hands of her husband' (Jain, 1998: 212). In many earlier novels dealing with the ruling princes the authors have shown and justified the 'moral' failings of the royal women. For example, the Maharani in Manohar Malgonkar's *The Princes* who walks away with the Muslim Prime Minister of the State of Begwad and Bhushan's mother in Nayantara Sahgal's *Mistaken Identity* who joins her Muslim Marxist lover in open defiance of traditions are interpreted as positive signs of empowerment. Jasbir Jain calls Bhushan's mother the 'bravest' of Sahgal's women (Jain, 2004: 122). In both these novels, the women are elderly with grown-up sons; in their situations they show remarkable courage to resist patriarchy and then justify their actions. In Jaya's case, she does not have the need to justify anything to anybody, not even to herself. But naïve as it appears, Jaya is singularly unaware that her three-day forays into the jungle with Arun Roy would create scandal, and it does. The British Resident's report to the Political office in Delhi contained full information of Jaya's 'intimate association' with Arun Roy. It angers and shames Jaya – as much for her personal image as for the interest of her state (421). However, the Jaya-Arun affair seems to be temporary if the ending of the novel is any indication when Jaya shows scant faith in Arun Roy. It is also significant to note that of her two friends – James Osborne and Arun Roy – Jaya is enamoured of Osborne, 'the blue-eyed Angrez boy' of her childhood dreams. But, they keep a respectable distance and Osborne though friendly and understanding never tries to take advantage of her vulnerability. It is arguable if Oaborne's cautious attitude has anything to do with his notions of racial superiority of the colonizer, or it is due to his duty-consciousness and personal self-restraint. Whatever it be, Osborne appears far more dignified than Arun Roy. One wonders why Jaya, even after understanding Arun Roy's motives, allows him to get closer, particularly when their relationship has no emotions involved. Is it Gita Mehta's tirade against the hegemonic control over women that objectifies them? Or is the author trying to project the 'new' Indian woman to the west?

In fact, Gita Mehta has attempted to project and explain many things to the west in this novel. For example, the question of sati. In 1987, the Roop Kanwar case had rocked the country and shocked the world. While there were questions and counter-questions and the condemnation games played by the media and the Hindu establishment, some scholars came out with the theory that the recent 'phenomenon of *sati* shows an ideological manipulation of women,' and it was a political move 'to mobilize support for forging a common identity (Bose, 2000: 29). Gita Mehta takes pains to demonstrate that a widow is not unclean or unholy and in progressive states like the Balmer kingdom sati was banned long since. She explains that sati means a 'woman of virtue' (127), one who can endure and continue even when her world falls around her. The concept of sati runs all through the novel in different forms like the prediction of Sati-mata, the *sati* prayer that Jaya seems to recite all through her life and the Balmer Maharani's transformation as Sati-mata. The Maharani of Balmer achieves the high status as Sati-mata not because of any occult power but because of her virtuous life which is strengthened by her philanthropic works – the service of the poor and the needy. Jaya recites the sati-prayer daily as a ritual but her concept of virtue is changed. She does not consider herself 'impure' after her affair with Arun Roy. This is an indication of the approaching social/cultural changes in the national psyche. While the Balmer Maharani, leading a 'pure' life, joins the Gandhian Salt March, her daughter (Jaya), segregating the private/personal from political/public forgets the Arun Roy issue and decides to join full-fledged politics.

The sub-text of the novel tackles the woman's question from many angles. That the woman's question was at the core of the nationalist discourse is an accepted fact which colonial studies scholars have considered as vital to the understanding of feminism in India. *Raj* has three strands running more or less parallel: (i) the condition of/in the native states, (ii) the rise of nationalism, and (iii) the woman's question in culture and in nationalism. Finally, these three strands are joined to the imperial colonial politics with its colonized-colonizer binary. Scholars in the fields of colonialism and the history of women's movement in India have recognized that by introducing the cultural notion of female inferiority, the imperialist forces perpetuated the notion of inferiority of men and thereby of the culture. 'The colonizers essentially drew upon gender as a tool to further their 'civilizing mission' in India and adopted the 'native' female social reform project to advance their larger imperialist designs' (Sen, 2001: 9). Interestingly, seen from another angle, Jaya is the central figure on whom the 'civilizing mission' is carried out: first by her father (who trains her in various aspects of governance), her mother (who makes her an Indian woman), and then her husband (who wants to teach her the 'intricacies of western society'). Life teaches Jaya much more. By the time the novel ends the Balmer princess stands out as a free, self-assertive and self-confident woman of free India.

Notes

1. Homi K. Bhabha feels that the aim of colonial discourse is to construe the colonial 'as a population of degenerate types on the basis of racial origin, in order to justify conquest and to establish systems of administration and instructions' (p. 295).To counter this, the decolonized communities try to assert themselves to establish their identity, which Simon During terms as the 'postcolonial desire' for identity (See Homi K. Bhabha, "The Other Question: Stereotype and Colonial Discourse," in K.N. Newton, ed. *Twentieth-Century Literary Theory: A Reader,* 2nd ed. 1988,

rpt.1997. New York: St. Martin's Press pp. 293–301). For Simon During see "Postmodernism and Post-colonialism Today," in *Textual Practice* 1 (1), 1987 and its rpt. in *The Post-colonial Studies Reader*. ed. Bill Ashcroft et al. (London/New York: Routledge, 1995, pp. 125–129).

2. Victor Jara was the Chilean poet, composer and singer. He also played an active role in New Chilean Song Movement and in Salvador Allende's Popular Unity Campaign. The quotation given here is cited in Joan Jara's *An Unfinished Song: The Life of Voctor Jara*. New York: Ticknor & Fields, 1984, p.121.
3. The native princes, though subdued by the British were not unwary of the emerging political trends; nor were they innocent observers of the political situation. As far back as 1944 the Chamber of Princes moved resolution requesting the British Government not to leave the rulers in 'No man's land' if independence was granted to India and to protect their interests. Many a time they even hindered the proceedings of important conferences, particularly the Round Table Conferences. They often played up to the British Government to forestall any move of the nationalist leaders towards the attainment of independence. After the British decided to hand over power to India, the princes were disturbed and 'used all foul methods' to avoid integration of their States. Diwan Jarmani Dass writes, 'It is my definite opinion that the ruling princes did not make any sacrifice for the independence of India .... Nearly all the States with 21 gun salutes revolted against integration. The Maharaja of Travancore resisted and the Maharaja of Baroda wrote in his own hand to Sardar Vallabhbhai Patel, Home Minister of the Government of India, on 2nd November 1947 that unless he was made King of Gujarat and the Government of India accepted his terms, he would not cooperate with them and would not help to subdue the revolt by the Nawab of Junagarh.' But the stern action taken by the Government of India made them realize that they had no choice but to seek protection in merger. (See Diwan Jarmani Dass. *Maharaja*. Delhi: Hind Pocket Books, 1970).
4. In his interview with Ramnath Jha, A.K. Ramanujan explains the significance of past in order to stay connected with the present. He himself explored the rich sources of Kannada and Tamil poetry, brought to the fore the folktales and showed their relevance to the present. What is so impressive about his attempt to explore this territory of his native literature is the fact that though he stayed all his life in the USA, he was always keenly aware of his rich native literary and oral traditions.
5. Jarmani Dass in his book *Maharaja* records how the British policy to keep the princes in good humour was in fact an ingenuous ploy:

"The British Government devised many tricky and tempting schemes to keep the ruling princes of India under their thumb. The most ingenuous schemes were gun salutes, conferment of honours and decorations, non-interference in the administration of the States and giving free hand to the rulers to dabble in the finances of the States. The rulers ruled without the sanction of the subjects, passed life and death sentences in accordance with their whims and helped themselves to the State revenue. Unlimited power was given to the ruling princes in the beginning of the 20th century to administer their States, as they willed. Some Maharajas began to act like Louis XIV, Emperor of France and copied him by proclaiming "L'etat C' est Moi" (I am the State).

"The salutes which glorified the rulers and of which they were most proud became sharp thorns and Bete Noir and wrecked the Round Table Conference and the Structure of the Federal Legislature" (pp. 302–305).

6. Jarmani Dass records how the British Government interfered with cricket and tried to debar the Maharajas from playing though some of them like Maharaja Ranji Singh and many others were ace cricketers. Captain Jardins resented the British Government's orders and took obstinate stand to include good players, be they English or Indian.

7. Partha Chatterjee notes the extent of resentment in nineteenth century Bengal towards women's education on the 'new' British pattern and the threat these 'overeducated' females held for the society. Many writers of the period caricatured the westernized Indian woman as an object of ridicule and rejection, seeing her as a threat to the culture. Chatterjee provides an example from literature where an educated woman is caricatured. She calls her husband a 'fool' and a 'rascal' (in English because she is educated), and wants to become a 'lady novelist' like Mary Correlli. This is how their daughter, Phulkumari, addresses her father:

   Phulkumari: Papa! Papa! I want to go to the races, please take me with you. Dhurandhar: Finished with your tennis?

   Phulkumari: Yes, now I want to go to the races. And you have to get me a new bicycle. I won't ride the one you got me last year. And my football is torn: you have to get me another one. And Papa, please buy me a self-driving car. And also a nice pony. And please fix an electric lamp in my drawing-room; I can't see very well in the gaslight

   Dhurandhar: Nothing else? How about asking the Banerjee Company to rebuild this house upside down, ceiling at the bottom and floor on top?

   Phulkumari: How can that be, Papa? You can't give me an education and then expect me to have low tastes? (p. 122)

Works Cited

Amin, Amina. "Claiming Space for Oneself: Politics of Gender and Imperialism in Gita Mehta's *Raj*". *Writing in Post-Colonial Space*. Ed. S.N. Panday. Delhi: Atlantic, 1999.

Bande, Usha. "Kamala Markandaya". *A Companion to Indian Fiction in English*. Ed. Pier Paolo Piciucco. New Delhi: Atlantic, 2004.

Bhabha, Homi K. "The Other Question: Stereotype and Colonial Discourse." *Twentieth-Century Literary Theory: A Reader*. Ed. K.N. Newton. 2nd ed. 1988. New York: St. Martin's Press, 1997.

Bose, Mandakranta. "Sati: The Event and the Ideology." *Faces of the Feminine in Ancient, Medieval, and Modern India*. Ed. Mandakranta Bose. New Delhi: Oxford, 2000.

Chatterjee, Partha. *Nation and Its Fragments: Colonial and Post-Colonial Histories*. Delhi: Oxford, 1994.

Deshpande, Shashi. "Interview" in *Indian Communicator*, 20 November, 1994, p.II.

During, Simon "Postmodernism and Post-colonialism Today." *Textual Practice* 1(1), 1987. Rpt. in *The Post-colonial Studies Reader*. Ed. Bill Ashcroft et al. London/New York: Routledge, 1995.

Fanon, Franz. *The Wretched of the Earth*. Trans. Constance Farrington. Rpt. 1961. Harmondsworth: Penguin, 1982.

Gardiner, Juliet. ed. *What is History Today?* London: Macmillan, 1988.

Jain, Jasbir. "Nayantara Sahgal." *A Companion to Indian Fiction in English*.

—. "Post-Colonial Realities: Women Writing History." *Interrogating Postcolonialism*. Eds. Harish Trivedi and Meenakshi Mukherjee. Shimla: IIAS, 1996.

Jain, N.K. "From Purdah to Polo to Politics: A Study of Gita Mehta's *Raj*." *Women in Indo-Anglian Fiction: Tradition and Modernity*. Ed. N.K. Jain. New Delhi: Manohar, 1998.

Jara, Joan. *An Unfinished Song: The Life of Victor Jara*. New York: Ticknor & Fields, 1984.

Jarmani Dass, Diwan. *Maharaja*. Delhi: Hind Pocket Books, 1970.

—. *Maharaja*. Rev. <http:// www.biblio.com/search.ph>

King, Bruce. *Modern Indian Poetry in English*. Delhi: Oxford University Press. 1987.

Krishnaswamy, Santha. *The Woman in Indian Fiction in English*. Delhi: Ashish Publishing House, 1984.

Malgonkar, Manohar. *The Princes*. London: Hamish Hamilton, 1963.

Mehta, Gita. *Raj*. New York: Jonathan Cape, 1989. New Delhi: Penguin, 1993. All references are to the Penguin edition.

Mukherjee, Meenakshi. "Marthand Verman and the Historical Novel in India". *Litt. Crit.* 18. 1–2 (1992): 1–18.

Nandy, Ashis. *The Intimate Enemy*. Delhi: Oxford. 1983.

Sangari, Kumkum. "Feminist Criticism and Indian Literary Theory". *Language and Discourse Writing*. 2. 4 (January–March, 2002): 33–49.

Said, Edward. *Culture and Imperialism*. London: Vintage, 1994.

Sarojini. "Gita Mehta's *Raj*: Alternatives to Sati." *Realism, Reality and Fiction: Essays on the Indian Novels*. Ed. Neelam Raisinghani. Jaipur: Best Book Company, 2006.

Sen, Indrani. "Devoted Wife/Sensuous Bibi: Colonial Constructions of Indian Woman, 1860–1900." *Indian Journal of Gender Studies* 8:1 (2001): 1–22.

Five

A River Sutra : Secular-Humanist View

> There is ... no end to the story of life. There are merely pauses. The end is the arbitrary events of the teller, but there can be no finality about his choice .... Life is a series of sequels to history.
>
> — Shashi Tharoor

A River Sutra (1993) is a simple story of the narrator-protagonist's vindication who thinks renunciation is all about withdrawal from the world and staying away from it; from another angle, it is an elucidation of Indian metaphysics presented in the traditional Indian narrative style; and from yet another perspective, it is an effort of the author to expound India specifically to the western reader with the result that it has often been critiqued as a pseudo-philosophical rendering of a sublime theme. In short, it is an 'exotica' manifesting the authorial assertion of cultural identity through a recognizable ethnopoetic discourse; a search of the diasporic writer to find moorings in the past so as to resist the present albeit comfortable yet emotionally void.

One of the most contentious aspects of interrogating *A River Sutra* as a resistant diasporic text is the challenge it poses with its thematic structure, philosophical stance and the 'exquisite tapestry of secular-humanistic' tradition of India (Wallia, 1997: 1). The eventful stories take place in quick succession, flowing smoothly like the River and are held together by the *Sutradhar*. While each tale provides framework for the epistemological as well as the ethical treatise, the problematic consists of concrete statements revealing the complexities of spiritual and mythical relations between the Elements and the human life. How do we then analyse a work representative of and indigenous to the culture on the diasporic agenda? The diasporic experience, which is integral here to the discussion of the novel, is one of flux, marginality, and the rankling sense of hybridity and ethnicity. The novel, on the contrary, probes 'the psychic depths of the conscious/subconscious/unconscious' (Khan, 1994: 7) and upholds the ideology that 'Man is the greatest truth,/ Nothing beyond.' What justification do we find then to apply the paradigms of diasporic discourse and the parameters of resistant aesthetics to the work?

Despite the fact that in the postcolonial discourse terms like marginality, hybridity and ethnicity have lost much of their negative signifiers, giving a new space for identity and recognition of difference, the diasporic consciousness emerges at times from the individual locations which inadvertently reflect some of the very differences within professed/apparent sameness and give rise to the resistant counter-discourse. The annoying experience that went into the writing of *Karma Cola* in which Gita Mehta takes a sardonic look at the western craze for instant spirituality (already referred to in chapter 1), is one of the examples of how the rhetoric of migrancy evinces a pattern of responses. Through literary articulation the diasporic writer becomes the spokesperson of his/her culture and the concept of cultural identity. In her conversation with Wendy Smith, Gita Mehta recounts, 'Trying to rise to the occasion and be a wisecracking American, I said, "Karma isn't what it is cracking it to be!"' (Smith, 1997: 53–54). This sharp reaction to an otherwise commonplace situation owes much to the question of ethnicity and hybridity as visible signs of racial difference and is indicative of resentment at being positioned as an 'ethnic' voice. The urge to cast backward glance and renegotiate the roots can be termed as the process to extricate herself from the conflicting and compelling demands of the diasporic ideologies and to re-write the narrative of the repressed dynamics of national tradition.

This strong inclination to look back to the roots, to reconstitute the past has embedded in it the imaginative possibility to find an aesthetic solution to the problematic of diasporic continuum. In *A River Sutra,* Gita Mehta draws heavily from her culture's metaphysics, history, geography, the arts, mythology and identity, to provoke us to rethink, through the migrant's experience, the structure of nostalgia and resolve the tension between 'home' and 'not home'. The diasporic longing is both retrospective and prospective – reaching deeper into the past and looking forward into the future to retrieve a time that is lost but still has a perennial hold and also innumerable possibilities. We have to consider two aspects of diaspora here – emotional-psychological and physical. Physical aspect relates to the inability to travel to the homeland or communicate with one's people, which generates a feeling of being trapped; however, it is much lessened in the present scenario. With communication technologies bringing remarkable changes in the global perspective, the diasporic experience is no longer what it used to be. For a metropolitan professional in particular since there is no monetary stringency mobility is not a problem.

As postcolonial professionals and upwardly-mobile migrants, the Mehtas are in a position to move about freely across continents and also extend their connection to the home country with unbroken regularity. This renewal of bonds after every visit is important to rejuvenate cultural memory. In her interview with Wendy Smith (already quoted in chapter 1), Gita Mehta categorically mentions the advantage she enjoys in moving about countries and cities. In short, diaspora does not connote for her the earlier, colonial migrant's impossible nostalgia for home, but only the need to appropriate a subject-position, challenge marginality and re-present the centre of her creative structure. As K. Satchidanandan notes the experience of 'otherness' need not necessarily be a 'crippling experience;' it has the potential to define one's 'Self' and reassure one 'about one's own distinct identity.' He further clarifies, 'The narrative product of home assumes many strategies according to one's relation to the place one came from, the place one came to and the place one belongs to' (Satchidanandan, 2001: 19). In *A River Sutra*, Gita Mehta simultaneously constructs and deconstructs her diasporic identity by implicitly fighting to go back to the cultural experience and claim the historical-mythological-textual tradition of her past.

To a casual reader, the novel is a charming piece of fiction with scintillating stories running like the river in their smooth telling. The initial focus being on the bureaucrat-narrator, one assumes that it is the story a man – a retired Administrative Officer who wants to renounce the world and live as a recluse, but who finally learns that only 'involvement' can really lead to detachment. With each story the novel gathers momentum revealing more facets: it becomes the story of Narmada, the symbol of our culture; the story of Shiva's penance and birth of Narmada; an exposition of tribal lores; and of man running around in search of life in its myriad aspects – Nirvana, love, peace, luxury, devotion, immortality and in fact all that humans long for. The novel becomes a variegated picture of life and life's philosophy. It provides a vast canvas: one could read it as an eco-feminist text, as a treatise on Indian concepts of animism, materialism and spirituality, as a work portraying 'imaginay' India and as a text propounding the oral tradition of story-telling.[1] But, as a diasporic experience, the novel inclines to displace the notion of a pre-given western/diasporic identity and desires to fix cultural difference thereby resisting the 'Self-Other' dichotomy. Desire is important in the postcolonial situation of power-resistance binary because it is the moving motor of the subject. Fanon puts it succinctly thus, 'As soon as I *desire* I am asking to be considered' (Fanon, 1967: 218). The 'desire' to be 'considered' can also be indicative of 'the anxiety of Indianness' (Mukherjee, 1998: 78–93).[2] To this point we shall return later.

When *A River Sutra* was published in 1993, it immediately caught the attention of critics and scholars, particularly for its unmistakable Indian cultural and spiritual ethos. Two of the early papers appearing in *The Literary Criterion* discussed the novel's narrative technique and its psychic depths. A.G. Khan, in his paper, calls it a significant contribution to 'the feminine writing' (as against feminist) and concludes that by restoring the saints to their pedestal, after debunking the conman of India, Gita Mehta has 'done her penance in a dignified manner' (Khan, 1994: 15). One cannot figure out, however, who Khan's 'saints' could be? Nag Baba or Uma, may be? One also does not understand how the saints are 'restored'. The critic has, nevertheless, tried to track the characters' quest and has classified them as 'fugitives,' 'mirror images,' and 'steadfast' characters. The same issue of *The Literary Criterion* contains a paper by C.N. Ramachandran who focuses on the Indian tradition of framed narrative technique. E. Galle, a French scholar, takes an all-inclusive view in an article again appearing in *The Literary Criterion* 1995 (Galle, 1995: 27–56). The scholar discusses the stories from the angle of animism, Hinduism, Islam, narrative technique and the use of imagery. The paper is interesting and analytical, though it states the obvious. In 1996, Pushpinder Syal took the postmodern view and saw the strength of the narrative in its ability to evoke continuity and inter-relationship but points out that Mehta is not able to coordinate her romanticism with the 'somber sophistication of language in which the narratives are told' (Syal, 1996: 93). Consequently, the characters peopling her novel lack depth and the 'ignorant' main narrator reduces some of the powerful passages to mere exoticism. Usha Bande in her paper "India of the Mind"[3] feels that by 'recreating the ancient myths in contemporary terms the author deconstructs some of the pre-defined Western notions about India,' and 'by interrogating the received mythologies she re-defines the self-image of the culture' (Bande, 2002: 146). Bande argues that *A River Sutra* creates a miniature India, which is 'India of the mind' because of which some of the vibrant factors of modern India are sidetracked. It can be argued that Mehta, as a displaced person, creates an India to affirm her Indianness by manoeuvring a mixture of the traditional technique with the western form. Discussing the present trends implicit in the writings of the cosmopolitan writers Meenakshi Mukherjee points out that many authors 'have successfully manipulated western forms of fabulist narratives and a post-modernist mode with local legends and popular fables as means of mythicizing contemporary reality' (Mukherjee, 1998: 89). This becomes their counter-point against the anxiety of 'Indianness.'[4]

Thematically, the novel has many focal points – renunciation, love, lust, ego and involvement and a number of others. It contains an eloquent commentary on Hindu myths, rituals and beliefs; it is an exposition of contemporary Indian psyche; it provides a useful dialogue on spiritualism vs. materialism, detachment vs. attachment, love vs. its various shades, and modernity vs. tradition, but finally and significantly, it eulogizes Narmada. The narrative technique is traditional Indian with story within the story told by the narrators – the bureaucrat, Tariq Mia, Mr Chagla and Nitin Bose's diary entries. The novel advances as discussion on each tale ensues. The analysis and the comments help in unifying the loose stories. Another unifying presence is the Narmada. All those who come to the Narmada whether in desperation or in quest get their due. Of the ten characters (including Tariq Mia the narrator) two commit suicide, one dies, two continue their quest, one enjoys worldly name and fame, and two seem to accept life after vindication (Prof. Shankar and the narrator) while Tariq Mia accepts life as it comes. This leads us to charter their demands/desires, analyse the result of their quest and study the strategies they employ to reach their goal.[5]

The first to set the story in motion is the bureaucrat-narrator, the manager of the Narmada Guest House. He has come to the guest house almost as a recluse, so he thinks. He calls himself a *vanaprasthi*, 'someone who has retired to the forest to reflect' (*River*: 1).[6] He has fulfilled his worldly obligations. A retired civil servant with no encumbrances (his wife is dead and he has no children), the narrator is in quest for peace and tranquillity. The location of the beautiful guest house, away from the town, is ideal. The narrator's love for the idyllic Narmada valley, the surrounding jungle, and his minute observations of nature are almost Wordsworthian. Also his remark, 'Bureaucrats belong too much to the world' (1), echoes Wordsworth's, 'the world is too much with us.' But the narrator is not a recluse. He has a lively interest in his surroundings and also in those questers he encounters. Their tales recounted by them personally or heard through Tariq Mia or others, affect him emotionally and whet his curiosity. For example, after hearing the Jain monk's story of renunciation he becomes almost melancholy. He seeks to probe deeper into the meanings of their enigmatic lives or actions and in the process the whole fabric of the novel is woven. When perplexed, he turns to Tariq Mia for his expertise. Not that everything the old Mullah explains appeals to his rational mind. Tariq Mia's remarks, sometimes serious and meaningful, sometimes vague or teasing, prick him. The bureaucrat's curiosity and confusion afford the author a befitting chance to knit another story into the fabric. And so one more story takes shape till we, the readers, realize that the narrator is in the thick of events. He is fully immersed in the lives of the men and women he meets or hears about. The narrator broods at the end of the novel, 'I stared at the flashes of illumination, wondering for the first time what would I do if ever I left the bungalow' (282). Obviously, he is so involved in life's vagaries that like the Jain monk he seems to be saying, 'Don't ask me to do this, my friend. I am to poor to renounce the world twice' (41). Professor Shankar's perceptive remarks, 'You have chosen the wrong place to flee the world, my friend ... . Too many lives converge on these banks' (268), set us thinking if the narrator really wanted to renounce the world or he was merely fleeing the monotony of the familiar.

Renunciation has always been an ideal in Indian metaphysics, culture, life and literature. Since the *Gita* has influenced the psycho-socio-cultural matrix of India, its philosophy is instinctively followed by the people. It is all-pervasive and it runs through Indian literature as a recurrent motif. One renounces material possessions, emotional bondage, love, lust, ego, desire, anger and passion. Discussing the concept of renunciation, Meenakshi Mukherjee points out that the ideal of getting divine bliss through detachment and of achieving the highest goal of self-realization is so fundamental to Indian thinking that it has cut across 'the boundaries of language and regional culture, and has become a motif that can be traced in Indo-Anglian novels profitably' (Mukherjee, 1971: 99). But in fiction, the concept poses several difficulties not only for the character who renounces the world but also to the author to carry it to its logical conclusion. At the metaphysical level the definition stresses on achieving inner calm, or being above pain and pleasure, and on developing the child-like qualities of playfulness. In the *Yoga*

Vashishtha, such a person is known as *jivan-mukta,* undisturbed by outside happenings. He need not have renounced the world to be a recluse but living within the world, among the temptations of life, he could still be non-attached. In Indian literature, both written in English and in regional languages, authors tend to deal with the traditionally venerated ideal of renunciation.

There are, however, instances to show that even if an author deals with it, he/she may not uphold it always; there is also another possibility that the characters or plot may slip out of the author's grip. Anita Desai's Harish in her short story "Surface Texture" leaves his family suddenly in his whim to renounce the world and becomes the cause of untold misery for his wife and children. In *Cry, the Peacock,* Gautama preaches Maya to strive for detachment, but since basically she is not prepared for it, the very ideal recoils on them – Maya becomes insane and kills Gautama. Not that this is the only cause of her madness, there are others too, but this is one of the many. In Shashi Deshpande's *A Matter of Time,* Gopal renounces the world. Part I of the novel begins with a line from *Brihad-Aranyaka Upanishad* 'Maitreyi,' said Yagnavalkya, 'verily I am about to go forth from this state (of householder).' Gopal goes away leaving a trail of problems for Sumi to face. Reading from the feminist angle, Usha Bande observes that in the patriarchal structure a man can shed responsibilities easily, but can a woman? (Bande, 2005: 194). In Arun Joshi's *The Strange Case of Billy Biswas,* Billy retreats from the civilized world into the tribal world, bringing suffering to his family. Examples galore in literature and in life too when renunciation, accepted as an ideal without being ready for it mentally, creates problems and the ideal itself becomes self-defeating. Generally, in reading the stories about renunciation the reader is carried away by the rhetoric and consequently, the other aspects like familial-social responsibilities, suffering caused to the family and the uncertainties the character faces half-way through are side-tracked.

Gita Mehta dexterously saves her characters from the possible allegation of having deserted the family – the bureaucrat-narrator makes it clear in the beginning of the novel that he has fulfilled his worldly duties. And Ashok, the Jain monk skirts the issue of suffering to family; as he reiterates, his father was proud of his decision to renounce the world, and his wife as too staid and passive to have felt anything. Thus, Gita Mehta not only absolves the two characters, but also guards the concept of renunciation from being exposed to western critical assessment. Moreover, the novelist quickly diverts the readers' attention to the surrounding wilderness, the tribal gods, and the ancient caves, in fact, to all the exotica and the reader does not get a chance to dwell on the pros and cons of renunciation. Nevertheless, on close reading one finds many chinks in the amour – the bureaucrat-narrator seems to harbor a secret wish to go back to the familiar after his interaction with Professor Shankar and his archaeologist assistants. He appears nostalgic and avoids going even to Tariq Mia whose company appears to him too primitive and rustic.

> I had not suspected that I would feel so lonely while they were away. I found I missed the noisy lunches with the young archaeologists and their infectious enthusiasm when describing the progress of their excavations. I found I missed Professor Shankar and the pleasure of talking to a companion who shared my own background of government service.
>
> Sitting on the terrace, meditating in the darkness before dawn, I admitted to myself that I envied the archaeologists for still belonging to a world I had given up.
>
> Now that I had the leisure I no longer had the inclination to visit Tariq Mia. I did not want to sit with the mullah of a small village that seemed frozen in time, untouched by the events of a larger world. With some alarm I realized I was becoming accustomed to that other rhythm the archaeologists had brought into the rest house, the rhythm of my previous life. (270)

In modern psychological parlance, detachment or renunciation of desire or possession means leaving one's 'having' orientation to embrace the 'being' mode of existence (Fromm, 1976). Eric Fromm explains that a man in the 'being' mode is free and non-attached; in our traditional concept too, the *jivan-mukta* has the same orientation. From the text of the novel the extent of the narrator's renunciation is not clear. He is not a recluse, he admits. He has neither the inclination to roam about in jungles nor the endurance to undertake penance. 'I know I was simply not equipped to wander into the jungle and become a forest hermit, surviving on fruit and roots' (*River*: 1). He admires the capacity of the pilgrims to endure hardships and reminds himself that the purpose of pilgrimage is endurance, but he admits that he cannot be one of them; city life has made him 'soft', so much so that he dared not 'enter the caves, for fear of snakes, unable to believe that even Narmada will protect me from a snake's fangs' (9). How can a person who is frightened to penetrate the heart of the jungle and who has no faith in the local tradition that Narmada will protect him from snake poison, penetrate the heart of darkness within to grapple with the 'real' self so as to march on the path to self-realization? The bureaucrat's view of *vananprastha* is simple and unassuming, to the point of being superficial and simplistic. A *vanaprasthi* is the one who has 'completed the first stages of life prescribed by our Hindu scriptures – the infant, the student, the householder – and who [has] now entered the stage of the *vanaprasthi,* to seek personal enlightenment' (7). [The narrator's and by implication the author's basic conception itself is erroneous. As Note No 6 in this chapter clarifies, *Vanaprastha* is the third stage when one prepares for renunciation by distancing oneself from the world.]

Going by the rhetoric of the book this is exactly what the narrator is striving for: 'personal enlightenment'. From his own account we surmise that having had nothing to look forward to after his retirement, the bureaucrat opted out of the modern consumer society where man as human has scant value. In retreating to the isolation of the Narmada valley, he has bargained to live in a better world, or let us call it a more 'humane' world. Here each individual who comes with his/her story is important. The tale is analysed and placed in the perspective of larger human experience. The epigraph asserts that 'Man is the greatest truth' and there is nothing beyond. The full significance of Chandidas's secular verses that sang of love and built bridges across Hindu-Muslim doctrines becomes clear when read against the backdrop of Rumi's poetry, the Jain monk's assertion that 'Jains follow in the footsteps of a man' (20); Professor Shankar's reiteration that he is an atheist and only a man, too puny to understand the intricacies of spiritualities. Elaborating how Gita Mehta reinterprets the great intellectual traditions of rationalism, reconciliation of religion and cosmic universalism, a critic says:

> Conforming with the Indian doctrine of the Samkhya ... Professor Shankar's humanistic position is an opportunity for Gita Mehta to extend her mediating action among the various doctrines that share her country, and also between Indian and non-Indian philosophies. Shankar's atheism may appears to Western readers as borrowed from their own thought system, even as an homage to their superior intellect. Gita Mehta suggests that it is in fact a re-surfacing of ancient Indian intuitions. (Galle, 1995: 32)

Humanism does not function just at the worldly level, it is woven in Indian thought system including its mythology. The River assures man:

> 'Bring your knowledge of mankind
> And follow me.
> I will lead you to the next Creation'. (278)

The novel reiterates that man is a learner all his life. The bureaucrat-narrator is the representative of us all, weighed down under the knowledge borrowed from the western education, trying to grapple with the inherent traditional lore and confused by our inability to assimilate the two. The narrator often repeats that he is seeking personal enlightenment. To the Jain monk he says, 'Do you know what the word Upanishad means? It means to sit beside and learn. Here I am, sitting, eager to listen. As a monk, can you deny me enlightenment?' (13). The rhetoric of the novel also suggests that he is a seeker, not an ascetic. Ignorant but with childlike curiosity, he is intent on being enlightened. When his ignorance is rubbed in on him by Tariq Mia, he gets piqued but becomes more eager to learn. Tariq Mia derives subtle pleasure in telling the narrator, 'How can you say you have given up the world when you know so little of it' (50). Or, 'you still know so little of the world .... But you have chosen the hard path to knowledge, little brother. Hearsay, not experience. I hope your education proves less painful than your musicians' (228). Obviously, the narrator is an apprentice – a disciple sitting cross-legged at the feet of a *Guru*. He is being initiated into the unique world of human experiences by Tariq Mia, Mr Chagla, Dr Mitra and Professor Shankar. Symbolically, the chess-board spread between Tariq Mia and the narrator signifies the world, human beings are the pawns and the two players denote the struggling consciousness trying to understand the mystery of life, love and death.

As against the narrator, Professor Shankar seems to have comprehended the mystery of life through his penance as an ascetic. For ten long years he delved deep into the jungle, roamed near the river banks performing extreme penance as a Naga ascetic. One wonders if he was really a seeker; or was he also running away from the protean realities of modern existence? He had a stern Guru who showed him the path to enlightenment through endurance, humility and social awareness. The Naga Baba alias Professor Shankar learnt the lessons of endurance the hard way – surviving in freezing cold of the Himalayas or the scorching heat of the desert; Naga Baba learnt to consider human beings as equals, not rich or poor, high or low. To attain this humanistic vision his Guru had enjoined on Naga Baba to beg at the houses of the untouchables, the unclean and the profane. This was his real 'graduation', his 'Diksha'. This led Naga Baba to learn to respect even the humblest and to see divinity in the most depraved of his fellow human beings. This was his initiation into real wisdom. Finally he proved socially enlightened when he rescued a girl from the brothel and gave her an identity besides giving her a clean life of spirituality. The girl is renamed as Uma, 'peace in the night' (252) and is transformed from her earlier identity as Chand, and led on the path of devotion. But this path is not an easy one. The Naga Baba knows it; so when he initiates the girl into it, he makes sure that the child learns it the hard way. This is a crucial time of her life – her 'other life' is to be annihilated before she acquires the new. It is hair-raising to read how the Baba treats her:

> The Naga Baba grabbed her, his breathing harsh above the stems breaking under his feet as he carried her through the darkness toward the river. ... Suddenly he gripped her arms and lowered her into the water. 'The Narmada claims all girls as hers. Tonight you become a daughter of the Narmada.'

> The paralyzed child stared into the ascetic's eyes. The ash from his hair was falling into her face, the cold current soaked her rigid body. Then the water closed over the child's head and she heard only the sound of her own blood pounding in her ears. She no longer even had the will to scream, knowing she could do nothing to prevent herself from being drowned, helpless in the grip of the Naga Baba's powerful hands.
>
> But the Naga Baba was already lifting her out of the river. Ignoring the child's tears, he began to burn his sticks of sandalwood ... and then drew three streaks of ash across the child's forehead. (253–54)

Savage as this treatment meted out to the child appears, it is an exposition of the fact that enlightenment has all the pangs of death and rebirth.

Between the story of the narrator and the Naga Baba, there are five stories of love, anguish, detachment and attachment seen from different angles. Love and renunciation are the main motif of the Jain monk's tale. The Jain monk begins his story with a meaningful but ambiguous statement, 'I have loved just one thing in my life' (14) and he ends it with, 'I am too poor to renounce the world twice' (41). On these two key sentences hinges the story of his renunciation which was an unimaginably gala event entailing a display of opulence. During the initiation ceremony Ashok realizes that it is easy to make a decision to renounce the world but it is hard to negate the self. One has to follow the principle of humility, understand the sacredness of all life and also the inviolability of humanity before attaining divinity. Ashok's life takes a summersault, as if, from one extreme to the other. His was the life of luxury. From his friends' remarks it is clear that he was given to sensuous pleasures – 'no more whisky, no more cards'; 'no more airplanes to take you to Gay Parties,' his friends teased him and added, 'Oh. Ashok repent your vanity! It is not human to give up those silken caresses.' 'Those long tresses!' (16). The road he has chosen is, on the contrary, beset with other extremes:

> You will be a social outcast.
> You will be insulted.
> You will be hounded. (57)

> You will suffer pain from constant walking.
> You will suffer loneliness. You will grieve for your choice. (38)

Once these formidable injunctions are drummed into the seeker, the next follow:

> You will be free from doubt.
> You will promise stability.
> You will protect life. (41)

The message of the above indoctrination is clear. One cannot run away from one's human duty towards the self and the others. The doctrine does not promise *Nirvana*, but one knows *Moksha/Nirvana* lurks on the horizon and is attainable through fellow-feeling, love and compassion. Somehow the rich details of his renunciation ceremony do not make an impact as we read on but the first and the last sentences keep on rankling – What has he 'loved'? How is he expected to renounce the world twice? Is he happy with his decision? Or is he regretting the loss? Reading between the lines it appears that so far Ashok probably loved only himself – his luxury, his wealth, his friends – everything in relation to the puny, worldly self. After induction into the cult he understands the value of fellow human beings and he asserts 'I am too poor to renounce the world twice' (41). He has renounced the world of his narcissistic 'self love' now he does not want to be deprived of the company of his fellow monks. Tariq Mia has no answer to the monk's intricate and ambiguous declarations. So, he tells the bureaucrat another story.

In the next four stories, Gita Mehta takes up the theme of love in its different shades to join them with the last story of selfless love. The music teacher's love for his blind pupil is in the Guru-Shishya tradition. Master Mohan is enthralled by the child's talent and despite opposition from his wife, he brings Imrat home and makes all efforts to take the boy to the pinnacles of glory. Do we call it 'selfless'? The answer is: to an extent 'Yes' because he has no ulterior motives in training the boy; to an extent 'No' because he wants to experience the self-satisfaction of having achieved glory. This would be vicarious satisfaction, though. A look at Master Mohan's life reveals his motives. As a child prodigy he had acquired a name 'as a child singer when he had filled the concert halls with admirers applauding the purity of his voice' (55). But poverty and lack of proper connections, or let us say the inability to find a 'godfather' to back him, stood in his way and no recording studio ever gave him a chance. He broods, '... It takes a very long time for a poor music teacher to cultivate connections with the owners of recording studio' (55). However, destiny was not in his favour. When a studio had finally agreed to record him, his voice broke and he was rejected. That was the end of Master Mohan as a musical genius; never recovering from this loss, he drifted into the life of an ordinary music instructor. Now he sees a great potential in the boy Imrat and he decides to support him because as a lover of music he would not like Imrat's talent to go waste; he would not like a repetition of his own misfortune. So he is magnanimous in helping the boy and even dares his wife. Somewhere in his psyche, the boy becomes a prop, a substitute for his 'lost' self and now he again hopes to re-live his own unfulfilled childhood dream. He would show his critics and detractors, particularly his wife, that after all he has not been an utter failure; that he still has the spark. When the boy is killed, something within him snaps; his innermost self is murdered and he becomes paranoid. He becomes a wanderer. Attachment leads him to detachment but this is not the healthy withdrawal of a self-realized man. It is a sick guilt-ridden psyche that prods him on, blaming himself for killing the child. Unable to bear the self-berating, he commits suicide. Prior to ending his life he hands over Rumi's lyrics to Tariq Mia. Unfortunate and a failure as he has been, he does not even possess the good fortune to commit suicide in Narmada. That probably would have absolved him of his sins as per the popular belief.

The next to commit suicide is the courtesan's daughter. Her death may be tragic but it is not pathetic because she jumped into the Narmada and as her mother asserts, she would 'be purified of all her sins' (190). The young woman opts to die because she does not want to fall in the hands of the police and be tortured and humiliated by them. As the famous and eminent courtesan's daughter and the wife of the legendary Rahul Singh, she finds it degrading to be locked up in the police custody and interrogated. The story of the Courtesan's Daughter has Robin Hood kind of adventure and romance – opulence, retreat into the jungle, the romance of tribal lore and passionate love. Rahul Singh, the dacoit abducts her from the busy bazaar in full view of the public in broad daylight. He considers her his beloved of previous birth and loves her passionately. Despite his rough manners and crude exterior he is tender to her. Staying in the caves, roaming around in the jungle and believing in the 'bee-lore' of the tribals the couple is in bliss. Gita Mehta has created for herself an opportunity to weave the hypnotic magic of the exotic wilderness – the 'black power' of Rahul Singh, life in the dark impenetrable jungle, the tribal ethos, the story of the bee and the warrior, and the description of the cave where they lived. This evokes a romantic atmosphere. Add to this the tribals' faith in him and their assertion that Rahul Singh is no murderer but a highly decorated soldier of the Indo-Pak war. The society turned him into a criminal. "'When his soldier's commission ended and he came home, he found his family dead and his lands stolen. No one dared help him. The man who took his land had the protection of the local politician. Denied justice, Rahul Singh only did what any man of honour would do. He swore vengeance on his family's murderers and killed them all. Of course he has become a hunted man. But he has never harmed anyone who did not deserve it'" (182). The movie *masala* is too obvious to be ignored by the Indian reader but for the western reader it might be evocative.

It would have been in bad taste had Gita Mehta let a criminal be above the law of the land. Despite their love and the tribal tale of the immortality of the warrior, Rahul Singh and his paramour's relationship cannot sustain. The dacoit is killed in a police raid and the Courtesan's daughter commits suicide. The author lashes out at the society for making criminals of simple people like Rahul Singh. The message is clear: People like Rahul Singh must be rehabilitated and given human treatment.

If the story of Rahul Singh and his beloved is one of sublime love, Nitin Bose's tale is of love as lust. Titled as "The Executive's Story" it gives a graphic picture of the modern sick society which consumes everything – love, finer sentiments, poise. Love is a game played with money. When love becomes a commodity to be bought and sold with money power, it degenerates into lust and damages the psyche. This is exactly what happened to Nitin Bose. His life in Calcutta was full of sensuous pleasures and when he joined the tea estate, he romanticized the outlandish atmosphere of the wilderness of the tea garden. Remembering the boasts of some of his friends just returned from the tea estates that life there was fantastic, he too imagined a paradise for himself – only that this paradise was full of forbidden pleasures. 'Our tea garden colleagues were young, good-looking Indians, bursting with alien energy. We listened to their boasts of rogue elephants tracked, man-eating tiger shot, hot-blooded women tamed, and envied the cowboy quality to their headlong pursuits of pleasure during the weeks they spent in the city' (111). But, true to his friends' fears, Nitin Bose found the loneliness oppressive. It was then that he prefigured Rima Bose and thought he was possessed. On reaching the Narmada Guest House in a frenzied state, he requests the Manager to take him to the 'shrine to the goddess in these jungles. A tribal goddess, who cures the madness of those who are possessed' (105).

In fact, Rima Bose is an extension of Nitin's own aberrations, and haunted by it, he turns schizophrenic. Narmada cures him, so the story tells us. And surprisingly, he is not only cured, he even attains enough mental equilibrium to write a treatise on Narmada. Rationally it could be argued that away from the corroding atmosphere of his office and friends, living in the soothing precincts of the river, and diverting his mind from sex to creativity (the researching and writing process), proves curative. Sublimating lust to creativity and study, Nitin Bose gets back his mental health. The story is told through Nitin's diary and it advances with Mr Chagla's comments and Dr Mitra's medical suggestions.

Sublimation works wonder in Nitin Bose's case, but not in the case of the musician's daughter on whom it is thrust. Music plays a significant role in the tale of the musician's daughter. The language is rhythmic and the ugliness of the woman is beautifully concealed by the lilting notes of music and her overwhelming response to the painting she sees in the bazaar. She explains the birth of veena to the bureaucrat-narrator who meets her by chance in the bazaar. Musicians believe that Shiva was so moved to tenderness, one morning, by the sight of Parvati's slender figure while she was asleep, that he created the Veena to immortalize her beauty (196). The description of the veena's parts in the painting has evocative sexual imagery: '... the two globes that provide the veena's resonance are the breast of Parvati. The neck of the veena is her slender arm, the frets of the veena her glass bangles, and the music of the veena the expression of Shiva's love' (196). According to the musician's daughter such great love as Parvati's love for Shiva gives birth to music (195). After this description starts her story of love and music and betrayal. The touch of music is in every word and every phrase in the chapter as the musician's ugly daughter describes her initiation into music.

Her father was a great and sensitive musician but he was not 'sensitive to the presence of other human beings unless they intruded on his music, so he never noticed me. But he noticed my despair' (202). She explains despair thus, 'You see, despair is an emotion, and the emotions were like shoals of brilliant fish swimming through his melodies. Or coloured gases floating through the ether in which his music dwelt' (202). The musician's daughter learns to listen to the music of the rippling waters, the whispering trees, the rustling leaves and the chirruping of the birds but unfortunately, she could not listen to the false tunes of another human being's heart. A young man, her father's disciple, callously arouses amorous feelings in her tender heart. She was just eighteen then. But as soon as his music lessons are over he quietly walks out of her life leaving her with a gaping wound. Her father advises her to consider herself married to her music and not to a musician. But the woman, jilted in love realizes that to accept a penance a person must be internally ready which she was not. She utters a great truth when she says, 'it is an impossible penance ... to express desire in my music when I am dead inside' (286). The river may or may not cure her, but the author is certain that time spent in the soothing company of nature may certainly heal her wounded heart. She was a loser in life not so much because of her ugliness as because of human deceit and conceit – deceit of her lover and conceit of her father. It is the failure of the father both as the patriarch and artist. Her father insists that she must meditate on the waters of the Narmada the symbol of Shiva's penance, until she was cured, but she rightly hints at the impossibility of detachment when the inner being is not ready. Let us consider three important facts: first that her love for her father's disciple was tinged with longing to escape her ugliness in the beauty of love; second, his love was coloured with selfishness and opportunism; third, it is only the sublime quality of love of nature that can be the redeeming feature. The chapter strikes a balance between Elemental Nature, human nature and art.

The persistent symbol of immortality, love, action and rationality is the river on whose banks the entire drama is enacted. Its eight hundred mile long course from Amarkantak to the ocean is a constant reminder to human beings to be useful:

> ... O Narmada:
> Defend me from the serpent's poison. (137)

Only that river has been given the power to cure. The snake here is the snake of desire that coils inside us and pre-empts our efforts to go towards self-realization.

The river's course and her name Narmada meaning laughter, exhort us to be optimistic and to laugh our way through life despite difficulties:

> The river is named after laughter.
> Narmada means the 'Delightful one'
> 'Soother of desires'.

The river teaches us to be repository of human experience and to give meaning to existence. The Naga Baba alias Professor Shankar tells the bewildered bureaucrat, 'If anything is sacred about the river, it is the individual experience of the human beings who have lived here' (267). He further asserts, 'it is an immortal river. It has never changed its course. It is a sustained record of human presence in the same place – that is immortality' (264).

Narmada is a palpable presence in the novel as also in the consciousness of the characters and concomitantly of the readers. The first few pages tell us that she is the daughter of Shiva, the Supreme Ascetic. 'It is said that Shiva, the Creator and Destroyer of worlds, was in an ascetic trance so strenuous that rivulets of perspiration began flowing from his body down the hills. The stream took the form of a woman – the most dangerous of her kind: a beautiful virgin innocently tempting even ascetics to pursue her, inflaming their lust by appearing at one moment as a lightly dancing girl, at another as a seductress loose-limbed with the lassitude of desire. Her inventive variations so amused Shiva that he named her Narmada, the Delightful One, blessing her with the words, 'You shall be forever holy, forever inexhaustible'.' (8–9).

The folklore of the region has it that Narmada protects one from snake poison and that suicide in Narmada is not a sin; she purifies all sins. The river is an object of contemplation to the narrator: playful and placid, dramatic during the rains, dark and fearsome at night and colourful at daybreak. His approach is of a rationalist, of a lover of nature who sees her physical form as geographical reality. To the minstrel singing the Sutra, Narmada is the 'grace of the earth', 'a dancing deer', 'the beautiful one', 'damsel of beautiful hips' and 'river born of love'. The whole of culture seems to have sprung around the river. She is associated with Kalidas, Shiva, Time, Ascetics, jungles and even bards, gamblers and cheats – all those who find refuge near her banks. Another timeless One is Shiva who pervades the pages of the novel. The author constantly keeps Shiva and Narmada in the consciousness of the reader.

It may be relevant here to recall Arun Joshi's *The City and the River,* published in 1990. Joshi's river is nameless but it is probably Ganga around which an entire civilization has sprung up. Joshi deals with the existential *angst* of the culture. It is a muffled portrayal of post-independence India, a kind of allegorical picture, where intrigues, nepotism, ostracism and violence are rampant. (Joshi, 1990). The river is the archetypal mother, the harbinger of peace and plenty. There is a constant tussle between modern point of view and traditional outlook. This tussle is a pointer towards the conflict going on in contemporary India – fast moving towards western rational approach yet tied down to the old beliefs. Joshi carries the question to the end of the novel when it assumes philosophical proportion and becomes a treatise on the question of man's allegiance 'to God or to man' (262).

In *A River Sutra* too, the sudden summersault taken by Professor Shankar and his denial of the divinity of the river reveal the same ambiguity in contemporary Indian thought. What is practical for us – abandoning our tradition and becoming rational or keeping both? Professor Shankar's views about the river are ambiguous and show that Gita Mehta seems to be on uncertain terrain – should she uphold her culture's animism or should she give in to the western notion? She chooses to show how our thought system is a pleasant amalgam of both. Narmada is the organizing principle of the novel. The six loosely knit tales give the novel multiplicity but the river vouchsafes its unity. The Narmada Guest House is mini-India where people from different backgrounds come and contribute to the richness of experience. The river with its mythology, religion, superstitions, spirituality and archaeology represents traditional, primitive and modern India. If the traditional wisdom chants, 'O Narmada defend me from the serpent's poison,' the rational mind interprets it as the 'serpent of desire;' if it stings, the result would be a schizophrenic state, symbolized by Nitin Bose.

The river sustains the concept of love in its higher form and teaches the lover not to be moved by puny human passion but to see love as divine incarnation. This is corroborated by the story of the musician who exhorts his daughter to meditate on the waters of Narmada, the symbol of Shiva's penance, 'until I have cured myself of my attachment to what has passed. ... He says I must understand that I am the bride of music, not of a musician ...' (226). The highest symbol of love is Lord Shiva and his love has many shades – it is sensuous towards Parvati, it is fatherly towards Narmada and yet it is unattached. The story does not condemn love but suggests that love needs to be uplifting. The tale of Naga Baba's love for the girl child, Chand, whom he rescues from the brothel is humanistic/philanthropic, while Master Mohan's love for his blind pupil is attachment in the Guru-Shishya tradition; Nitin Bose's love is corroding; and the love of the musician's daughter is in the form of longing. Thus the aesthetic framework moves round love. Apart from these worldly images, there are rich motifs of divine love – the references to Kama, allusion to Parvati's penance to get Shiva's love, the stories about the origin of veena and the seven notes of music – uphold the divinity of love. The lyrics of the great Sufi poet Rumi strengthen the image of love, a purifying emotion above the narrow worldly barriers of cast and religion.

In *The City and the River*, the Yogeshwara tells the story to the Nameless-One to enlighten him, and He wants him to try and prevent the periodic disintegration of culture. The Nameless-One signifies a period of future hope for humanity. In *A River Sutra* the movement is forward which denotes the march of time but since time is seen in its variety of forms as historical, mythological, narrative and contemporary time, its movement back and forth cannot be overlooked. It is significant to note that by keeping the bureaucrat-narrator 'nameless,' she is trying to keep the possibilities open for interpretation. There is hope, too, for humanity in the movement of the river with the lamps flickering on its dark waters. After a brief spell of bewilderment at his inability to grasp Professor Shankar's revelation, the narrator goes to his favourite spot on the terrace. It was time for the evening prayer at Mahadeo.

> The temple bells were clanging in the distance at Mahadeo. Behind me the servants were switching on the lights in the bungalow.
>
> I leaned over the parapet to look at the river. Below the terrace the water flowed black under a moonless sky.
>
> At the bend of the river the clay lamps were still flickering as the current carried them toward the ocean. (282)

The novel is both praised and criticized for stirring up an Indian ethos. The novelist's descriptive power is evocative and graphic and some of the early reviewers appreciated the graphic and suggestive descriptions and the cultural contexts. Some of the Internet reviews, obviously by western readers are relevant to be quoted in the present context. A *Publisher's Weekly* review says that the novel beautifully embodies the art and craft of storytelling and that music is an important narrational prop. In it 'the music of India, the raga, figures prominently in some of the chapters.' As characters reveal the pleasure and pain that have shaped their lives, Mehta discloses the wonders of this country – the Jain religion;

savoury samosas and pickled mangoes; bazaars where one can choose from 'glass bangles,' 'clouds of spun sugar' or a bar of soap with a film star's face on the wrapping.' The review ends with the assertion that it is a charming book not only for its stories that reveal the complexities of India but also for its 'fascinating' and 'irresistible' text (*Publisher's Weekly*, 1993: 33).

Another in the *Library Journal* points out that the novel 'evokes the profound presence of tradition and desire along the banks of the holy river Narmada.' The reviewer speaks of the river's bright and dark powers, and of the surprising range of stories. 'For all the horror and passion of the tales, the bureaucrat remains little moved until book's end. Readers too may be more intrigued and edified than moved. As in folktale, the stories' dynamics dominate their characters, who serve primarily to illustrate cultural and religious forces.' One customer reviewer feels that *A River Sutra* is 'kind of like a primer to India's often ignored jungles.' This reader appreciates the book's flow and its detailed portrayals that are far from being 'sketchy' (http://www.amazon.ca/river-sutra/gitamehta).

In fact, the river and the multi-faceted subjectivity created through the inter-related tales repeatedly drawing attention to the main themes of love and renunciation and the powerful impact of the Indian ethos so dominate the narrative that criticism has overlooked some of the important issues like the use of myth, the portrayal of women, the residual colonial culture and the implicit sexual imagery. The revival of myth in the twentieth century manifested itself in writers' attempt to use it to look back and reconstruct the past. It offered a supportive base to build up a new creative perspective on recognizable images. Particularly in the case of the diaspora, which brings about dislocation and loss of identity, the restoration of a collective past implied a shift towards redefining the self. Critics of myth criticism like Leslie Fiedler supported the view that myths made literature accessible to the general reader. In one of his essays he contends that the common reader does not look for intricacies of the plot or the credibility of characters or the style. What he enjoys is the familiar elements like myths or fantasy. That accounts for much of the appeal of *A River Sutra*. Gita Mehta makes profuse use of myths and takes support of popular legends and beliefs and mythological stories. The river is inseparably associated with Shiva and allusion to one brings in allusion to the other. Towards the end, in her attempt to be rational, she suddenly lets Professor Shankar repudiate the myth of the Immortality of the river and twists the definition of immortality to suit the contemporary mind. But will she be able to erase the strong impact the river has left in the novel? The minstrel is there to sing of the river; the Sutra has been in the collective unconscious of the race; and even a person like Nitin Bose performs the tribal ritual of immersing the idol in the Narmada. Probably, it is because the 'will to live is stronger than the longing for death' (180).

The novel is replete with archaic beliefs and superstitions – the legend of the tribal hero and the bee sting; the tribal faith in the goddess who can cure the possessed; and the conviction that a man can become mad if he walks out into the jungle during the eclipse of the moon (134–35). It is interesting to read the account of Nitin Bose's foray into the jungle after Rima on a dark night and Rima, a tribal from Assam tea garden working black magic spell on him. Moreover, one unlikely myths is that the priest of that remote area of Assam should tell Nitin's servant, 'If your sahib wants to recover his mind he must worship the goddess at any shrine that overlooks the Narmada River. Only that river has been given the power to cure him' (137). The bureaucrat-narrator does not question these beliefs/stories nor does he seem to believe them. He is just confused and at best amused by the rigmarole. Another belief is that the grey-green oval stone found in the river are Shiva-lingam. 'For some reason only the rocks in the Narmada riverbed carry the mark denoting the third eye of Shiva and the three lines of his ascetic's ashes, becoming the smooth lingams worshipped in family altars and mighty temples alike with the prayer "In the living stones of the Narmada, God is to be found"' (174). He repeats the prayer but he does not seem to have deep faith in it. Professor Shankar, who refuses to believe the divinity of Narmada may have some scientific explanation for this particular phenomenon, but he is never asked this question. Obviously, it is too mysterious to be explained with scientific expertise or maybe, Gita Mehta does not want to expose the Professor's scant knowledge despite his stint as a Naga ascetic.

Professor Shankar's character is rather mystifying, not because he sheds the ascetic's garb and materializes as a knowledgeable archaeologist, but because of the inscrutability of his motives. Why did he become an ascetic? Why after attaining a particular high ascetic stage did he decide to come back? What happened to his family in the meanwhile? Well, the decision to come back may be explained and justified, but then after coming back we do not find him engaged in any useful/fruitful social activity. Above all, how could he get back into his Government job after so many years? His coming back is almost regression not progression on the path of spirituality. Gautam Buddha wandered from one ascetic to the other in search of true knowledge; he was often disappointed but he did not abandon the search. Swami Vivekananda travelled from guru to guru till he found Swami Ramakrishna; he attained enlightenment; and through spiritual knowledge he explicated the rational. If the Naga Baba has to reincarnate as Professor Shankar only to repudiate the immortality of Narmada, it is too heavy a price he is paying. He is really a 'trishanku' who is neither fully of this world nor of the spiritual.

Whether the river is Immortal or not depends on how one explains the concept; then, whether we accept it as Immortal or not is of no consequence because the river has had a powerful impact on our collective psyche, it is an archetypal symbol of an entire culture – not only the classical/Brahminical culture but also the tribal ethos. In fact, Gita Mehta need not have been so apologetic about her loving portrayal of the river. Since the diasporic experience is one of nostalgia and alienation there is always an explicit urge to re-establish the bond with the native culture. Geography of the homeland often impinges on the mind and the familiar landscape, with its rivers, mountains and trees becomes the metaphor for home. Uma Parameswaran has cited two examples from her personal experience to elucidate how an immigrant tends to look back at such 'territorial markers' (Sura P. Rath's term). In *Saclit* she evokes a beautiful picture of the landscape of her adopted home but finds it unable to stimulate those sentiments that the native scenery does:

> Though the landscape around me has been cedar and spruce for the last twenty-five years, the landscape I am most familiar with is trees with mango and jasmine. I can describe without effort the tender yellow blossoms and the hailstorm showers that brought green mangoes to the ground but cannot be as effortless when it comes to the pine cones that have been raking off my yard for the last so many years. The endless skies and the vastness of prairie fields recur frequently in my poems and with a single change of adjective I communicate the person's feelings of alienation that turns to love, but the details are not there. (Parameswaran, 1996: 40)

In her paper entitled "Ganga in the Assiniboine" she speaks of the process of transference when one can see, as she does, the merger of her native river with the river of the adopted home (Parameswaran, 1985: 79–80). If the Indian mind personifies and even deifies the rivers, it need not be disclaimed. Postmodernism, in rejecting the western notions of master narratives of progress and accepting a more democratization of knowledge, has opened up the portals of debate in favour of the traditional animistic approach. Studies conducted during the later half of the twentieth century acknowledge the ecological prudence of the traditional folk practices and scholars are trying to work out alternative paradigms to integrate folk wisdom with modern technological perceptions. Professor Shankar's (by implication the author's) refutation of the local myths and practices may give him/her an enhanced status as a rational, educated, westernized mind but it cannot obliterate the tribal ethos that is ingrained in the individual psyche.

Geographically, the area of Madhya Pradesh from where Narmada flows is the tribal belt. The setting of the novel gives a convincing glimpse into the tribal lore. One of the scenes that is vivid in its evocative images is the picture of the Vano tribal women collecting fuel in the jungle and enjoying typical female humour. Teasing each other they laugh and speak of Kamadeva, the god of love. 'The sahib finds your face pretty today, Rano,' says one, and the other replies, 'It must be the season. Spring arouses even old tigers from their rest' (92). This occasions beautiful descriptive passages about Kamadeva and his legendary sugarcane bow and arrows of blossoms and the maddening sandalwood scent from the south. The narrator's mood lightens by the Vano women's sonorous laughter and we realize that with a few deft touches the author has been able to give us an exposé of tribal women.

The portrayal of women in the novel is, however, not its mainstay. They are by far stereotypes – scheming, grabbing, sensuous, arousing man's lust and hence dangerous. What does Rima do to Nitin Bose? If she is a reality, as Nitin thinks, and not a figment of his abberrated psyche (as we surmise), she is the dangerous type. Her influence is as poisonous as the serpent's. On the same analogy, Master Mohan's wife is also venomous from yet another angle. She is ill-tempered, uncompromising and greedy – almost inhuman. Not only that she turned her children into little devils who ill-treat the blind boy and in one instance 'force pork into his mouth' (68). Master Mohan's life would have been tolerable had he had an understanding wife. The musician's lovelorn daughter is a pathetic figure. She has no verve and is an epitome of failure – unable to use the power of music to withstand puny human passion. Her father too is a failure as his music has no sustaining power – if he was a genius as his daughter reiterates several times, his music should have evoked ennobling feelings in the young man, who instead of jilting the girl could have uplifted her. The courtesan's daughter is just a passionate doll, the shadow of Rahul Singh; as for the courtesan, she has no independent identity; she is bound within her social role to make the princes immaculately stylish. She voices the reality of her life when she says, 'The city is owned by men who believe every human being has a price, and a full purse is power. Trained as scholars, artists, musicians, dancers, we are only women to them, our true function is to heave on a mattress and be recompensed by some tawdry necklace flashing its vulgarity on a crushed pillow. When they come to our haveli they throw cigarette cases, watches, dirty bank notes at our feet as we dance, oblivious to the frigidness of our salaams' (167–68).

Uma, the minstrel, stands apart from these women but then she is an ascetic and she has a limited function. She appears towards the end of the novel and sings the Sutra. She has no distinct personality but her song helps us to know more about the river and she saves the narrative from being disrupted. Gita Mehta could not have given the Sutra fully without interrupting the flow of her stories. Uma's presence supplements what the author had been giving us in bits and pieces. With her song, Narmada assumes many dimensions and becomes a palpable presence.

River Narmada is, thus, the most enduring female figure. It is, however, worth noting that she is seen as a 'dangerous' female who can tempt even the ascetics by her innocent laughter and frolicsome ways. Probably that is the reason why Shiva turns her into a divinity, blessing her thus, 'You shall be forever holy, forever inexhaustible' (8–9). One more significant point comes to the fore: Narmada Sutra has various appellations for the river – Delightful one, Damsel of beautiful hips, Surasa, Rewa and Laughter but not 'Mother.' Ganga is the primordial mother but Narmada is the enticing female. However we look at it, Narmada has history, a female identity and above all it has sustained the culture. On its banks there has evolved a tradition of secularism when the Nawab of Shahbag would come to honour the river for her holiness and sing in her praise: 'Bathing in the waters of the Jamuna purifies a man in seven days, in the waters of the Saraswati in three, in the waters of the Ganges in one, but the Narmada purifies with a single sight of her waters. Salutations to thee, O Narmada' (163).

After thus sentimentalizing the culture, Gita Mehta turns her attention to the India fifty years after her independence in *Snakes and Ladders*. She is astounded to see that even after half-a-century of freedom, the country is still irresolute, vacillating between the old and the new, not knowing what to choose. The failure of vision leaves her frustrated – a frustration which she vocalizes through her ironical tone, satirical comments and mock-serious style. It is a multicultural India with catchy slogans, colonial continuities, and postcolonial anxieties that we see in our next chapter.

A Chart Showing the Quests of the Characters and the Ultimate Result

Character	*Quest for*	*Escape from*	*Solution sought*	*End result*
The Narrator	Peace/ Tranquillity	Fed up with city life/void/ aimlessness	Flees from reality, settles in a remote place	Involvement towards fulfillment
Ashok, Jain monk	Nirvana	Duplicity, life of luxury	Renunciation	Quest continues
Master Mohan	Lost chance, fulfillment through music	Filial vacuum, family vacuum, self-effacing	Vicarious satisfaction	Detachment/ suicide
Nitin Bose	Mental satisfaction, psychological health	Schizophernia	Primitive cure	Sublimation, name and fame
Rahul Singh	Beloved of previous birth/venge-ance on society	Superstitious belief	Reckless love, rehabilitation	Death
Courtesan's daughter	Life of luxury, love and immortality	Weak, inability to face life	Return to society	Death by suicide
Musician's daughter	Beauty/ selfless love	Fear of ugliness/fear of rejection	Sublimation	Puzzled
Naga Baba (Prof. Shankar)	Enlightenment /Rationality	Fed up with modern life	Escape, renunciation/return/ excavation work	Back to society, involvement, towards fulfillment
Uma	Devotion/ peace/purity	Not belonging, fear of male	Sublimation/ devotion	Quest continues
Tariq Mia	—	—	—	Accepts life as it is

Notes

1. C.N. Ramachandran discusses the Indian tradition of framed narrative technique used in recounting the tales in *A River Sutra*. Ramachandran avers that almost all our ancient texts are told by the framed narrator/s

whether we take the *Mahabharata* or the *Ramayana, Kathasaritsagar* or *Panchtantra*. We often have 'double or triple framing' as in *Mahabharata*. Moreover, the 'narrative mode in the Indian (Oriental) tradition is non-realistic and fantastic. Thirdly, the framed stories are often variations of certain broad human experiences, no attempt being made to particularize either the characters or incidents in time and space.' Framed narratives have two strands: passive or dynamic. *A River Sutra* uses both passive and dynamic technique and the inset stories provide the 'work multiplicity of point of view.' See "Gita Mehta's *A River Sutra*: Two Views". *The Literary Criterion*. Vol. XXIX (1994) pp. 1–7.

2. Meenakshi Mukherjee, in her essay, "The Anxiety of Indianness," places before us two paradigms: the Indian writer in English and the writer in Indian languages. She maintains that the choice of English as the language of creative writing generates the problem of defining a national identity, which produces the anxiety of Indianness. To overcome it some writers manipulate the western forms with the postmodernist mode using local legends and fables to depict contemporary reality, while others, particularly the diasporic, take advantage of the concept of cultural hybridity to describe their experiences of displacement. The diasporic writers betray the anxiety of Indianness more than the writers in Indian languages because for Indian language writers India in not a 'discursive place' to be used as a metaphor, it is 'the first world' where he/she lives. This gives them a firm footing and a sound sense of belongingness. See Meenakshi Mukherjee, "The Anxiety of Indianness," in Nilufer Bharucha and Vrinda Nabar, ed. *Mapping Cultural Spaces*. New Delhi: Vision Books, 1998
3. Usha Bande remarks in her paper "India of the Mind" that Mehta creates an imaginary homeland within contemporary homeland. The paper entitled "'India of the Mind' – A Study of Gita Mehta's *A River Sutra*" was read at a conference in Ludhiana, in 1995 and was later published in *Modern Indian English Fiction* in 2002.
4. Uma Parameswaran in *Saclit* studies *A River Sutra* but she does not seem to have high opinion about the novel. She appreciates the author for creating a viable symbol in Narmada which is not simply a backdrop to the novel but a living presence; she finds the prose rhythmic and the final scene esoteric. Uma Parameswaran records her experience of reading the novel thus: 'Drawn to identifying oneself with the main character in each story, one dies with him/her and rises anew with an awareness of some essential truth' (*Saclit*, 1996: 256).
5. A chart is provided at the end of this chapter to give a bird's eye view of the quests and their ultimate results in the lives of the characters.

6. The four stages of a man's life as expounded by Indian metaphysics are: Brahmacharya (stage of celibacy and studentship), Grihastashram (householder), Vanaprasta (retiring to the forest to loosen all worldly bonds), and Sanyas (renunciation). These stages are meant for man, the male. Interestingly, women do not seem to need these and there is no reference to women taking Sanyas. In Shashi Deshpande's *A Matter of Time*, Gopal tells Sumi, his wife, that women are not troubled by existential angst as they are fulfilled through child birth whereas a man is not. In *A River Sutra*, there appears to be a kind of confusion as to the state of *Vanaprasta* which is called renunciation, even Tariq Mia and Professor Shankar believe that the bureaucrat has decided to renounce the world which, in effect he has not. The narrator admits several times in the course of the novel that he is not psychologically equipped to take *Sanyas* and retreat into the jungle.

Works Cited

Bande, Usha. "Resistance and Reconciliation: Shashi Deshpande's *A Matter of Time* and *Small Remedies*." *Writing Difference*. Ed. Chanchala K. Naik. New Delhi: Pencraft, 2005.

—. "'India of the Mind' – A Study of Gita Mehta's *A River Sutra*." *Modern Indian English Fiction*. Eds. T.S. Anand et al. New Delhi: Creative Books, 2002.

Fanon, Franz. *Black Skin, White Masks*. New York: Grove Press, 1967.

Fromm, Eric. *To Have and To Be*. New York: Bantam Books, 1976.

Galle, E. "Gita Mehta's *A River Sutra* – An Analysis." *The Literary Criterion*, Vol XXX (1995) No. 3 pp. 27–56.

Internet entry, http://www.amazon.ca/river-sutra/gitamehta.

Joshi, Arun. *The City and the River*. New Delhi: Vision Books, 1990.

Khan, A.G. "Gita Mehta's *A River Sutra*: Two Views." *The Literary Criterion*. Vol. XXIX (1994) No. 3. pp. 7–15.

Mukherjee, Meenakshi. *Twice Born Fiction*. New Delhi: Arnold-Hienemann, 1971.

—. "The Anxiety of Indianness: Our Novels in English." *Mapping Cultural Spaces: Postcolonial Indian Literature in English*. Eds. Nilufer E. Bharucha and Vrinda Nabar. New Delhi: Vision Books, 1998.

Parameswaran, Uma. "Ganga in the Assinibonie: Prospects for Indo-Canadian Literature." *A Meeting of Streams. A Meeting of*

Streams: South Asian Canadian Literature. Ed. M.G. Vassanji Toronto: TSAR Publications, 1985.

—. "Literature of the Indian Diaspora in Canada: An Overview." *SACLIT: An Introduction to South-Asian-Canadian Literature.* Madras: East West Books, 1996.

Ramachandran, C.N. "Gita Mehta's *A River Sutra*: Two Views." *The Literary Criterion.* Vol. XXIX (1994) No. 3, pp. 7–15

Review in *Publishers Weekly*, Vol. 240, No. 13, March 29, 1993, p. 33.

Satchidanandan, K. "That Third Space: Interrogating the Diasporic Paradigm." *In-Diaspora* Ed. Makarand Paranjape. Delhi: Indialog Publication, 2001 pp. 15–23.

Smith, Wendy. "Gita Mehta: Making India Accessible." *Publisher's Weekly*, 12 May 1997. pp. 53–54.

Syal, Pushpinder, "The Threads of Narrative: Gita Mehta's *A River Sutra*." *The Postmodern Indian English Novel.* Ed. Viney Kirpal. Bombay: Allied, 1996.

Wallia, C. J.S. "Gita Mehta: An Interview" www.indiastar.com/wallia.html.

Six

Snakes and Ladders : Snapshots of a Nation

I am a camera and the reader can see through my eyes.

— Gita Mehta (in an interview)

Snakes and Ladders, published in 1997 came as a surprise to Mehta-fans, not because it marked any significant breakthrough in her art of writing prose, but because it was a big letting down. It failed to evoke the sense of a collective past coherent with the present. The vignettes of the nation in the making – she subtitles her book: *A View of Modern India* – though recognizable, have something of the touch of a tourist viewing the country with a bemused gaze. The concerns are many – national/individual – history, political leaders, the environment, Indian villages, literature, art, culture and lifestyle, in fact, dozens of things a keen observer cannot miss. The present challenges vis-à-vis the inherent cultural paradigms create a sharp contrast and are portrayed from the point of view of a nostalgic romantic who reflects upon the situation without being able to communicate the constraints. Finally, there is a sentimentalized looking back as the time for departure comes and a hasty and uncritical acceptance of the paradoxes of a culture that is complex yet simple, pre-colonial in the post-colonial era and 'meaninglessly meaningful.' One cannot question the author's knowledge of her culture and her cinematic vision but somehow, the interconnectedness between what Lucas called the 'quasi-time' – the visible moment of a work of art – and 'quasi-space,' which gives spatial momentum to literature – is missing. A diasporic consciousness looks for redemption when with one's own community or in home; creativity has the power to give that redemption; for achieving this the author has to be a conscious mediator between his/her diasporic view and the rapid socio-politico-cultural changes taking place as a consequence of decolonization and the current globalization.

In all fairness to Gita Mehta, *Snakes and Ladders* is not a poor book, but it *did* disillusion both the Indian and the western readers, precisely because it is a weak presentation. Moreover, as a diasporic writer Gita Mehta has to juggle with two cultures and being astride two cultures makes one vulnerable; it is a position that Bhabha terms 'third space' and Sura P. Rath calls 'trishanku.' When the book came out, the Indian scholars/critics thought she wrote for the west; the western readers thought it was a 'patch-work India' that she was peddling. One critic in particular, using pun with peddle and paddle remarks that in *Snakes and Ladders*, Gita Mehta seems to be 'frantically paddling around India'[1] to finish the manuscript before the fiftieth anniversary of India's freedom, so that she could peddle India for the west. The reviewer observes that she managed it because of the current inclination to believe that distance brings objectivity. The reviewer sounds bitter:

> The formula is simple. You go away. You write a book. The book is about India, the specific India of your childhood filled with details about the rektakarobi that bloomed outside the window and the still-cherished taste of raw amla. Or an imaginatively recreated India. Any kind of India. You become a minor celebrity. You give an interview in which you claim that distance has lent you objectivity, and you would never have been able to write about India inside the all-engulfing maw of the experience. This gives the interviewer a warm feeling because they were right to allow you to live there, and not slam the door on you ... Maybe it works too well. In Mehta's case it gave her the courage – some might say the

> overweening arrogance – to think that she could pack it all into 225 pages. But it certainly hasn't given her what it takes to sum up India for Indians. (www.indiatravelogue.com)

Such acerbic comments apart, there are critics, both Indian and western who appreciate her 'rapier wit,' and staggering frankness in portraying modern India. Barbara Crossettee remarks that the essays in the book are written 'with a frankness and incisiveness still in surprisingly short supply among many who write about India. Mehta's years in London and New York add interesting dimensions to the sense of what India has become in the past 50 years and what Indians have come to expect from the rest of the world' (Crossettee, 1997: 1). C.J.S Wallia remarks that the public reading at Black Oak Bookstore, in Berkeley, California was 'very well received' by the audience. Interestingly, a few of the 'customer reviews' I found in some internet sights also choose to take both positive as well as negative view of the book.[2]

Snakes and Ladders opens with the description of Gita Mehta's family background and woven within the fabric is the story of the freedom struggle from 1943 (the year of Gita's birth) to 1947 (new India's birth). From chapter two through chapter thirty-five, there are sketches of India struggling all these fifty years (1947–1997) to understand herself. It cannot be denied that India has both bewildered and attracted the west. The epigraph to the book eloquently shows how each generation, each individual has tried to understand India:

> I should be sorely tempted, if I were ten years younger, to make a journey to India – not for the purpose of discovering something new but in order to view in my own way what has been discovered. (Goethe, 1787)[3]

That is exactly what Mehta is doing – viewing India in her own way, almost 210 years after Goethe's statement. Another point worth taking note of is that the book is dedicated to 'India' via America, through Mark Twain's words. Significantly, in 1897 (one hundred years ago), Twain called it a unique land 'all men desire to see.' One wonders is it possible that India has remained the same? Has not the country changed in these three centuries 1787 to 1897 to

1997? The answer to these questions can be: yes and no! In the flux of time nothing can remain static but it is equally true that nothing changes in India.[4]

Independence has been the beginning of a process of social and political transformation for us but somehow, there has always been a baffling mixture of western, rational approach and the traditional, ritualistic mediation. The title of the book (already discussed in chapter 1 of this book) is meaningful as the essays appropriately show how each step forward is forestalled by a couple of steps backward, how each political assertion is marred by vested interests and how the common man lives in blissful ignorance amid contradictions – the desire for order, freedom, status and privilege fortified by a tacit complicity and the pretext of ideology. The author looks at her country both as an anxious onlooker and a bemused insider-outsider – distant, pained and confused. Gita Mehta sums up her confusion in the last paragraph of her foreword:

> Perhaps historians can make sense of India's early years of freedom. I find myself able only to see fragments of a country in which worlds and times are colliding with a velocity that defies comprehension. These essays are an attempt to explain something of modern India to myself. I hope others may also see in them facets of an extraordinary world spinning through an extraordinary time. (vii)

Coming back to the opening chapter, the author portrays with expert strokes, the period between 1943 and 1947. It is not a chronological view of the history of our freedom struggle, but it is history all the same and it is connected with her personal life. Born in 1943 to parents active in India's struggle for freedom, she defines herself in relation to the history of the nation. History was recounted and re-created for her by those who lived it, and they reconstructed the time through memory. Memory is a selective process, and as Rushdie says in *Midnight's Children*, it has its own truth and everyone likes to trust his/her own version of that truth. 'Memory's truth, because memory has its own special kind. It selects, eliminates, alters, exaggerates, minimizes, glorifies, and vilifies also; but in the end it creates its own reality, its heterogeneous but usually coherent version of events ...' (Rushdie, 1982: 211). Gita Mehta notes that once she asked her mother and later her father about their 'worst memory during the British rule.' To her surprise each recounted events that had nothing to do with personal sense of humiliation or pain. On the contrary, both in their peculiar way created the reality that minimized the hurt and poured scorn on the colonizers. Gita asked her mother, 'What is your worst memory ... your absolutely worst ... of living under the British rule?' Her mother told her of an incident when she was sixteen and was boarding a train to Lahore. At the railway station an old Englishwoman pulled off the turban of her old retainer. Furious at the insult to the venerated old man, Gita's mother shouted at the Englishwoman, 'How dare you? You old hag?' At this the woman looked out of the carriage window and said, 'My dear, one day you will be an old hag too' (8). That was her worst memory of the Raj. Here a kind of relationship evolves between individual memory and collective history. The incident reminds us of Gandhiji's experience in South Africa which changed his life and brought him into the freedom struggle. For that matter, one can also recall Khushwant Singh's short story "Karma" in which two drunken British soldiers throw out a renowned advocate from a first class compartment, just because he happens to be an Indian. Gita Mehta's mother probably did not have to undergo this kind of humiliation or may be memory did the work of sifting.

Gita's father had something more challenging to relate. 'Once I was asked to fly a British colonel and his adjutant to the North-West Frontier. As I was climbing into the cockpit he said, very loudly, 'My God! I'm not going up in an airplane flown by a bloody native!' Of course, he didn't have any option.' So they flew and Gita's father landed the plane in a field a hundred miles from Quetta, on one of the hottest summer days and left the officers sweating and cursing while he coolly told the colonel to find someone who was not 'a bloody native to fly him,' and getting into the plane Gita's father took off, 'leaving him [the officer] to walk to Quetta' (9).

In retrospect, and more so in a postcolonial situation, the narrators of these experiences seem to have dyed the two incidents with due heroism but what appears potentially liberating in the new historical setting must have been threatening and insulting in the colonial context when the events took place.

Gita Mehta's third narrator to tell his personal history under the British Raj is her uncle who was sent to Kala Pani (the cellular jail in Port Blair) at the tender age of 14. This uncle, now in his seventies (in 1997), was incarcerated for 17 years. When asked if he wasn't frightened, the septuagenarian admitted that it really was a frightening experience to be tortured and flogged 'by British jailors in knee socks and starched white shorts cracking their whips on the sand, shouting, "this is where we tame the Bengal tigers"' (11–12).

Freedom fighters like Gita's parents and her uncle were fearless and selfless individuals motivated by a noble vision. They had no 'self-aggrandizement, or ideological dogma or religious fervour' (11). Mehta has an obvious regret that though freedom came with the sacrifices of numerous people, the real freedom fighters have been pushed into oblivion and power politics has taken every care to wipe off the names of those who 'genuinely fought for freedom' (12). Decolonization, instead of bringing freedom in the real sense has landed the country into another colonization – the internal colonization with despotic and dynastic rule in the offing.

The hint is clear – Mrs Indira Gandhi's political tactics had created a vicious atmosphere, particularly during the National Emergency. 'Wholesale imprisonment' of all those who dared to go against her views and were fearless enough to defy her or raise their voice against her 'intense obsession' to induct her son to 'imaginary inheritance' of power came as a shock to the right-minded people. India was evolving, not as a nation of fearless citizens, the likes of her parents and myriad others, who faced the British ire stoically, but as a nation of sycophants and fawning coteries all out to please those in power. It would not be out of place to mention Arun Joshi's *The City and the River* in this context. Written in 1997, the novel is allegorical: the story of the Grand Master and his obsession to perpetuate dynastic rule. In his 'monstrous egotism' (65) the Grand Master orders that the entire city should 'owe allegiance' him. The scenario is one of mass imprisonment and civil strife and the ruthless silencing of those who resent the orders. Finally the deluge comes washing away the entire civilization. That, however, is not the end. It is indicative of a new beginning as the Great Yogeshwara prepares the Little One for another evolution and cautions him that recurrence of such events will be the law till man learns to purify himself of his greed and egoism. As T. Vijay Kumar observes, *The City and the River* is a 'collocation of the strange and the familiar,' of the ancient and the modern, the old and the new (Vijay Kumar, 1996: 146).

On the same analogy, the colonial and the postcolonial, the old and the new remain side by side in the psyche of modern India. At the political level, the public ethics has gone down the drains. Within less than fifty years of freedom, the regime of 'fear', sycophancy, nepotism and shenanigan has surfaced. But, there is always the game of "Snake and Ladders" to remind us that if moving up implies sliding down, there is also the possibility of moving up the ladder again. Despite the curb imposed on freedom of expression during the National Emergency, Gita Mehta is surprised to come across a senior bureaucrat sitting in his office a couple of rooms away from the Prime Minister's office and openly criticizing the Prime Minister. He also has the courage to assert, 'She doesn't bloody employ me .... The people of India employ me. Don't you ever forget it. This is my damned soil' (13). This astounds the author and makes her brood over the paradoxes and contradictions ingrained in the Indian soil that makes India endearing. The author puts it thus, 'Such bad humour is enough to make you want to cling to your Indian passport for another fifty years of freedom' (13).

Despite substantial changes in the political and economic concerns between the colonial and postcolonial situations, there are important and obvious threads of continuity in the two conditions. Discussing the continued impact of colonialism in the field of economy in India, Ashis Nandy points out that 'the colonial political economy began to operate seventy-five years before the full-blown ideology of British imperialism became dominant,' and 'the ideology of colonialism is still triumphant in may sectors of life,' thirty five years of after the formal ending of the Raj (Nandy, 1983: 2).

Gita Mehta's attention is drawn to the subhuman conditions of the poor in the country. In the chapters entitled "Banish Poverty" and "Banish Charity" she provides a gruesome picture of the poor – the jetsam and flotsam of the society – living in bondage and in dismal conditions. The rag-pickers' tales are of displacement, impoverished existence and fear – the fear of being displaced again. For them freedom means the slogan from "Garibi Hatao" to "Garib Hatao", and broadly, their problem lies in their economic exploitation by the contractors, the paper tycoons, the apathetic government officials and the government itself – all those who take charge of their lives and their livelihood. The selfishness and superficiality of their attitude is obvious in their approach to the problems faced by these poor people. While speaking to Gita Mehta, one paper tycoon appreciates the 'faceless, nameless' rag-pickers for making 'a valuable contribution to the recycling industry' (41), but the spuriousness of his sympathy is revealed by his condescending observation that the rag-pickers are in a way 'used to' such living conditions because they are all scavengers and are engaged in a work which was 'only an extension of the kind of work they have always done.' In other words it means they are not worth a thought nor do they deserve any betterment. A telling image in this chapter is that of puppies nestling for warmth in a bundle of rags, probably better off than the human beings (40). It may be argued that by equating the rag-pickers to animals and perceiving them as emotionally deficient and lacking in intellectual development, Gita Mehta is playing the game of the 'Orientalist' looking at them from the position of authority and superiority. However, that would be stretching it too far because Gita Mehta's aim here is to expose the 'new colonizers'. But, the irony of the situation is that the colonizers' lobby is so strong that there are no chances of the despicable rag-pickers being heard.

It would be of academic interest to refer to Leonard Woolf's short story "Pearls and Swines" set in colonial Sri Lanka. The imperialist logic of controlling the economy is simple: 'We rule India and the sea, so the sea belongs to us and the oysters are in the sea and the pearls are in the oysters. Therefore of course the pearls belong to us ...' (Woolf, 1983: 269–70).

Likewise, the economic advantage of the rag-pickers' labour goes to those who employ them. Further, the irony of the situation is that these unnamed, unrecognized beings – children and women – are not the flotsam and jetsam of the earth as the paper tycoon conveniently believes. Some of them are from the Bhat clan, others from the Bhumihar tribe of Rajasthan. They are the displaced and the dispossessed who try in their own way to keep alive their traditions. As the mother of the Bhat child laments, 'Once our recitation began a royal coronation ... . Now look at my child's fate. We teach him the historical poems, otherwise they will be forgotten. And he shouts them aloud to frighten the vultures away while he looks for rags' (37–38). The humour intended here is too grim even to smile. Here one may recall the ballad-singers in Gita Mehta's *Raj* who come to the Maharajah's Durbars on every significant occasion to sing of Queen Pushpavati's valour and get handsome rewards. After the independence when these singers are told that they are as important as the kings now, one senior bard pushes it aside lighty, feeling self-important in the fact that they have always had a voice. One realizes soon how unrewarding has been independence for the poor like these Bhats-turned-rag-pickers.

One more picture of human cruelty is provided in Chapter Five "Banish Charity." But in this case, the efforts of organizations like SEWA and Dastakar have given hope to the women textile workers. Earlier, these women were working as bonded labour, in the grip of the money-lenders who purchased their products at negligible price earning enormous profits for themselves. SEWA and Dastakar did considerable work to help these women. These organizations introduced the goods produced by the women weavers in the export market and engineered substantial profits for them thus improving their economic condition. When their products got recognition for their high quality, the textile women workers' erstwhile employers changed their strategies. They were now ready to buy their products at export rates. The economic exploitation in the neo-colonial period reminds us of the veracity of Edward Said's words:

> Even though India gained independence ... in 1947, the question of how to interpret Indian British history in the period after decolonization is still, like all such dense and highly conflicting encounters, a matter of strenuous, if not always edifying, debate. There is the view, for example, that imperialism permanently scarred and distorted Indian life, so that even after decades of

> independence, the India economy, bled by British needs and practices continued to suffer. Conversely, there are British intellectuals, political figures, and historians who believe that giving up the empire ... was bad for Britain and bad for 'the natives', who both have declined in all sorts of ways ever since. (Said, 1993:163)

In India some Non-Government Organizations are working for the betterment of the subalterns and Gita Mehta extols their efforts. At the same time, she subtly pokes fun at the superficialities and the overbearing attitude of the high-brow men and women associated with voluntary works whom she meets at the party. The atmosphere at the grand party was charged with energy: men engaged in discussing economy and profits and the women busy hovering round the buffet table. Gita Mehta's friend (or rather acquaintance whom she had given the dollars for the poor weaver women) was more interested in stuffing her plate with the gourmet delicacies than in discussing the real issues pertaining to the weaver women. And when she talked about them, her tone was rather patronizing as if she was the only one responsible for the amelioration of the poor. Mehta felt hurt at her dismissive attitude. 'I was rather hurt. I felt she could at least have acknowledged my gift as being helpful. I didn't know that her organization was into self-reliance, not gratitude' (48). Thus again the contradictions in India continue to exist.

The concept of "Food for Work" leads Mehta to title her chapter "Food for Thought." In 1973, Maharashtra faced acute drought conditions bringing untold misery to the farmers, their children, livestock and crops. There was mass exodus from villages to the cities, particularly to Bombay (Mumbai). The government sprang into action and floated the "Food for Work" scheme whereby the farmers were employed to dig canals or build roads for which they were paid in kind. Imported grain from the USA was distributed to them but unfortunately, the wheat was mixed with Dhatura, and was fit for 'animal consumption, poisonous to human beings' (59). The farmer women sifting assiduously wheat grains from the poisonous Dhatura grains make a pathetic picture of poverty and want.

The contrast becomes more prominent when Mehta tells how she, a member of the foreign Media team was over-fed while here were the children of the soil dying of hunger. 'I, on the other hand, was being given more than I could possibly consume. Enough to keep ten families fed at every meal. Enough liquor to keep ten men intoxicated for a week. A private plane to fly me around the state. Cars to drive me to the worst sites of the drought. I was working for a British television company, you see. ... Because of our foreign employers we were honorary foreigners, traveling with the foreign journalists. So we shared in all the luxuries by which we in the Third World seduce the First World into paying attention to our problems' (59–60) Mehta laments that the exploitation continues; earlier it was the British colonizer, now the USA is the new colonizer. The condition of the Third World poor has not improved over the years.

Gita Mehta has discussed three famines in her works: the famine of 1898 in Rajasthan, 1943 famine of Bengal and 1973 drought in Maharashtra. In *Raj*, it was the 1898 famine in Rajasthan when the kingdom of Balmer was affected and the Maharajah took quick measures to set up relief camps. At that time the vested interest groups sold arable land to the British for railways and factories. The Maharajah expresses his impotent rage at his greedy ministers: 'Dead cattle litter the country-side, yet my ministers want to lease land to British companies to build Railways and factories. They say it is for Balmer's progress, but the ministers will become partners with the Englishmen, fattening on the misery of Balmer's starving farmers' (*Raj*: 29). In *Snakes and Ladders*, Mehta first refers to the Bengal famine of 1943[5] and British villainy in withholding the supply of food-grains. 'That winter of 1942 (sic), while tons of food rotted away, nearly three million people starved to death, most of them on the streets of Calcutta' (9–10). Mehta is crisp and brief in her description because of the requirement of a prose piece. We know from Bhabani Bhattacharya's novels the grimness of the situation. Even R.K. Narayan comments through Gopal, in *Waiting for the Mahatma*:

> 'See what the British have done to our country: this famine is their maneuvering to keep us in enslavement. They are plundering the forests and fields to keep their war machinery going, and the actual sufferer is the child'. ... 'Everyone is engaged in this war. The profiteer has hoarded all the grain beyond the reach of these

growers. The war machine buys it at any price. It's too big a competitor for these poor folk'. (Narayan, 1955: 82–83)

Gita Mehta too holds the complex structure of colonial power politics responsible for the suffering of the masses. In Balmer, the ministers, playing into the colonizer's hands were at fault; in Bengal, British injustice was responsible and in free India, the purblind officialdom. By looking back to the past, the author tries to explain the present in relation to the past. The problems of droughts and deaths cannot be simply reduced to the formula that since there were no rains there was famine. It is a more complex issue and it required futuristic planning. The author is not very sanguine about the policies of Nehru who placed his faith in industrialization at the cost of agriculture.

Industrialization of a predominantly agricultural country and rapid urbanization has been a grave mistake of our leaders. Pandit Nehru wanted India to be progressive and rich on the lines of the west. From his writings and speeches it is clear that Nehru was emulating the west that had become wealthy through industry. Mehta comments, 'Prime Minister Nehru and his advisors came up with a bold new plan to take India's bullock-cart economy into the machine age of the twentieth century' (60), which resulted in the neglect of agriculture. It was Lal Bahadur Shastri who brought back the focus to agriculture and within a few years the Green Revolution made it possible for us to export food grain. But, Mehta regrets that the policies of the successive governments have been detrimental to the welfare of the farmers and the benefits of the new laws always went to the rich landholders, leaving the middle-level and small farmers in debt. She quotes the instance of the Land-sealing Act whereby the prosperous farmers became money-lenders and the poor farmers, 'instead of being exploited by large landlords, our landless labourers were being exploited by small landlords, their condition deteriorating as the price of farming increased' (63). Once again in the game of snakes and ladders, the country and its economy went sliding down the mouth of a huge snake.

But the snakes and ladders board has its bright moments too. In our socio-political setting everything is not gloomy, the author seems to say in her tongue-in-the-cheek style as she narrates how because of unchecked urbanization agricultural land was sold and the landowners living near metropolises and big towns became rich overnight. This is how a landholding farmer sums up the situation: "'... isn't it wonderful? I worked so hard for so many years but the land gave me so little. Now I get up every morning and just smile at my field. And each day I get richer'" (64).

Gita Mehta is pleasantly surprised to see rapid urbanization in India by 1996. Small and medium towns sprung up to life and there was mushroom growth of shops; the bazars looked unruly and congested as the purchasing power of the buyers increased. Mehta looks at a typical Indian Bazar – crowded, filthy, loud and disorderly. Coming from the neat western Shopping Malls, the vibrant bazars attract her yet jar on her senses. Mehta's description is vivid, 'The stench of badly cured leather competed with the smell of food being fried in corner cafes where customers had stopped for snacks after renting their evening's entertainment from video shops. Racks of garments collected dust in crowded corridors next to rows of shoes piled in precarious pyramids that could not be crammed into the tiny shops. Loud film music emanated from record stores, drowning civilized conversation, disturbing the students pounding away their rented keyboards in their Computer Course schools consisting of two tables, two chairs, two machines' (79–80).

Somehow, a discerning reader can feel that despite being evocative, the description of the bazaar lacks sense of locale. Both the town and the bazaar are nameless and thus devoid of personality. Conversely, let me mention that some of the British travel-writings of the colonial era have given graphic description of our cities or towns. Travelling in India was by no means an easy proposition for them. They were often frustrated by Indian loudness and garish colours; despite that they managed to give authenticity to their portrayal by their use of suggestive language and gripping illustrative power. For example, G.W. Forrest in his work *Cities of India: Past and Present* describes Bombay's Byculla thus:

> We leave London club life, and plunge into the native city, a paradise of luxury and splendor, stench and squalor. The richness and variety of the outlines of the narrow and curving, but not crooked streets, take hold of our imagination. The many-tinted

> houses, the colours white, yellow, and red, the luxurious or wild carving lavished on the pillars of wood, the balconies, rosettes of windows, and the architraves of the roofs, give an air of refinement, of subtle grace which defies description or criticism. ... It is a world of wonder .... With much trouble and much shouting the driver works his way through the enchanted street, and we see ... rows of bakers' shops with large ovens, and vast round loaves of unleavened bread. There are long lines of confectioners', in which the sweetmeats are piled up in all sorts of fantastic shapes, and behind his pile sits the fat, greasy, half-naked confectioner. Then come shops of *bunias,* which are crowded with baskets filled with pulse and grain; and the oriental grocer kindly chatters to three or four women as he weighs their flour in a pair of primitive scales, and after much bargaining they purchase for a farthing a lump of salt and two green chilies, which are their sole luxuries in life. Long and sharp is the ting-ting that proceeds from the shops [selling brass vessels]. They are filled from floor to roof with large pots and small pots; for as the Hindu eats and drinks only from vessels made of brass, the brazier's art is an important one in the land. There are shops of the money-changers, who are seated square-legged on their carpet, with heaps of rupees and shell before them. (Forrest, 1999: 32)[6]

Usually a diasporic writer in his/her attempt to forge links with a distinctive cultural heritage and to place his/her experience within an acceptable historical framework is often careful with the description of the place. Perhaps, Mehta's objective in keeping the location of the town or the city flexible is to make it ubiquous. Landscape always plays a significant role not only in evoking the mood but also in reaching beyond the creation of a setting. In India each city or town has an unmistakable local flavour but when it becomes the centre of the author's preoccupation it becomes a part of the direct experience of being in India. The local appeal of the landscape helps the reader in connecting it with the broader national consciousness.

In some of her pieces, however, Gita Mehta describes the topography and the rich flavour of the states she visited during her journalistic assignments. Such passages display her powerful observations and descriptive skills. For example, she visited Assam in 1975 to do a piece on the non-violent agitation there to check the inflow of Bangladesh refugees. She writes, 'Its rice fields stretching to Bangladesh on one side, its wooded hills rising to China's border on the other, Assam is connected to India only by a narrow corridor of land' (114). Later standing on the hill in the courtyard of the temple (probably it is the Kamakhya temple though she does not name it) she looks down at the Brahmaputra River and writes, 'In the temple courtyard a frangipani tree was dropping white blossoms on the black stones, the slender petals spinning like hexagons against the darkening sky. Below the temple, the setting sun was throwing the islands in the vast sweep of water into red relief. River streamers from the days of the British Empire, still bearing their battered old Jardine Henderson signs, crossed the crimson water of the great river as mist closed over fishing villages on the distant banks. Inside the temple the priest had begun the evening devotions, chanting a melancholy melody that seemed to evoke Assam's separation from the rest of India' (115).

The passage catches attention for its three distinct characteristics: first, its descriptions of nature that have the unmistakable English Romantics' fervour; second, it juxtaposes the immutable with the present flux; and third, it hints at the Government's failure not only to give a sympathetic ear to the problem of the land but also their failure to bring the province at par with progress seen in other parts of the country. The poverty and the blockage of development are obvious from the example of the old-time dilapidated streamers still running. It is foreboding to think of the disintegrating trends but then by the end of the chapter the message is reassuring that people do understand that safety lies in being a part of India than being cut off from her. What a teacher tells his students is important to be recorded here, 'I tell my students, once you think you belong only to a particular part of the country you deprive yourselves of the wealth of the whole country' (118). Misplaced emotionalism is fuelling provincialism and it has to stop if we wish to enjoy safety, security and the rich national wealth.

Her continual exploration of the paradoxes of India and her confusion on finding it both traditional and modern is postcolonial and diasporic in essence. The decolonized India is fast competing with the consumer-oriented societies of the west. She observes the changes in life patterns with accuracy. The India of 1996 baffles her – it has modernized rapidly. Cars, telephones, computers and air-conditioners are no longer considered luxury items, they are the necessities and they have found their way even in villages. This can be contrasted with what M.V. Kamath observed in the 1970s when he came back to India to take over the charge of *The Illustrated Weekly* as its Chief Editor. After his stay in the US for over two decades, he was confused to find the slow movement of things in India. For example, even to get a telephone connection one had to wait for years; and getting a car was out of question, you had to wait any length of time from two years to five years. Not so now, in the last decade of the twentieth century; change within these twenty years is tremendous. The Indian youth are no longer interested in the security of government jobs but are looking westward for high-profile placements; Indian universities are churning out computer, management and engineering graduates; India has its silicon valley in Bangalore; and people have become aware of the need to educate their children. And within this milieu of the old and the new, Indians still preserve a way of life in which man does not become a machine (85); this is probably a gift from India's ancient pragmatism.

Gita Mehta begins Chapter Ten on an amused note. Her French companion shouts, "It's a scandal!" when she observes people worshipping gadgets. Gita's response is rather blatant, "What's the big deal? I thought to myself. Worshipping videos? Get a grip. This is India. We worship air-conditioners and computers and cash registers and bullock carts – in an annual ritual called Weapon Worship" (80). These thoughts are not as innocuous as they appear. The author is adopting a satirical posture while describing the progress India has made. Modernization and ritualistic attitude stay cheek by jowl in India and that is probably her beauty or let us say her postmodernism – displaying panache for ethnicity. Mehta's view is clearly of an outsider looking in; she swears by the colonial's standards and decries everything native. As Fanon avers, "... in the colonial context the settler only ends his work of breaking the native when the latter admits loudly and intelligibly the supremacy of the Whiteman's values" (Fanon, 1990: 33).

Interestingly, in the adopted "homeland", a diasporan flaunts his/her "otherness" by looking *back* to the home culture, but in the familiar native milieu the same person flaunts his/her "otherness" by looking *down* at the same culture (emphasis added). This is a complex psychological mindscape that both likes to cling to a past and yet disown it. In response to the colonial psychology of the "elite" Indian, Gita Mehta too is posing as an ideologue of the rational superiority of the west. The existence of modern materialism with the traditional ritualism can best be comprehended if we read it in the light of A.K. Ramanujan's 'context-sensitive' and 'context-free' paradigms. For Ramanujan borrowing from the west and vice versa and then accommodating the concept to the 'prevailing system' is a perfectly normal phenomenon in every culture. There are two situations: when the western culture borrows our ideas they turn them into highly individualized and universal form to agree with their context-free cultural pattern; whereas when we adopt some idea or concept from the western cultural context, we convert it to fit it into our context-sensitive needs and make it our own. This, Ramanujan says, has happened with regard to the English language, in sciences and in many other disciplines/fields. What happens when we borrow is that 'the new ways of thought and behaviour do not replace, but live along with the older 'religious' ways. Computers and typewriters receive *ayudhapuja* ('worship of weapons') as weapons of war did once. The 'modern', the context-free, becomes one more context, though it is not easy to contain' (Ramanujan, 1990: 56–57).

From gadgets, Mehta's attention now shifts to the trends of 'marketing India'. 1997 was the silver jubilee year of our Independence. The celebrations provided a platform to the vested interest groups to market India. Not only do the Hippies and the Rolling Stones come and go with their 'Hare Rama, Hare Krishna' chants but more harmful and persistent marketing strategy comes from the Government tourism promotion programs. I am tempted to quote here Graham Huggan's observation at some length. He discusses the western trend, supported by India, of 'marketing'

India not only with regard to its culture, tourism and mysticism but also its academic and literary products. Huggan shows how the Indian Tourist Office in London was trying to project India as the Shangri-la capable of exuding its exotic flavour.

> On 5 October 1997, the British weekend newspaper *Observer* carried a full-page spread devoted to the fiftieth anniversary of India's independence. The display, tastefully arranged (and no doubt handsomely paid for) by the Indian Tourist Office in London, features a series of marketing blurbs by British-based tour operators. The centerpiece blurb, to which the others refer, announces reasons to celebrate, not least of these being that "the attractions of India as diverse as the tour operators who organize holidays there." The familiar Orientalist icons are then dramatically unfurled, with a "profusion of romantic palaces, impressive forts and extraordinary temples" counting among the many wonders of India's fabled shores. The operator blurbs are similarly gushing, with emphasis on the exclusive, offering "classical tours" escorted by well-heeled "guest lectures" ... or holding out to "the discerning traveler" the chance to relive the opulence of the Maharajahs. Here again then, the skillfully marshaled, is the Orient as exhibition; and here is a further example of the twisted logic of the tourist industry, more than capable of turning the occasion of a half-century of independence into a fanfare for colonial nostalgia and the invented memories of imperial rule. (Huggan, 2001: 245)

The India of 1990s is influenced by the wave of globalization. Our notions of freedom, money, and energy have continued to develop as per our decolonized, postcolonial setting and these are now supported by free economy and other changes in the wake of globalization to which the country has responded with enthusiasm. Gita Mehta is baffled by the 'other-worldly' approach of the Indian culture and 'this worldly greed' of the individuals. In Chapter Ten, the boom of the new-era gadgets and an ever-expanding commercialization of the country leave her wondering at the readiness of Indians to seize the first opportunity to grab the new advances of science and technology.

In the earlier two chapters namely, "New Money" and "An Embarrassment of Riches" she throws a glance at the affluent urban middle-class and the entry of the western entrepreneurs on the Indian soil bringing riches to the land of detachment and renunciation. The change from the austerity of the past decade to the vulgar show of wealth in the present decades leaves the author wondering at the new sense of identity the nation has acquired. She compares the ethos of the 1950s and 1960s with the changed perceptions of the 1990s. In the years following the independence of the country there was a conscientious display of austerity and a glorification of everything Indian. A decade or two later more austere measures like state control over industries, nationalization of banks and insurance and ban on 'imported goods' landed the economy in conflicting situation. Some critics called it 'the Land of Permit Raj' while others thought that it was making the country self-reliant and independent from western commercial imperialism.

The older generation of nationalists who accepted with dignity the usable past and traditions to assert the cultural identity of India against the colonizers' notion of superiority was fast vanishing. Probably, as a reaction to the humiliation of clinging to the past, the new generation leaders, Rajiv Gandhi in particular, opened the economy and further accelerated the process of decolonization by ousting the 'Homespun' and welcoming the Luxury Goods of the West. Assessing the trends of India's economy during Rajiv Gandhi's tenure Gita Mehta says, 'For the first time in independent India it was politically correct to be rich' (69). This opening up brought in the sudden spurt of flashy neo-rich who reveled in pretentiousness. They liked to make an exhibition of their 'gold watches, German cars, Italian clothes, yachts and airplanes, Crystals and Dom Perignon champagnes, reserved tables for sprawling families in the most expensive restaurants and discotheques. An awful lot of caviare congealing uneaten in an awful lot of Lalique bowls signals the new Indian attitude: if you've got it, flaunt it' (65). This is contrasted with the older attitude, 'if you have it, you hid it.'

To appreciate the significance of Gita Mehta's observation, let us make a passing reference to Nayantara Sahgal. In *A Time to be Happy* Sahgal hits at the double standards of the high society women who discard all Indian furnishings and household items in 'shame' during the colonial period because the Indian things were not what the British approved of. Immediately after the Independence the same elite society replace all their furnishings with handloom curtains, and shift their attention to ethnic brass items like diyas (lamps), and Natraj and Buddhas. But then, this urge to parade their affluence and taste was limited to the rich; it has now percolated to the middle-classes. This is the demonstrative use of consumer goods and is associated with the *nouveau riche*. In consumer society the consumption of material goods is a dominant drive. The term also carries an undercurrent of criticism as it stifles the higher values and creativity.[7]

The description of the lavish party Gita Mehta attended is one of the examples of the vulgar display of wealth. It was a high-level dinner where the representatives of the Third World countries had assembled. Mehta observes that not only India, but almost all the Third World countries are guilty of excesses when their poor population is living below poverty line. The dinner she describes is the ultimate in consumer greed, 'Over dinner our silver platters were constantly replenished with kewabs, curries, Indian breads, vegetables; our glasses filled to the brim with wines, champagnes, liquors to keep us busy until the band came on' (77–78). This crudeness appears more offensive and unpardonable when we remember our hungry millions, particularly the farmers hit by droughts. To cap it all, Mehta refers to a repulsive turn the conversation takes during the dinner. One cabinet minister from Thailand sitting next to her, who had earlier that day addressed the gathering on Population Control in Third World, showed her a key ring he possessed which had an electric blue condom inside the glass case. This is not only offensive to her sense of propriety, but it also shows the callous approach to the most significant problem of population control.

Mehta is unable to understand how in the land of spirituality, so much of greed and extravagance could stay cheek by jowl. 'The new enlightenment is money,' says Mehta in one of her interviews (Neelakanthan, 1997. forbes.com. interview). And she is right. The avarice of the contractors who are thriving on the labour of the rag-pickers (as she reveals in "Banish Poverty," Chapter 4); the employers of the weavers who treat them as bonded labour ("Banish Charity," Chapter 5) are uncouth examples of blackmailing. It would not be out of place here to mention Ashis Nandy's observation about the bewildering gap between the metaphysical tenets and the real life approach of the Indians:

> True to the description of ethnocentrism in some contemporary studies of the authoritarian personality, the British colonial attitude to Indian culture was always inconsistent. On the one hand the British saw the Indian overly this-worldly – exceedingly shrewd, greedy, self-centered, money-minded. On the other hand, they also despised the Indian as overly other-worldly – not fit for the world of modern science and technology, statecraft and productive work. ... This is a split which has persisted in India's modern sector. Once other explanations of India's problems are exhausted, the modern Indian is always tempted to fall back upon either the stereotype of the spiritual Indian or on that of the pseudo-spiritual. (Nandy, 1983: 80–81)

Indian democracy draws Gita Mehta's attention several times: a multi-coloured affair consisting of the big show called elections, colourful and wasteful displays to please a leader, the dark years of the emergency, the demonstrations and strikes over issues like cow-slaughter and price-rise and the current waves of violence over non-issues. These things are happening in a country founded on the principles of simplicity and on the dreams of non-violence. Mehta narrates how Prime Minister Nehru's reception arranged in the North-East turned into a fiasco. It goes back to 1957 when Pandit Nehru visited the North-East. An impressive gathering of tribals was 'arranged' to welcome him but when the Prime Minister arrived, instead of the 'colourful guard of honour' the tribals all turned 'with regimental precision and lifted their colourful sarongs. The Prime Minister of India found himself taking the salute of hundreds of naked tribal behind' (96).

We Indians have an idiosyncratic panache for pageants and strikes and demonstrations. Our democracy, says the writer, is one of the funniest spectacles of the world. Consider thousands of naked sadhus, all armed with iron tridents, marching to the Parliament; hermaphrodites dressed in brilliant saris staging a demonstration against Family Planning, the hue and cry over cow slaughter and the *Thali* Revolution of Gujarat against rising prices. The price index rose to an alarming height in 1975. To attract attention of the government, thousands of women armed with *thalis* (stainless steal or brass plates) came out on the streets and created 'such a din that the state echoed with their displeasure' (121). This was necessitated because of the inaction of the administration/the government. Prices were rising rapidly and 'finding it impossible to make ends meet and feed their families, the housewives waited until street lamps came on. Then they beat their metal platters, their *thalis*, with wooden rolling-pins to express their dissatisfaction with rising prices' (121). Gita Mehta laughs at this unique method to display women's solidarity and to draw the attention of the dumb and deaf administration to the real problems of the people. On the one hand, it is a residue of the colonial psychology; fifty years after we ceased to be a colony, 'we still bristle with the over-sensitive antennae of a colonized people' (94); and on the other hand, such demonstrations have become necessary to raise the administration from its torpor. 'Modern India is a fiction. A fiction in search of an administration' (97), says Mehta.

With the new crop of political leaders more interested in personal economics than in the welfare of the people who elected them and the bureaucrats engaged more in sycophancy and less in governance, the public scenario is one of corruption, indolence and other harmful practices. The vision of the makers of our constitution is shattered in the political muddle that we have created for ourselves. 'The chaos is enough to intimidate anyone. Rather than undertake the duties of their office, our leaders have too often settled for redefining the privileges of office, making political corruption so endemic that winning an election in India today is tantamount to winning a lottery for the family' (98). Gita Mehta alludes to Nirad Chaudhari's writing and feels that he has chosen an apt title for his book *The Continent of Circe* describing India. There are so many baffling happenings, weird ideas floated by politicians and so many magic cures found for the ills of governance that we all seem to be under the thrall. It would be relevant to refer to V.S. Naipaul at this point because he too is a sever critic of India's political, administrative and democratic failings. Naipaul feels humiliated and defeated by the weakness and the exploitation of the system. In *An Area of Darkness,* he resists the traditional Indian passivity and fatalism and feels splintered when instead of finding the signs of a 'great culture' that he had expected as a diasporic visitor to his native land, he encounters corruption, incompetence, self-centeredness, lack of concern for others and the existence of the dehumanizing customs like the feudal-system and economic exploitation. He is rather critical of the socio-cultural-religious ostentations he encountered during his pilgrimage to Amarnath. His 'discovery' of India was disillusioning for him and he records that 'It was a journey that ought not to have been made; it had broken my life into two' (Naipaul, 1965: 266).

Like Nirad Chaudhari and Naipaul, Mehta too is disenchanted by the land of her birth turned into a dirty and decayed land, not the paradise of her dream. But Mehta is less acerbic than both Nirad Chaudhari and Naipaul. Probably because she does not see her country from an immeasurable distance in time as the first generation diaspora searching for a home, do. For her the 'home' is always there, but the return every year is marked by the sights of further deterioration; and herein lies her anger and dejection. Whereas Naipaul is critical of colonialism and he refuses to sentimentalize England, Gita Mehta has no such stipulations. She sees India as she is, half a century after independence, and she spots India's weaknesses which are the creation of her own politicians and political system. Throughout her travel, Mehta is saddened by the spectacles she sees but she has the knack of deriving fun out of the idiosyncrasies of people and the absurdities of situations. Like Naipaul, she too is ashamed and angry at the filth, greed, decay and passivity and she wants her country to be rational, efficient and progressive like the west without losing her cultural authenticity, her base of rich heritage and healthy traditions. This aspect can be substantiated by the vision she gives of the culture in *A River Sutra*. Just as Naipaul says in *A Way in the World*, 'we cannot understand all the traits we have inherited. Sometimes we can be strangers to ourselves' (Naipaul, 1994: 9). Similarly, Gita Mehta too feels that no one theory is adequate for a diasporic consciousness to understand the inheritance and the mysterious connections that the diaspora has to the past.

Appearance and reality existent in the present system are contradicted in *Snakes and Ladders* at several places. The first casualty in modern India is the concept of non-violence. Mehta remembers her visit to Assam to collect material for her write-up about the agitation against the infiltration of Bangladeshis in the state. When Mehta talked to one young engineer he was rather bitter, 'We are fighting another invasion and Nehru's daughter sends the Army to fire on us! Is she mad? Is it our fault that millions of foreigners who are over-running us today don't speak Chinese?' (115). Such comments are searing pointers towards the mishandling of the North-East problems by the central leadership. What Gita Mehta records is authentic and it can be validated by M.V. Kamath's editorials in *The Illustrated Weekly of India* way back in the 1970s. The Assam problem took an ugly turn and violence has become a frequent feature now. Mehta expresses her concern succinctly, 'Non-violence may have expelled the British from India but our first lesson in freedom was the violence of Partition, and in Assam I discovered that we have not learned our lesson well' (114). She laments further when she learns that twenty-eight villages were put to torch, 'Why indeed? Whatever happened to India's proud pluralism? Whatever happened to non-violence?' (119). Unfortunately, pluralism, non-violence and such like terms have only become concepts with their original connotation gone berserk in the maze of self-centeredness, separatist tendencies and continued in-fighting. At every level – social, cultural, ideological and political – the inherent idealism of the pre-independence days has been subverted by violence, nepotism and shenanigans.

It would be relevant to give some space to Sasthi Brata, who in his *India: The Perpetual Paradox* looks at India 'from two sharply opposed perspectives' (Brata, 1986: 18). Sashti Brata was a journalist who stayed for twenty-five years in London and New York and his views are totally contrary to those of Naipaul or Chaudhari or even Gita Mehta. In reassessing India, he finds it refreshingly open which allows an assimilation of all religions, where there is no beggary in villages and where there is 'new self-confidence' in the people. He has, in fact, full-throated praise for the multifaceted India. While Gita Mehta finds the political scene one of utter disgust, he finds Indian political system unique. He particularly speaks of the election of 1984 when Rajiv Gandhi was voted to power. Mehta calls it "The Greatest Show on Earth" and misses no opportunity to see the chinks in its armour. 'The sheer force of the Indian electoral process has introduced a new word into the dictionary of democracy – Wave – to decide such furious display of voter preference that sweeps all calculations before it' (151). She gives a resume of the various elections held since the inception of democracy in India, the emergence of various political parties particularly the party meant for the lower castes. Everything is a big joke, a gimmick in India – secularism, religion in politics, division of the country on caste basis, sectarianism and a whole gamut of activities that pass for democracy. The author laughs at the stunts and recollects the line that had appeared in the *Financial Times* of London, 'The democracy of India is a wonder of the world' (159). Mehta concludes her chapter with a mock-serious remark, 'And its guardian is not the politician so beloved of feature writers but the faceless, nameless, all-enduring Indian voter' (159). Interestingly, while Sashti Barta appreciates the voter for his political acumen in voting, Gita Mehta has her doubts.

The faith that some prose writers reposed in the emerging nation seems to have been splintered by the time Mehta looks at it. Pt. Jawaharlal Nehru's euphoria in *The Discovery of India* for India's multiculturalism, her 'unity in diversity', secularism, and her tolerance turn out to be only catchwords in the scenario of the present day India. It can be argued though that Nehru was the first to use the terms indigenization and Indianization. Indigenization means the act of making something native. He uses it to denote the process whereby cultural artifacts are incorporated into an existing civilization. Thus the English language and the material culture, including machinery becomes indigenous. He uses the term Indianization to refer to cultural assimilation and lays much stress on synthesis. Thus we get a picture of the emerging Indian identity.

Sunil Khilnani explicates that Nehru's idea of Indian identity 'could emerge only within the territorial and institutional frame of the state' (Khilnani, 1997: 167). Gita Mehta looks at these facts from her position as a media person roaming India during the silver jubilee year – 1997. She perceives the shattered dream and she does not hide her dissatisfaction at the way things work. India has traditionally described herself as *Karma Bhoomi,* the Land of Experience, with a hoary past, but Mehta laments that nothing of her previous experience has taught her any lesson. Referring to Alex Aoronson's ascerbic remarks that India was a civilization and 'civilization is always a process' she observes, 'half a century later that observation still proves astute. Somehow India has managed to stay a civilization, still unpredictable, still surprising, still defying definition. Maybe India's indolence preserves her. Or her traditional fascination with unifying what appears fragmented. In any case, in a world of perpetual motion India remains a perpetual becoming, a vast and protean sea of human improvisations on the great dance of time' (164).

All through the work, Mehta's tone is one of resentment camouflaged as sarcasm. As stated in *The Discovery of India*, Nehru wanted to create the right kind of modernized India by replacing the colonial power with the centralized national state. That ideological premise, however, appears spurious, simply a matter of rhetoric now because when power came in the hands of the Congress it soon turned into personal aggrandizement, communalism, corruption and nepotism. The notions of Indianization, unity in diversity, and what Aijaz Ahmad calls the 'civilizational ethos' got diluted in the fragmented psyche. Even Gyanendra Pandey in one of his articles on Hindu-Muslim riots recounts how the concepts such as 'unity in diversity' fail to stand as a national ethos.[8] Yet India has successfully countered the divisive trends and remains, partially though, a peaceful, democratic nation.

Snakes and Ladders also focuses on Indian literature, art and cinema, the reading culture and the home décor. In dealing with topics such as these she seems to enjoy the simple pleasures of Indian life, like the pavement book stalls. She appreciates the simplicity of our homes because for an Indian 'home is neither his castle nor a stage set by his decorator. By necessity it is organic' (173). But living in the west her personal sense of home décor differs from the Indian sense of aesthetics, which she finds lacking in imagination, with no artistic sense; only given to chaos and decay. Mehta's scribbling on Indian literature and cinema are unfortunately not thought provoking and are rather trite like entries in the general knowledge books meant for students.

Despite its obvious drawbacks, *Snakes and Ladders* is considered an agreeable contribution to India's prose writing in English. It may not be as organized and strong as Naipaul's travelogues or as acerbic as Nirad Chaudhari's works but it has simple jottings on our postcolonial history in everyday language. The observations have a grain of truth in them whether we like it or not. On the flip side of it, the book has some factual errors that put a question mark on its authenticity. As one reviewer points out, the book has more than its fair share of mistakes that cannot be condoned, 'the Bengal Famine is timed a year early, the annexation of Tibet nine years later. Tashkent is located in Russia, the politician Rajmohan Gandhi is called Ram Mohan Gandhi. Ashoka's wheel at the centre of the Indian flag is mistaken for a spinning-wheel' (symbol that was dropped in 1947). Further, the review corrects another mistake. Mehta says it was Mahatma Gandhi who 'insisted' that Mountbatten should remain as governor-general of free India; 'in fact, it was Pandit Nehru and Sardar Patel who made the decision. Gandhi played no part in it' (http://www.amazon.com. customer review). The errors are disconcerting and one does not expect such a perfunctory work from an author of Mehta's standing.

As a travelogue, *Snakes and Ladders* takes upon itself the onus to provide us the camera view of our own recent history; as a memoir it gives the author's viewpoint of her motherland which she does with genuine concern. Both travelogue and memoirs are history in that they are based on evidence. What she sees, she presents and in recording her anger and resentment she is not deriding the culture but is certainly voicing her resistance to the present that has made a mockery of the past, the vision of freedom and of the high ideals that motivated the freedom fighters. Scholars of postmodernism and postcolonialism would agree that a postmodernist work does not portray the past as past, but it portrays the present which includes the past; a postcolonial text resists the imperialist/colonialist tendencies of the political set up. *Snakes and Ladders* performs both these functions. Maybe the links between chapters are tenuous, but the mixture of the factual and the personal and the ability of the author to maintain her distance as an onlooker, give the work its postmodern, postcolonial position. The book has history and it puts across the detrimental forces that have changed the ideas about the making of the nations, the ideas that motivated the early visionaries like Gandhi. But whatever the political crisis or disconcerting happenings, which she records in the course of her narration, it is the perennial India that holds. Mehta is mesmerized by the sound and smell of the land. She admits 'God made India at his leisure,' and we too agree with her notwithstanding the present scenario.[9] This brings to mind the words of Ernest Renan with which I venture to conclude:

> A nation is a soul, a spiritual principle. Two things, which in truth are but one, constitute this soul or spiritual principle. One lies in the past, one in the present. One is possession in common of a rich legacy of memories; the other is present-day consent, the desire to live together, the will to perpetuate the value of the heritage that one has received in an undivided form. (Renan, 1990: 19)

Notes

1. See John Maria's book review published in "Travelogue India" @www.indiatravelogue.com. According to the reviewer the book begins with memorable image: Gita Mehta's father training his wife (Gita's mother) in various outdoor activities – something that was out of bounds for women in the early decades of the twentieth century. 'Mehta's father decides to teach his wife some of the accomplishment of the new woman (circa 1930) and starts off with bridge and ballroom dancing. With a fine sense of alliteration, the next course is bicycling. Mehta writes: 'Then he put her on a bicycle, pushed it until she peddled well enough to retain her balance, and deserted her. She cycled halfway around Delhi before she had the courage to dismount ...' I wonder whether Gita Mehta felt that way when she was writing this book, hailed on the jacket as 'a key to

modern India'. Was she paddling frantically around India, wondering whether she would ever get off, whether she would ever have the courage to send the manuscript off to the publisher in time for that milestone, the 50 years of the nation state of India?'

2. A few customer reviews that appeared in amazon.com make an interesting reading and give a fairly good idea of the different views. They may not have much literary or academic value but they are a good indicator of the general readers' reaction. Some extracts are given below:
   (i) "An Objective Review of Indian Politics," Sept 2 1997: The book *Snakes and Ladders* is indeed a very nice book which introduces (the) reader to various facets (...) over the last fifty years. The choice of title is very appropriate as (the) author tries to take stalk of progress over the years and the factors that hinder growth. It is not an easy job to write an objective book without personal bias. The book can be said to be an outsider's view yet the author understands India .... However, I feel the twenty-one month emergency rule deserved a little more space .... .
   (ii) "This Non-Student of India Found the Book fun to read," April 30 1997: As someone who has never loved reading serious, academic, historical studies, I found this book delightful. My knowledge of foreign cultures and history comes from traveling, from reading fiction, and from studying art. And when I wanted to learn more about India, a country of huge size and population, of countless religions and traditions, and of a mystifying political history, I couldn't even imagine attacking the tomes it would take to gain even a small understanding of this country. Though a slim confection of ... 'dinner party anecdotes,' I enjoyed reading it .... .
   (iii) "Too Many Factual Errors to be Condoned". April 20 1997: It is baffling that a writer with Mehta's reputation should have turned out such a book [with so many factual errors]. I am tempted to think it might be an elaborate spoof, a satirical sequel to *Karma Cola*, developing the theme that westerners will buy any old tripe provided it bears an Indian label.
   (iv) "Poor Perception of Indian Realities". May 9 1997: The author has not taken time to see things as they are. India's pristine past and poor present stands further aggravated with such a hotchpotch of facts as the author has projected. The book does not capture the real spirit of its time and theme.
3. See epigraph to the book. The quotation is from Johann Wolfgang von Goethe.

4. A.K. Ramanujan feels that Indian way of thinking is context-sensitive and since everything is placed in a context, there is continuity. He takes up one sentence and placing his stress on different words answers the question, 'Is there an Indian way of thinking?' The four paradigms he takes are: (i) *Is* there an Indian way of thinking? (ii) Is there *an* Indian way of thinking? (iii) Is there and *Indian* way of thinking? (iv) Is there and Indian way of *thinking?* He also relates to our old texts to illustrate their continuity. 'Texts may be historically dateless, anonymous; but their contexts, uses, efficacies, are explicit. The Ramayana and Mahabharata open with episodes that tell you why and under what circumstances they were composed. Every such story is encased in a metastory. And within the text, one tale is the context for another within it; not only does the outer frame-story motivate the inner sub-story; the inner story illuminates the outer as well. It often acts as a microcosmic replica for the whole text.' Ramanujan goes on to narrate briefly the stories of Nala-Damayanti and Yudhishtra to explain how context within the context is built unendingly in which the contained and the container become one. '... the microcosm is both within and like the macrocosm, and paradoxically also contains it' (see A.K. Ramanujan. "Is There an Indian Way of Thinking? An informal essay" in *India Through Hindu Categories*. Ed. Mckim Marriott. New Delhi: Sage, 1990. 41–58).
5. This is a chronological mistake. Bengal famine took place in 1942.
6. G.W. Forrest was the Director of Records to the Govt. of India between 1857–1858. The present book is a selection from his letters, dispatches and other state papers preserved in the Military Department of the Imperial British India. Forrest collected information about the cities he visited as a part of his official duties. He tried to capture the charm and spirit of the Orient. As the Preface says, 'he has endeavored to give life to old scenes, and to reproduce sentiments unfamiliar to the present generation.' He writes about his visit to Cuddalore in the South. 'At break of dawn we start with our Marhratta friend to visit the city of Cuddalore. The air is fresh, the road is lined with noble trees, and the country is rich with maize, corn, and rice, spreading as far as the eye can scan. Before we reach the town, we skirt the broad river, lit with the scarlet shafts of sunrise, and here nature grows even more rich and lavish. But man has not been lavish in his bounties on the city of Cuddalore. The streets are extremely narrow and dirty, and with some difficulty we thread our way through them, in order to reach the old factory' (p. 344).
7. Consumer society emerged as a result of modern industrial advances; it is the ultimate reward of wealth and progress. Consumer society is influenced by the glamour and glitter of advertisements and it takes to vulgar

display of wealth. Many critics objected to the consumer display of wealth on the premise that it establishes a nexus with the profit motives of the producers in catering to and stimulating conspicuous consumption by artificial means. The needless consumption is detrimental to available resources. In literature, Margaret Atwood's novel *The Edible Woman* in particular succeeds in depicting the psychological debacle of the heroine due to the consumer-oriented approach of her society. Eric Fromm also condemns this approach in his *To Have and To Be.*

8. See Gyanendra Pandey, "In Defence of the Fragment: Writing About Hindu-Muslim Riot in India Today." *Economic and Political Weekly,* March 1991, 559. Pandey emphasizes the local and particular as against the national and laments the loss of the ethos of "unity in diversity."
9. Shailaja Neelakanta, in her *Forbes Magazine* interview records that Gita Mehta's faith in India is reflected in her message to a fellow Indian. She inscribed in the copy of *Snakes and Ladders,* presented to the interviewer(Shailaja Neelakanta), 'With many thanks and don't rush with the Green Card. The next century is ours.'

Works Cited

Brata, Sasthi. *India: The Perpetual Paradox.* 1985. Rpt. Calcutta: Rupa, 1986.

Corsellee, Barbara. "After the Raj." www.nytimes.com/books/97/07/06. reviews.

Fanon, Franz. *The Wretched of the Earth.* Harmondsworth: Penguin, 1990.

Forrest, G.W. *Cities of India: Past and Present.* Delhi: Shubhi Publication, 1999.

George, T.J.S. Comp. *The Enquire Dictionary.* New Delhi: Harper Collins India, (PB) 2000.

Huggan, Graham. "Consuming India." *Post Independence Voices in South Asian Writings.* Eds. Malashri Lal, Alamgir Hashmi, Victor J. Ramraj. New Delhi: Doaba, 2001.

Khilnani, Sunil. *The Idea of India.* London: Hamish Hamilton, 1997.

Maria, John. "Bookshelf" *Snakes and Ladders* – Gita Mehta. http://www.indiatravelogue.com.

Naipaul, V.S. *An Area of Darkness.* London: Andre Deutsche, 1965.

—. *A Way in the World.* London: Heinemann, 1994.

Nandy, Ashis. *The Intimate Enemy*. Delhi: Oxford, 1983.

Narayan, R.K. *Waiting for the Mahatma*. Michigan: University Press, 1955.

Pandey, Gyanendra. "In Defence of the Fragment: Writing About Hindu-Muslim Riot in India Today." *Economic and Political Weekly*. March 1991: 559.

Ramanujan, A.K. "Is There an Indian Way of Thinking?" *India Through the Hindu Category*. Ed. Mckim Marriott. New Delhi: Sage, 1990.

Renan, Ernest. "What is a Nation?" (1882). *Nation and Narration*. Ed. Homi K. Bhabha. London: Routledge, 1990.

Rushdie, Salman. *Midnight's Children*. London: Pan, 1982.

Said, Edward. *Culture and Imperialism*. London: Vintage, 1994.

Vijay Kumar T. "Allegory and the Negation of History: Arun Joshi's *The City and the River*." *The Postmodern Indian English Novel*. Ed. Viney Kirpal. Bombay: Allied, 1996.

Wallia, C.J.S. *Indiastar* interview. http://www.indiastar.com wallia4.html.

Woolf, Leonard. "Pearls and Swines." *Stories from the East: Three Short Stories on Cylone*. Rpt. Leonard Woolf, *Diaries in Cylone 1908–1911: Records of a Colonial Administrator*. Dehiwela: Tisara Prakashkayo, 1903.

Seven

Conclusion

> India with all her infinite charm and variety began to grow upon me more and more, and yet the more I saw of her, the more I realized how very difficult it was for me or for anyone else to grasp the idea she had embodied.
>
> — Jawaharlal Nehru

As a casual reader of Gita Mehta, little did I recognize her subtle kind of diasporic leaning. On close reading, however, I became aware that when she looks at her country with the bemused gaze of an outsider, she is indeed, trying to recover the lost essence and that her return to roots is not meant to flaunt her "otherness" but is an effort to write the difference so as to come to grips with her past with a wistful recapitulation of India that *was* and India that *is*. We have argued that Gita Mehta is not an exile in the sense of having lost her moorings. Taking the twentieth century migrant's voluntary decision to go abroad for education or for professional reasons, and also the possibility of visiting the 'home' country often, the sense of loss has mitigated, though not overcome. The need to belong, the urge to relive old memories and the longing for the familiar cannot be denied as these psychological prerequisites surface occasionally with the experiences of daily living. Similarly, the awareness of difference is always there, at conscious or unconscious levels. And when 'difference' is felt, the search for identity inevitably emerges. Considering this, the question that needs to be answered is how much diaspora is discernible in her works and with what force? And again, how much of that diaspora is linked with the present process of globalization which underscores the centralization of culture. Terry Eagleton, in her *The Idea of Culture* feels that the current cultural consciousness instead of solving the problems of identity for the diasporic or the ethnic communities has become a part of the problem (Eagleton, 2000: 86ff). It is generally agreed that through literary articulation a migrant becomes the spokesperson of his/her distinct identity and thereby puts forth the notion of cultural distinctiveness.

A diaspora needs to reconcile two cultures and many diasporic persons achieve it by seeking the past and making sense of it in the present. The aim of literary production is to negotiate the diaspora's position in twain cultural realities and to legitimatize the cultural diversity. The endeavour is to create conditions conducive to assimilation as well as to end his/her isolation by validating his/her objective of recognition and acceptance. Gita Mehta is well established in the U.S. society with her high profile husband; and consequently, her diasporic condition is not one of alarm. But the tendency to look back and to be aware of one's country and culture and its ideologies is a natural outcome of distance and Mehta, in recreating the shaping forces of her background neutralizes the influence of her migrant status by reclaiming her space, and reliving her collective and individual past.

The present study argues that Gita Mehta looks at her country with the ambivalence of an outsider and yet she is possessive about it. She deglamorizes it but at the same time she valorizes it for its enduring values and strong traditional base. This is obvious in *Karma Cola.* While the author makes fun of the ridiculous situations created by the Karma-craze, taking in her sweep both Indian duplicity and the western absurdity, the travelling narrator-observer intrudes at intervals to provide serious and authentic information about Indian culture and traditions wherever she feels too stifled by the visitors' erratic view of the culture. Thus, in trying to show what Indian culture really envisages and what it is made out to be in the present she upholds the perennial values. But in the flow of the satiric language, much of its seriousness eludes a casual reader.

However, Mehta does not always use satire, nor has she chosen the satiric mode for her other works. In *Karma Cola* she uses it profusely because it lends itself aptly to the literary representation of the chosen theme: the call 'Eastward, Ho!' of the alienated western youth, their nausea amid plenty and their isolation among the teeming humanity that India is, the improbable groups thrown together and finally making a mess in which the high philosophical term like 'karma' becomes a substitute for flimsy pseudo-spiritual fulfillment. The entire scenario is peopled with those who have nothing better to do, which includes both the gurus and the seekers.

Let us remember that Gita Mehta wrote this non-fiction work in three weeks; she was then in the USA. She not only looks back at India but looks into the country as she roams around with the Hippies in an imaginary journey. The roving observer is not nostalgic; in fact she has no time to brood as she shifts from one situation to the other in quick time; moreover, if not physically, mentally she is in India; it is the western expatriates in India who feel lost/uprooted and long for the familiar. In one incident a new-comer from California and two of the earlier Hippies engaged in conversation reveal their homesickness thus:

> "Where are you from?"
> "California," she replied.
> "Oh yeah?"
> "Yeah. You know. Cokes. Tacos. Surfing."
>
> "And you?"
> "California, babe. Just like you. Tell me more. Remind me."
> "Okay. Popcorn? Jacuzzis? Redwoods?" (31)

Trivial as these allusions sound, they evoke the sense of familiarity and oneness; the two Californians build a bond which helps in warding off the cultural void for a short while. A short while, because the Hippies are so immersed in the newness of their experience that they soon start speaking the guru's tongue and make fun of the newcomer for her name Joanie. For them the simple Christian name makes no sense; because now they are Abhimanyus, and Buddhas, and Saraswati. They conveniently overlook that while they have lost their identities, the Californian girl has not.

In *Karma Cola*, the author seems to have relied heavily on some of the first person narratives of the rehabilitated drug-addicts and the glossy foreign travel magazines inviting tourists to Goa. Cleo Odzer's *Goa Freaks* contains first hand information about smuggling, drug-dens, police apathy, criminal activities, the smuggler boss (called "The Man" in *Karma Cola*), the Flea market and the concentration of the Hippies near Anjuna beach. I would not suggest that Gita Mehta has presented a rewritten version of the narrative of Cleo Odzer but her work certainly has situations that those familiar with *Goa Freaks* can identify.

Mehta uses mythology and religion along side the geography of the country for the structure of *A River Sutra*. This defines for her her inheritance and affirms her identity, not as an individual but as an Indian. Thus the individual memory merges into the collective one and by mythification of the land of her birth she paves the distance created by her migrancy. The India she creates is lively, pristine and metaphysically strong. This is the poetic mode of expressivity in which the author engages in an articulation of the past with confidence and seems at ease with her ethnic background. The dominant motif of the discourse is the River Narmada, symbolically unifying India. It bridges the social, religious and economic differences among the people and offers a gentle picture of the unity and continuity of India. It seeks to depict in the romantic sense the shared mythology of the River, Shiva and Parvati, of our music and cultural unity, and of our common spirit.

But is not this poetic vision of India too lyrical to be recognizable today? This can be a question, instead of a statement, and the answer can be found in both *Karma Cola* and *Snakes and Ladders* where the author sternly interrogates the rapid materialism and consumerism of the present culture. So far as *A River Sutra* is concerned, it never takes us to the now-familiar scenes of twentieth century India; it keeps the reader mystified by its fairyland ambiance. The author romanticizes the landscape, the people and the native/tribal scenario and thus creates almost a fantasy.

It is generally agreed that fantasy is one of the modes of putting 'reality in parentheses' so as to find an imaginary solution to real challenges and that the diasporic writers turn to this mode to make life in the present bearable. Ien Ang, in his study of some of the American soaps argues that fantasy 'does not function in place of, but beside, other dimensions of life (social practice, moral or political consciousness). It is a dimension of subjectivity which is a source of pleasure *because* it puts 'reality' in parentheses, because it constructs imaginary solution for real contradictions .... Fiction and fantasy function by making life in the present pleasurable or at least livable ...' (Ang, 1985: 135).

In *A River Sutra*, the pristine beauty of the Narmada valley cannot be questioned but our disagreement is with Professor Shankar's rationality vis-à-vis the mythology associated with the river. How can the mythology be justified with so many excavations going on around the river (a la Professor Shankar) and how far can Professor Shankar's rationality hold when he acknowledges the sanctity of the Sutra being sung by Uma in the same breath as he denies the immortality and sanctity of the river? The shift between fantasy and reality appears rather intriguing. In denying the immortality of the river the author gives Professor Shankar a chance to defend the excavations, on the same analogy she herself gets an opportunity to put across for the readers the rationality of the Indian thought system. In his study of science fiction and fantasy, Karl Kroeber opines that 'the use of fantasy in a work of literature involves the fantast in an act of intense self-reflexivity, enchanting himself so that he enchants others' (Kroeber, 1988: 1). Somehow, the *modus operandi* to enchant the reader recoils on Professor Shankar who appears as flimsy in his approach to spirituality as do the Hippies in *Karma Cola*. That palpable presence of the cultural-spiritual duo with which Raja Rao's works throb or which A.K. Ramanujan explains in unambiguous terms is missing here.

The historical aspect of Mehta's works shows the efficacy of the view that one rewarding way of understanding and recovering the past is through the creative works. *Raj* tells us a great deal about the colonial period and its implications for postcolonial times, thus re-creating India's history. It cannot be claimed that *Raj* is a unique work because there are several works dealing with the Indian royalty and also with the colonial period but Gita's approach is different and since there are more than one ways of seeing and interpreting historical events, *Raj* stands vindicated. However, one question needs to be answered here: is Gita Mehta consciously trying to revive the past to attract the west? Is she following the usual agenda of the diaspora? Probably, this assumption would be unfair to the author and would tantamount to denying Mehta her due. But it cannot be overlooked either that Gita Mehta tends to explicate Indian ethos to her western readers in this work and as she glamorizes the traditional Indian tenets of democratic governance, she just connives at the other side of the reality – the debilitated rulers, their dissipated life style and the suffering of the masses. The dichotomy between the traditional principles of *Rajniti* and the then present colonial realities leave a gaping void. The gap is concealed temporarily by Jaya's efforts to bridge it at human level. But one realizes that rulers like the Maharajah of Balmer and the Regent Jaya were few and far between and they were powerless. The diasporic consciousness works through Jaya, to an extent who is uprooted from her traditional home and thrown into an environment (of Sirpur) that is not conducive to Indian culture. The British stronghold and the weakness of the royalty impinge on us in this novel with redoubled force and make us aware of colonialism's logic.

How colonialism intrudes even in independent India becomes obvious when we turn to *Snakes and Ladders*. Lost in the present global politics and the consumer-oriented market economy we are passing through a confusing phase as the colonial, the postcolonial and the decolonized forces on the one hand and the traditional approach on the other, work on us with bewildering intensity. Since the past cannot be separated from the present, so India has to carry a double burden of tradition and modernity. On the eve of her fiftieth anniversary, Independent India marches forward with poverty and affluence, caste factors and liberal policies, feudal attitudes and modern rationality – full of paradoxes as ever yet India all the same.

In dealing with Mehta's works one explores a varied territory of different literary genré – a non-fiction-fiction (often termed faction), a historical novel, a novel in the Indian aesthetics of story-telling, and a collection of prose writings. The analysis of their style, techniques and structure yields the author's vision of certainty and faith in her own culture and traditions. But she is not unaware of the latent tensions, the overt materialism and the fast disintegration of values. She looks at these problems from different stand points: in *Karma Cola*, the internal rifts between the old freaks and the new-comers is not much different from the caste divisions we have; their superior-inferior syndrome causes tension and violence; in *A River Sutra*, the author looks at the violence of suicide which she condones if suicide is committed in Narmada, but she inveighs against the society for creating the likes of Rahul Singh and condemns the violence perpetuated by the administration. In *Raj*, the colonial violence to the native rulers and the freedom fighters draws her attention. *Snakes and Ladders* provides her a better scope to look at degeneration of values in modern India which disillusions her.

Somehow, Gita Mehta camouflages her disappointment in her usual flamboyant optimism. This is probably the logical attitude: since you cannot change India, it is better to accept her. The formidable shaping influences are active and the traditional structure is jeopardized by their assault but somehow in her discursive strands she accepts them as they go into the making of both real and 'imagined' India. Our view of India is shaped by the rhetorical tropes, the ideologies and the generic expectations when India gets inscribed and re-inscribed in postcolonial setting. And as the polytemporal time shifts from past to present to future, we realize that in the Indian cultural context there exists a strong sense of existential time too, which allows an escape from time-history and in which things tend to take their own course as time, history and reality cease to be. Overwhelmed by the timelessness of India, one would like to conclude with the story of the teacher who waits for decades for his glass of water, little realizing the march of time.[1]

Notes

1. In *Rich Like Us*, Nayantara Sahgal's Sonali recounts an interesting old tale to Rose. The story befits Indian sense of existential time which allows us to transcend time-history:

   Once a teacher asked his young disciple to fetch him a glass of water and the young man went off to get it, but on the way he met a beautiful girl whom he fell in love with and married. They lived happily together, had three children and cultivated their fields. Before long floods came, and later drought, and they had to work very hard to recover from these calamities, but finally all was well again. Their children were growing fast and in good health, and the whole family was prospering when one day the teacher arrived in the village, looking for his disciple, and said to him, 'Where is the glass of water, my son? I have been waiting half an hour for it' (See Nayantara Sahgal. *Rich Like Us*. London: Hienemann, 1985, p. 208).

Works Cited

Ang, Ien. *Watching Dallas: Soap Opera and the Melodramatic Imagination*. London & New York: Methuen, 1985.

Eagleton, Terry. *The Idea of Culture*. Oxford: Blackwell, 2002.

Kroeber, Karl. *Romantic Fantasy and Science Fiction*. New Haven: Yale Univ. Press, 1988.

Sahgal, Nayantara, *Rich Like Us*. London: Hienemann, 1985.

Bibliography

I. Primary Sources

(i) Works:

Mehta, Gita. *Karma Cola*. London: Simon & Schuster, 1979. New Delhi: Penguin, 1993.

— *Raj*. London: Jonathan Cape, 1989. New Delhi: Penguin, 1993.

— *A River Sutra*. New Delhi: Penguin, 1993.

— *Snakes and Ladders*. London: Random House, 1997.

— *Eternal Ganesha*. Vendome Press, 2000. (This information was taken from internet, www.amazon.com. The book could not be procured).

(ii) Interviews and other articles:

Mehta, Gita. "Neon India: A Song Celestial for Rock and Sitar." *Harper's Magazine*. August 1979: pp. 41–60.

Mehta, Gita and Cutler, Anne. "Detection of Target Phonemes in Spontaneous and Read Speech." *Language and Speech*. 1988 April-June; 31(2): pp. 135–156.

Neelakantan, Shailaja. "The Next Century is Ours" (*Forbes* magazine internet forbes.com 06.16.97).

Smith, Wendy. "Gita Mehta: Making India Accessible." *Publisher's Weekly*, 12 May 1997. pp. 53–54 (Interview) "Voices from the Gaps." http://voices.cla.umn.edu/authors/gitamehta.html

Wallia, C.J.S. "*Indiastar* Interview."http://www.indiastar.com/ wallia4.htm

2. Secondary Sources

Aaron, Daniel. "The Hyphenate Writer and American Letters." *Smith Alumnae Quarterly,* July 1964: pp. 213–17.

Amin, Amina. "Claiming Space for Oneself: Politics of Gender and Imperialism in Gita Mehta's *Raj.*" *Writing in Post-Colonial Space.* Ed. S.N. Panday. Delhi: Atlantic, 1999.

Ang, Ien. *Watching Dallas: Soap Opera and the Melodramatic Imagination.* London & New York: Methuen, 1985.

Ashcroft, Bill, Gareth Griffths and Helen Tiffin, eds. *The Empire Writes Back: Theory and Practice in Post-Colonial Literature.* London: Routledge, 1989.

— eds. *The Post-Colonial Studies Reader.* New York: Routledge, 1995.

Bande, Usha. *The Novels of Anita Desai.* New Delhi: Prestige, 1988.

— "*Raj*: a Thematic Study." *Indian Women Novelists,* Set I, Vol. 5. Ed. R.K. Dhawan. New Delhi: Prestige, 1991.

— "Is Sita Mad?" *Indian Literature* (Sahitya Akademi), 139 (Sept-Oct 1990): pp. 179–184.

— "'India of the Mind': A Study of Gita Mehta's *A River Sutra.*'" *Modern Indian English Fiction.* Eds. T.S. Anand et al. New Delhi: Creative Books, 2002.

— *Cultural Spaces and Diaspora: Journey Metaphor in Indian Women's Writing.* Shimla: Indian Institute of Advanced Study, 2003.

— "Kamala Markandaya." *A Companion to Indian Fiction in English.* Ed. Pier Paolo Piciucco. New Delhi: Atlantic, 2004.

— "Resistance and Reconciliation: Shashi Deshpande's *A Matter of Time* and *Small Remedies.*" *Writing Difference.* Ed. Chanchala K. Naik. New Delhi: Pencraft, 2005.

— *Writing Resistance: A Comparative Study of the Selected Novels by Women Writers.* Shimla: Indian Institute of Advanced Study, 2006.

Baral, K.C. (a), ed. *Humanities and Pedagogy.* New Delhi: Pencraft International, 2002.

Baral, K.C. (b), ed. *Interpretation of Texts: Text, Meaning and Interpretation.* New Delhi: Pencraft International, 2002.

Bhabha, Homi K. *The Location of Culture.* New York: Routledge, 1994.

Bhabha, Homi K. "The Other Question: Stereotype and Colonial Discourse." *Twentieth-Century Literary Theory: A Reader*. Ed. K.N. Newton. 2nd ed. 1988. New York: St. Martin's Press, 1997.

Bhaskaran, G. "Bureaucrat's Quest: A Study of Gita Mehta's *A River Sutra*." *Critical Essays on Indian Women Writing in English*. Ed. A.S. Ratnam. New Delhi: Harman Publishing House, 1999.

Bhatt, Indira. "Shobha De's *Sultry Days* and Gita Mehta's *A River Sutra*: A Study in Orientalism." *Indian Women Novelists*, Set III, Vol.1. Ed. R.K. Dhawan. New Delhi: Prestige, 1995.

Bose, Mandakranta. "Sati: The Event and the Ideology." *Faces of the Feminine in Ancient, Medieval, and Modern India*. Ed. Mandakranta Bose. New Delhi: Oxford, 2000.

Boym, Svetlana. *The Future of Nostalgia*. New York: Basic Books, 2001.

Brata, Sasthi. *India: The Perpetual Paradox*. 1985. Rpt. Calcutta: Rupa, 1986.

Chatterjee, Partha. *Nation and Its Fragments: Colonial and Post-Colonial Histories*. Delhi: Oxford, 1994.

De Quincey, Thomas. *The Collected Writings of Thomas De Quincey* in 14 vols. Ed. David Masson. Edinburg: A&C Black, 1889–1890.

Desai, Anita. *Journey to Ithaca*. New Delhi: Minerva, 1995.

Davis, Rocio G. "Gita Mehta's *A River Sutra*: Discovering India in a Postcolonial Short Story Cycle." Ed. and introd. Guardia, P. and J. *Stone Proceedings of the 20th International AEDEAN Conference*. Barcelona, Spain: Universitat de Barcelona, 1997.

Deshpande, Shashi. "Interview" in *Indian Communicator*, 20 November, 1994.

During, Simon "Postmodernism and Post-colonialism Today." *Textual Practice* 1(1), 1987. Rpt. in *The Post-colonial Studies Reader*. Ed. Bill Ashcroft et al. London/New York: Routledge, 1995.

Eagleton, Terry. *The Idea of Culture*. Oxford: Blackwell, 2002.

Fanon, Franz. *Black Skin, White Masks*. New York: Grove Press, 1967.

Fanon, Franz. *The Wretched of the Earth*. Trans. Constance Farrington. Rpt. 1961. Harmondsworth: Penguin, 1982.

Forrest, G.W. *Cities of India: Past and Present*. Delhi: Shubhi Publication, 1999.

Fromm, Eric. *To Have and To Be*. New York: Bantam Books, 1976.

Galle, E. "Gita Mehta's *A River Sutra*: An Analysis." *The Literary Criterion*, Vol. XXX (1995) No. 3 pp. 27–56.

Gardiner, Juliet, Ed. *What is History Today?* London: Macmillan, 1988.

George, T.J.S. Compiled. *The Enquire Dictionary*. Rpt. 2000. New Delhi: Harper Collins, 1988.

Gohain, Hiren. "On Interpretation: A Necessary Evil." *Interpretation of Text*. Ed. K.C. Baral. New Delhi: Pencraft International, 2002.

Gooneratne, Yasmin. *Diverse Inheritance*. Adelaide: Centre for Research in the New Literatures in English, 1980.

Hogue, W. Lawrence. *Race, Modernity, Postmodernity: A Look at the History and the Literature of People of Color Since the 1960s*. Albany: State University of New York,1996.

Huggan, Graham. "Consuming India." *Post Independence Voices in South Asian Writings*. Eds. Malashri Lal, Alamgir Hashmi, Victor J. Ramraj. New Delhi: Doaba, 2001.

Hutcheon, Linda. *A Poetics of Postmodernism: History, Theory and Fiction*. New York and London: Routledge, 1988.

Kondo, Dorinne. "The Narrative Production of 'Home,' Community, and Political Identity in Asian American Theatre." *Displacement, Diaspora, and the Geographies of Identity*. Eds. Smadar Lavie and Ted Swedenburg. Durham: Duke University Press, 1996. pp. 97–118.

Jacquemont, Victor. *Letters from India: Describing A Journey in the British Dominions of India, Tibet, Lahore and Cashmere, During the Years 1828, 1829, 1830, 1831*. London, 1934.

Jain, Jasbir. "Post-Colonial Realities: Women Writing History." *Interrogating Postcolonialism*. Eds. Harish Trivedi and Meenakshi Mukherjee. Shimla: IIAS, 1996.

— "Postcoloniality, Literature and Politics.," *Contesting Postcolonialism*. Eds. Jasbir Jain and Veena Singh. Jaipur: Rawat, 2000.

— "The New Parochialism: Homeland in the Writing of the Indian Diaspora." *In-Diaspora*. Ed. Makarand Paranjape. New Delhi: Indialog 2001, pp. 79–92.

— "Nayantara Sahgal." *A Companion to Indian Fiction in English*. Ed. Pier Paolo Piciucco. New Delhi: Atlantic, 2004.

Jain, N.K. "From Purdah to Polo to Politics: A Study of Gita Mehta's *Raj*." *Women in Indo-Anglian Fiction: Tradition and Modernity*. Ed. N.K. Jain. New Delhi: Manohar, 1998.

Jara, Joan. *An Unfinished Song: The Life of Victor Jara*. New York: Ticknor & Fields, 1984.

Jarmani Dass, Diwan. *Maharaja*. Delhi: Hind Pocket Books, 1970.

Jhabvala, Ruth P. *Heat and Dust*. London: John Murray, 1975.

Jhabvala, Ruth P. *A New Dominion*. 1972; rpt, London: Granada, 1983.

Joshi, Arun. *The City and the River*. New Delhi: Vision Books, 1990.

Kalanmani, N. "Soul-Questers & Spiritual Bedlams: a Study of Gita Mehta's *Karma Cola." Indian Women Novelists*, Set III, Vol. 4. Ed. R.K. Dhawan. New Delhi: Prestige, 1995.

Kalanmani, N. "Soul-Questers & Spiritual Bedlams: A Study of Gita Mehta's *Karma Cola* and *A River Sutra." Indian Fiction of the Nineties*. Ed. R.S. Pathak. New Delhi: Creative, 1997.

Keenan, Brigid. *Travels in Kashmir*. New Delhi: Permanent Black, 1989.

Khan, A.G. "Gita Mehta's *A River Sutra*: Two Views," *The Literary Criterion*. Vol. XXIX (1994) No. 3. pp. 7–15

Khilnani, Sunil. *The Idea of India*. London: Hamish Hamilton, 1997.

King, Bruce. *Modern Indian Poetry in English*. Delhi: Oxford Univ Press. 1987.

Kroeber, Karl. *Romantic Fantasy and Science Fiction*. New Haven: Yale UP. 1988.

Krishaswamy, Santha. *The Woman in Indian Fiction in English*. Delhi: Ashish Publishing House, 1984

Lavie, Smadar and Ted Swedenburg., eds. *Displacement, Diaspora, and the Geographies of Identities*. Durham Duke University Press, 1996.

Malgonkar, Manohar. *The Princes*. London: Hamish Hamilton, 1963.

Mukherjee, Arun. "Interrogating Postcolonialism: Some Uneasy Conjectures." *Interrogating Post-Colonialism*. Eds. Harish Trivedi and Meenakshi Mukherjee. Shimla: IIAS, 2000.

Mukherjee, Bharati. *Jasmine*. New York: Viking/ Penguin, 1989: 21

Mukherjee, Meenakshi. *Twice Born Fiction*. New Delhi: Arnold-Hienemann, 1971.

— "Marthand Verman and the Historical Novel in India," *Litt. Crit*. 18. pp. 1–2 (1992): pp. 1–18.

— "The Anxiety of Indianness: Our Novels in English." *Mapping Cultural Spaces: Postcolonial Indian Literature in English*. Eds. Nilufer E. Bharucha and Vrida Nabar. New Delhi: Vision Books, 1998.

Naipaul, V.S. *An Area of Darkness*. London: Andre Deutsche, 1965.

—*A Way in the World*. London: Heinemann, 1994.

Nair, Rama. "The Myth of Redemption in Gita Mehta's *A River Sutra*." *Fiction of the Nineties*. Eds. Veena Noble Dass and R.K. Dhawan. New Delhi: Prestige, 1994. Also in *Indian Women Novelists*, Set III, Vol. 4. Ed. R.K. Dhawan. New Delhi: Prestige, 1995.

Nandan, Satendra. "The Diasporic Consciousness: From Biswas to Biswasghat." *Interrogating Post-Colonialism* Eds. Harish Trivedi and Meenakshi Mukherjee. Shimla: IIAS, 2000

Nandy, Ashis. *The Intimate Enemy*. Delhi: Oxford. 1983.

Narayan, R.K. *Waiting for the Mahatma*. Michigan: University Press, 1955.

Nasta, Susheila. *Home Truths: Fictions of the South Asian Diaspora in Britain*. London: Palgrave, 2002

Nehru, Jawaharlal. *The Discovery of India*. Calcutta: Signet Press, 1946.

Nityanandam, Indira. "Gita Mehta's *A River Sutra*: the Threads of Life." *Fiction of the Nineties*. Eds. Veena Noble Dass and R.K. Dhawan. New Delhi: Prestige, 1994. Also in *Indian Women Novelists*, Set III, Vol. 4. Ed. R.K. Dhawan. New Delhi: Prestige, 1995.

Pandey, Gyanendra. "In Defence of the Fragment: Writing About Hindu-Muslim Riot in India Today." *Economic and Political Weekly*. March 1991, 559.

Parameswaran, Uma. "Ganga in the Assinibonie: Prospects for Indo-Canadian Literature." *A Meeting of Streams: South Asian Canadian Literature*. Ed. M.G. Vassanji. Toronto: TSAR Publications, 1985.

— "Gita Mehta: *A River Sutra*." *Saclit: An Introduction to South-Asian-Canadian Literature*. Ed. Uma Parameswaran. Madras: East West Books, 1996: pp. 257–68.

Paranjape, Makarand. "One Foot in Canada and a Couple of Toes in India: Diaspora and Homeland in South Asian Canadian Experience." *In-Diaspora*. Ed. Makarand Paranjape. New Delhi: Indialog, 2001.

Parasuram, Laxmi. "*Karma Cola:* Another Version of East-West Encounter." *Indian Women Novelists*. Ed. R.K. Dhawan. Vol. 5. New Delhi: Prestige, 1991.

Pathak, R.S. "Gita Mehta's *A River Sutra* and Its Concentric Polysemy." *Indian Fiction of the Nineties*. Ed. R.S. Pathak. New Delhi: Creative, 1997.

— "*A River Sutra*: Thematic, Narrative & Semantic Structure." *Modern Indian Novel in English*. Ed. R.S. Pathak. New Delhi: Creative, 1999.

— "Tribal People, Locales & Values in *A River Sutra*." *Modern Indian Novel in English*. Ed. R.S. Pathak. New Delhi: Creative, 1999.

Radhakrishnan, R. *Diasporic Mediation: Between Home and Location*. Minneapolis, MN: University of Minnesota Press, 1996.

Ramachandran, C.N. "Gita Mehta's *A River Sutra*: Two Views." *The Literary Criterion*. Vol. XXIX (1994) No. 3. pp. 7–15.

Ramanujan, A.K. "Is There an Indian Way of Thinking?" *India Through the Hindu Category*. Ed. Mckim Marriott. New Delhi: Sage, 1990.

Rath, Sura, P. "Home(s) Abroad: Diasporic Identities in Third Spaces." *Theory and Praxis*. Eds. Prafulla C. Kar, Kailash C. Baral and Sura P. Rath. Delhi; Pencraft International, 2003.

Ray, Mohit Kumar. "*A River Sutra:* a Gyno-ecological Perspective." *Women Writers in the Twentieth Century Literature*. Ed. Monika Gupta. New Delhi: Atlantic, 2000.

Renan, Ernest. "What is a Nation?" (1882). *Nation and Narration*. Ed. Homi K. Bhabha. London: Routledge, 1990.

Root, Deborah. *Cannibal Culture: Art, Appreciation, and the Commodification of Difference*. Boulder: WestView Press, 1996.

Rushdie, Salman. *Midnight's Children*. London: Pan, 1982.

— *Imaginary Homelands*. London: Granta/Viking, 1991.

Safran, William. "Diaspora in Modern Societies: Myths of Homeland and Return". *Diaspora: A Journal of Transnational Studies,* 1(1), 1991: 83–99.

Sahgal, Nayantara. *Rich Like Us*. London: Hienemann, 1985.

Said, Edward. *Culture and Imperialism*. London: Vintage, 1994.

Sampat, Manju. "Old and New Expatriate Indian English Novelists." *Mapping Cultural Spaces: Postcolonial Indian Literature in English*. Eds. Nilufer E. Bharucha and Vrinda Nabar. New Delhi: Vision Books, 1998.

Sangari, Kumkum. "Feminist Criticism and Indian Literary Theory." *Language and Discourse Writing*. 2. 4 (January–March, 2002): 33–49.

Sarojini. "Gita Mehta's *Raj*: Alternatives to Sati" *Realism, Reality and Fiction: Essays on the Indian Novels*. Ed. Neelam Raisinghani. Jaipur: Best Book Company, 2006.

Satchidanandan, K. "That Third Space: Interrogating the Diasporic Paradigm." *In-Diaspora*. Ed. Makarand Paranjape. Delhi: Indialog Publication 2001.

Schneller, Beverly. "Visible and Visitable': The Role of History in Gita Mehta's *Raj* and Rohinton Mistry's *A Fine Balance*." *Journal of Narrative Theory*. 2001 Summer; 31(2): pp. 233–54.

Scott, Paul. *The Jewel in the Crown*. 1966; rpt. London: Granada, 1980.

Sen, Indrani. "Devoted Wife/Sensuous Bibi: Colonial Constructions of Indian Woman, 1860–1900." *Indian Journal of Gender Studies* 8:1 (2001): pp. 1–22.

Steadman, John M. *The Myth of Asia*. London: Macmillan, 1969.

Syal, Pushpinder. "The Threads of Narratives: Gita Mehta's *A River Sutra.*" *The Postmodern Indian English Novel.* Ed. Viney Kirpal. Bombay: Allied Publishers, 1996.

Tololyan, Khaching. *Diaspora: A Journal of Transnational Studies*, 1 (1), 1991: pp. 4–5.

Trikha, Pradeep. "Gita Mehta's *The River Sutra*: a Pilgrim's Progress." *Fiction of the Nineties.* Eds. Veena Noble Dass and R.K. Dhawan. New Delhi: Prestige, 1994. Also in *Indian Women Novelists*, Set III, Vol. 4. Ed. R.K. Dhawan. New Delhi: Prestige, 1995.

Trivedi. Harish. "India and Post-colonial Discourse," *Critical Theory: Western and Indian.* Ed. P.C. Kar. New Delhi: Pencraft International, 1997.

Vijayasree, C. "The Politics and Poetics of Expatriation: The Indian Version(s)." *Interrogating Post-colonialism.* Eds. Harish Trivedi and Meenakshi Mukherjee. Shimla: IIAS 1996.

Vijay Kumar T. "Allegory and the Negation of History: Arun Joshi's *The City and the River*". *The Postmodern Indian English Novel.* Ed. Viney Kirpal. Bombay: Allied, 1996.

Woolf, Leonard. "Pearls and Swines." *Stories from the East: Three Short Stories on Cylone.* Rpt. Leonard Woolf, *Diaries in Cylone 1908–1911: Records of a Colonial Administrator.* Dehiwela: Tisara Prakashkayo, 1903.

Young, Robert J.C. *Colonial Desire: Hybridity in Theory, Culture and Race.* London: Routledge, 1995.

Young, Robert J.C. *Postcolonialism: A Very Short Introduction.* Oxford: Oxford University Press, 2002.

3. Internet Sources

Corsettee, Barbara. "After the Raj." < www.nytimes.com/books/97/07/06. reviews>.

Customer Reviews. <www.amazon.com/customer/reviews>

Gita Mehta. <www. people.virginia.edu. html.>

Maria, John. < http://www.indiatravelogue.com> "Bookshelf" *Snakes and Ladders* – Gita Mehta.

Review. *Maharaja.* <http:// www.biblio.com/search.ph>

V.G. Artist Biography. <voices.cla.umn.ed/vg/Bios/mehat_Gita.Html>.

Index